FEEDING BACK

CONVERSATIONS WITH ALTERNATIVE GUITARISTS FROM PROTO-PUNK TO POST-ROCK

DAVID TODD

CHICAGO
REVIEW
PRESS

Published by Chicago Review Press Incorporated
814 North Franklin Street
Chicago, Illinois 60610
ISBN 978-1-61374-059-0

Library of Congress Cataloging-in-Publication Data
Feeding back : conversations with alternative guitarists from proto-punk to
post-rock / [interviewed by] David Todd.
p. cm.
Includes index.
ISBN 978-1-61374-059-0
1. Guitarists—Interviews. 2. Rock musicians—Interviews. I. Todd, David, 1971–

ML399.C66 2012
787.87'1660922—dc23

2012002144

Cover design: Jeffrey Scharf
Interior design: Jonathan Hahn

Printed in the United States of America

"Question the heroic approach."
—BRIAN ENO AND PETER SCHMIDT

"Take the only tree that's left and
stuff it up the hole in your culture."
—LEONARD COHEN

CONTENTS

Introduction

The Quine Machine

Robert Quine was born in 1942 in Akron, Ohio, into a middle-class family and prospects of a straight life. He grew up on Link Wray and James Burton and played guitar eight hours a day, yet by the mid-1960s he found himself in a St. Louis law school "just out of inertia." In 1969 he drifted farther west to San Francisco, but instead of the local strychnine, it was the death-meth of the Velvet Underground he sampled during their visits to town. "When I first heard the V.U. . . . I thought it was the worst," he told *Perfect Sound Forever*. Nonetheless, "I became a total fanatic." After following the Velvets to New York City, he suffered there for years writing tax law and being received on the music scene "very condescendingly." It wasn't until 1975 that he met a relative youngster named Richard Hell and fermented his strange mix of Albert Ayler, Chuck Berry, and the Stooges in a group called the Voidoids.

Robert Quine didn't look like a guitar hero—he looked like a deranged Doonesbury character—and he didn't play like one. "Quine's fixed idea was brutality," his collaborator Jody Harris said in the oral history *No Wave*. But Quine's was a particularly deep brand of negativism that encompassed the stranglebilly of the Voidoids' "Blank Generation" and the severed nerves of Lou Reed's "Waves of Fear" and the noise-pop of Matthew Sweet's "Girlfriend," to name but a few of his excursions. If one premise of this book is that the alleged "alternative rock guitar tradition" can be encapsulated as what funnels into bands like the Stooges and then funnels out of bands such as Sonic Youth, Quine is at the center of the intervening pipeline. "From my own selfish point of view, it was perfect for me," he said of the Voidoids' early days at CBGB. "I happened to have all these influences that were suddenly hip and fit into what was going on. By many people's standards, my playing is very primitive, but by punk standards, I'm a virtuoso." Thus Quine, as he was known even to his wife, was an anti-saint in a lineage that stretches from the neon Beat jazz of the Magic Band to the gothic punk of the Birthday Party, from the Krautrock of Neu! to the un-rock of Public Image Ltd. to the post-rock of Slint. Within the larger world we call alternative music, a more specific tradition runs back and forth among these groups and their guitar conceptualists, as evidenced by a series of connections inscribed in invisible ink. The point to this book is to shine a black light on their informal but vital exchange.

But what filters into the Stooges? Out of Sonic Youth? And what else does Quine have to do with that? With so many different ways of looking at the big picture, you just have to start by throwing a dart somewhere. The first lands on John Coltrane, just one notch away on this particular board from John Cale. Along with other free-jazz wildings such as Ayler and Archie Shepp, Coltrane and his counterpart Miles Davis represented music as a high sonic art—that is, a virtuosity not for its own sake but matched with ambitious ideas. As Miles famously put it, "The difference between a fair musician and a good musician is that a good musician can play anything he thinks. The difference between a good musician and a *great* musician is what he thinks." These alternative guitarists saw free jazz as a figurative Carnegie Hall, but recognizing that they needed some other way to get there besides practice, they dug their own subway tunnels. "I found that if I played my best Chuck Berry solo as fast as I could, with as much velocity—if you just moved what he was doing over an inch—it started to turn into those sheets of sound that Trane was playing," Wayne Kramer of the MC5 recalls herein. In true Warhol fashion, the art-punk guitarists probably did a better job on the frames than on the paintings themselves, but even with their shortcuts they achieved the dark magus potency of their heroes. "That's right, Iggy and the Stooges were every bit as good as Archie Shepp," Lester Bangs proclaimed in his 1979 article "Free Jazz/Punk Rock." "And John Coltrane could have played with the Velvet Underground."

The influence of the Velvet Underground on alternative music has been well documented, as has the impact of other seminal bands such as the New York Dolls. This book gathers plenty of the usual suspects, but another part of its goal is to pick up where previous treatments of alternative rock leave off. Looking at the Velvet Underground that way, one of their main contributions to these guitarists was the link they presented, via John Cale especially, to the minimalism of composers La Monte Young, Tony Conrad, Steve Reich, and Philip Glass. Just as free jazz and wild punk converged as shared noise-on-sound, so did Reich and the Ramones meet at the vanishing point where all overtones become indistinguishable—again, respective training be damned. This fusion led to the work of direct descendants such as Glenn Branca and Rhys Chatham (basically New Music with rock gear) and the next-level guys such as Sonic Youth (rock in just intonation), and even trickled down to Bob Mould (and his "bag of dimes" sound). Cale and Young's Theatre of Eternal Music is perhaps the true prehistoric source for all of this music, by virtue of being the first ensemble to cross serious art with rock electrification. Also known as the Dream Syndicate, its low-flying-plane drones echoed through the guitar of the Stooges' Ron Asheton, who rode them into his own shimmering trances. Different dronings leaked into this scene from the folk music of Davy Graham and the ragas of Ravi Shankar, just as different approaches to noise filtered in from improvisers Derek Bailey and Keith Rowe. Still, it made karmic sense that it was John Cale, sent by fate to produce the first Stooges album in 1969, who banged out the famous one-note piano line on their repetitive classic "I Wanna Be Your Dog."

Cale also produced the debut album by the Patti Smith Group, whose guitarist Lenny Kaye assesses how songs such as "I Wanna Be Your Dog" differ from garage rock, the genre he codified with the 1972 anthology *Nuggets*. The garage aesthetic is another major strand in these guitarists' DNA: the songs were fun to play and reproducible with cheap gear, and as a whole the movement composed a proto-DIY circuit to prefigure later undergrounds. Almost as important, *Nuggets* helped hold down the fort during a lull period within this lineage, that tenuous phase in the early 1970s when stadium shows and prog rock drowned out the Dolls in the United States and the Krautrock bands that were emerging in Germany. However, somewhere in there a shift took place, and the idea behind the Seeds' "Pushin' Too Hard" took a step punkward with the Stooges' "No Fun," one more step with the Patti Smith Group's own "Rock n Roll Nigger." "If the last cut on *Nuggets* was from 1968 and the Stooges came out in 1969, the Stooges weren't influenced by those bands—they were the evolvement of them," Kaye says. These evolutionary steps are essential, because while garage rock played straight up might not have been so radical after its initial life span, its spirit was transformed by Pere Ubu's "avant-garage" modifications and the thrash of Joy Division's "Interzone" and the Sex Pistols' return to "Steppin' Stone." As a defining trait, these alternative guitarists are bent on seeking new ways to modulate the content of whatever they're working with, to taint the form or perversify the tone. They are not retro in orientation but *futuro*.

There are so many other musical currents circling through this whirl-pool that it's not feasible to address them all at length. (Just one that will have to get shorted for now is the curious effect of German bands such as Faust, Can, and Neu!, whose reinterpretations of music coming from England and America wound up reversing the influence back toward those countries.) But one of the last essential sources of the alternative thread is the noisy rock of the early Yardbirds, Kinks, and Rolling Stones. If you think of the fastest jangling rave-up, the Davies brothers romping through "You Really Got Me," the two-guitar Stones playing out of their heads, you can imagine how those bands were a British analogue to the American garage groups. But while the Yardbirds featured some of the most celebrated guitar gods—Eric Clapton, Jeff Beck, and Jimmy Page—their impact on the alternists had more to do with the sheer rhythm and energy of their playing, the visceral as opposed to virtuoso qualities. From these groups, the guitarist most cited by this book's subjects is Pete Townshend, especially at the peak of the Who's "maximum R&B" auto-destruction. (Not for nothing did a teenage Ron Asheton run away to England and catch the Who at the Cavern Club, where in the midst of a scene he described in *Please Kill Me: The Uncensored Oral History of Punk* as a "primitive" yet "mesmerizing" riot, he realized, "This is definitely what I wanna do.") As gifted a lead guitarist as Townshend is, I suspect his appeal stems from his larger role as a rhythm player, songwriter, sound manipulator, and bandleader; this is the type of creative scope to which all of this book's interviewees aspire, each in his or her own deceptively ambitious way. Finally, of the many folk and folk-rock artists who also affected this outsider lineage—including Bert Jansch, who was a little less electric than suits our purposes, just as Townshend is a little less underground—one of the most routinely acknowledged among them is another not-quite-alternative figure, Roger McGuinn of the Byrds. Like Townshend, McGuinn was more than a lead player or songwriter; he was the auteur behind lush soundscapes with overtones ringing out of twelve-string guitars and three-part harmonies alike.

Putting some of these influences together, you could say that for many alternative guitarists, garage rock, Bo Diddley and Chuck Berry, and those fevered British Invasion groups provided the tools for what could be played. (This is one reason these alternists fit the "rock" designation as opposed to being better classified as jazz like Bill Frisell or experimental like Keiji Haino; those artists are also a half-step outside this domain.) As to what these guitarists did with those tools, the first move was to infuse them with aspirations of free jazz, minimalism, Karlheinz Stockhausen, Iannis Xenakis, and other highbrow abstractions. In reduced terms, there were ideas and there was a language, and where they met was what one might call the musical concept. And for most of this book's subjects, that concept was where they were at their most sophisticated—not the craft of their songwriting, necessarily, not always the skill of their playing, but the sparks inherent in their ways of, to use composer Edgard Varèse's definition of music, "organizing sound." I think this is what Asheton's bandmate Iggy Pop meant when he told the *Los Angeles Times* that with the Stooges, "I started out just wanting to front a musically adventurous band which would of necessity work with very, very basic skills." Thus, when Asheton took a terse up/down strumming break in the Byrds' "Tribal Gathering" and boiled it down to the most bare-bones chord construction, mummified it in feedback, and repeated it until his amps bled as "1969," the genius wasn't in the latter song's formal complexity but in its charged simplicity. As with Townshend and McGuinn, guitarists like Asheton acted as their own funnels of existing sonic possibilities on their way to discovering new ones. Their expectation was that, as Rowland S. Howard explained a generation later to *Rip It Up*, "The way you played your instrument should be a direct extension of certain aspects of your personality."

As I've already suggested, the alternative lineage is best conceived of as a series of intersections, with many ways of equal merit to view the big picture. Begin with John Coltrane or John Cale or John Cage; you'll eventually encounter all three as you skip from Johnny Thunders to Johnny Ramone to Johnny Marr. Thus, no single view will be perfect, and there are a few internal inconsistencies to contend with, such as a split over Chuck Berry vs. Bo Diddley that, it seems, has created a lasting riff/groove opposition. But I started with the Stooges-to-Sonic Youth corridor because it strikes me as the most irreducible framework within this chaotic phenomenon. As just one reason for this, there's the curiosity that if punk "broke" twice—in 1977 and again in 1991—each of those ruptures came eight years after one of those bands' first albums. I don't think this was coincidence, as in both cases these groups were the progenitors of those next waves, setting up resonances that sounded when the Sex Pistols covered "No Fun" and when Quine and the Voidoids covered "I Wanna Be Your Dog," or when Sonic Youth covered "I Wanna Be Your Dog" or chaperoned a young Dinosaur Jr. on their early tours or referred Nirvana, for better or worse, to Geffen Records.

Until the Stooges, it seems, alternative guitar didn't really become a "thing"; to that point the outsiders were cropping up somewhat randomly— in New York City; in Canterbury, England; in Austin or Houston, Texas; in Detroit—whereas afterward they were more clearly part of some greater phenomenon that was taking shape. And the Stooges themselves, because of their completely fucked-up history, which involved rising and falling three times like a Sophoclean trilogy, underwent a few generations of their own musical stakes-raising, which only heightened their impact. The Stooges' respective Ron Asheton and James Williamson incarnations represented hot-and-cold poles within alternative rock—as if over in the metal world, Black Sabbath had replaced power-chording Tony Iommi with neoclassicist Randy Rhoads, instead of switching in vocalist Ronnie James Dio for Ozzy Osbourne. These dueling visions even neatly encapsulate the aforementioned Chuck Berry/Bo Diddley divide, with Ron picking up on Diddley's beats and James on Berry's shuffles (and only magic Stooges drummer Scott Asheton bridging the gap between them). And that's not even including the lost period when Asheton and Williamson played psychotic mega-riffs together that could've led to who knows what else.

Sonic Youth, on the other hand, might be the last group to pull together a vast amount of what preceded them within this alternative landscape while still having a clear impact on what followed. There is continuity among later guitarists, of course, but less of a sense that any one group or artist possesses that seminal godparent quality, so that when you look at Dinosaur Jr. you see the connections to Sonic Youth right away, but by the time you get to Christian Fennesz you find that even though his music was informed by them, it reflected a much more fragmented musical climate. What makes Sonic Youth so pivotal is that they were such an agile and sophisticated filter of so many things, from minimalism to Raymond Pettibon; they were simply capable of embracing more, incorporating more into their work, than pretty much anybody else. (Spacemen 3 were a bit like this over in England, distilling "Stooges? Velvets? Stones?" among other questions.) Alternative guitar was definitely a thing by the time Sonic Youth got to it, and they were sensitive to all its permutations, including the MC5, whose Fred "Sonic" Smith helped provide their name; the "no wave" bands they lived among; noise before and after—everything up to Neil Young, the most popularly successful patron for the guitarists in this tradition. At times, the Youth swelled to include three guitarists—first with Jim O'Rourke, who was a full-time member from 2001 to 2005, and then with Kim Gordon, pulled over from her original spot on bass—but for most of their lifespan, it was the original duo of Lee Ranaldo and Thurston Moore who were behind their innovative tunings and forms. (Of the two, Ranaldo is interviewed herein; Moore is not, partly because after Ron Asheton passed away I realized that one guitarist per group was enough, and partly because after beginning to hound him anyway I asked myself, Does Thurston Moore really need an interlocutor to bring out his thoughts on anything?) When you think of how ingeniously that pair transformed ideas taken from gallery rock, folk, and hardcore, with such awareness of mixing melody and abstraction or rhythm and noise, of sensing where sound meets structure, of balancing the past while still breaking from it . . . they are simply an ideal of conceptual art within the medium of rock guitar.

So that's the logic behind the Stooges/Sonic Youth premise. But there is room for other viewpoints as well. For instance, there's the notion that the post-punk period is the zenith of a totally reconceived rock guitar (as

Johnny Marr says in his interview, "No R&B rhythm playing, no distortion, no lengthy solos, no blues, no bending"). Or you might build around the "quintessential outsiders" such as Rowland Howard and Keith Levene, those who led by being their complex selves and taking risks (Levene on Public Image Ltd.: "We were so free, post-punk punks getting away with fucking murder"). Another contender is the "conceptualist" thread already touched on, which includes those more consciously conceptual and those winging it with proto-snot precocity (Ranaldo: "Everybody was experimenting, Teenage Jesus and DNA and the Contortions . . . it seemed so normal"). Equally legit are the "resistant virtuosos" such as Tom Verlaine and John Frusciante, who combine the craftiness of the most interesting simpletons with the command of the master craftspeople (Frusciante: "I think of myself as somebody who put the same amount of time into guitar playing as a guy like Steve Vai would, but I used that time completely differently"). And finally for now is the "guitar player turned songwriter" school of Richard Thompson and Bob Mould—a particularly useful alternative in that it reflects how these artists evolved beyond sideperson status, either widening the term "guitarist" to include singing and composing or breaking out of it completely. ("It's a singer-songwriter style," Mould says. "I'm not a big rock guy doing bar chords; I'm writing in a folk motif that delivers a story.")

Each of these alternate theories illuminates something essential about the larger milieu that might be missing without it. For instance, that last "turned songwriter" thread helps explain why the overdriven interviewees often identify the folky Richard Thompson as one of their true inspirations. ("He's not so much an anti-hero, more an aversion hero," Colin Irwin wrote in *Melody Maker* long ago. "Denies it, of course.") The shortest rationale for this is that being half guitar genius and half songwriting great, Thompson produces wholes of such uniformly high quality. When you factor in his virtuosity as a solo performer, the way his prodigious electric chops combine with acoustic open tunings in a style that's oddly contemporary at the psych folk moment, his career-long indifference in the face of public indifference . . . all of these are further evidence of his ability to lead by inscrutability. Sure, Thompson is not often lumped in among the art punks or the alternists, whatever you want to call the members of this alleged conspiracy; he isn't often lumped in with anybody. But I think he captures the way his outsider nature meets those of the others in this book when he says, "If you're going to be a writer of any kind, you have to be alienated from your own generation, and from society as a whole, or you'll never have enough perspective. I try to be an independent thinker . . . and of course independent thinkers find each other, sooner or later." That, in short, accounts for much of how this whole loose movement fits together.

If you go a step past Richard Thompson into the types of songs that other alternative guitarists in this book write, you find their music often harks back to the plaintive, simple style of Leonard Cohen, who in his own somber way is one of their strongest archetypes. This may be because not only is Cohen a songsmith in the "resistant virtuoso" mold, combining a fully realized approach to craft with the highest aspirations as to content, but he also offers a suggestion for what these guitarists could do with all the punk anger that fueled their youths as they got older. Namely, they could convert it to a kind of aching sadness, what the once-crazed Nick Cave cites in his lecture "The Love Song" as *duende*. Derived from poet Federico García Lorca—who himself was keenly studied by Cohen—this fetching term refers to a vast soul-emptiness that needs to be spanned lest an artist default on the challenge of his or her life, a void that should be documented in the artist's chosen medium with brutal, antimaudlin honesty. ("As far as my playing sounding 'frustrated' or 'angry,' sometimes it was," Quine recalled to *Vintage Guitar*. Alternatively, in *Perfect Sound Forever*: "There's a ballad [Lester Young] does, 'These Foolish Things.' The feeling is resignation beyond sadness, self-pity. That has affected my playing.") One could develop the idea of a sadness that comes from alienation that's deeper than "punk"— although I use that term myself, almost none of these guitarists are what you'd call textbook punks—but as with other viewpoints, it would be rendered moot, because if you enter the network via *duende* you get to Rowland S. Howard pretty quickly, and from Howard you get to Fred Frith, and via Frith you get to French Frith Kaiser Thompson, and via Thompson you get into one type of alternate tunings, which leads to another with Sonic Youth, and both echo into overtones, which goes back to minimalism . . . and so on.

In some ways, this whole discussion is dependent on the existence of something only hinted at thus far: an implied *mainstream* guitar pantheon, be it real or imagined. Now, I'm not naïve enough to suggest that while the alternative legacy is too complex to pin down, the mainstream one is simple enough to stereotype. On top of that, many of the conventional heroes such as Jimi Hendrix, Jeff Beck, and Duane Allman are obviously great musicians, deserving of the praise they've received (and unlike people like Quine—or, for that matter, his interlocking counterpart in the Voidoids, guitarist Ivan Julian—they've received a lot). I would be content to say that that there might not even be any three-dimensional human being who fits the mold of the stock guitar god, that the image only exists as some vague caricature for players of every variety to circumvent.

Still, I can hear a scoffing: "How can you talk about the alternative to something when you can't even establish the original thing?" So I'll quote Andre Millard, who wrote in *The Electric Guitar: A History of an American Icon*:

> Who is a guitar hero? Many of us who grew up in the 1960s would simply answer "Eric Clapton." Others, coming of age in the 1970s, might say "Carlos Santana" or "Peter Frampton." Still others, youngsters in the 1980s, would respond, "Eddie Van Halen." Virtually all great guitar players, regardless of age, sex, or national origin, would say "Jimi Hendrix." The list would grow as we asked more people: Peter Townshend, Les Paul, Jeff Beck, Jimmy Page, Slash, Steve Vai, Ritchie Blackmore, Eric Johnson, Yngwie Malmsteen, Joe Satriani, Stevie Ray Vaughan.

That gets to the heart of it for me: the gallery of conventional guitar heroes, broadly assessed at that. No Johnny Thunders, no John McGeoch, no Quine, no Michael Karoli, no Sonic Smith, no Bryan Gregory, no D. Boon, or any other people who died within the outsider strain as I see it. No T-Bone Walker, no Guitar Slim, no Ike Turner, no Lou Reed, no Verlaine, none of the dots Robert Palmer connected in his essay "The Church of the Sonic Guitar," the closest thing to a precursor to this book, which traced the weed of distortion from its roots in early rock to "the punk art wing." For present purposes, then, let Millard's summary stand as our definition of the mainstream trajectory. It is what it is.

Millard also supplied a list of essential traits for guitar heroism. They're worth reviewing if only to see how the alternative tradition counters them:

> There must be virtuosity, certainly, but skill at playing the guitar is not the only qualification. There is a heroic dimension . . . the guitar hero emerged in the 1960s when electric guitar technology merged with an English interpretation of African American blues traditions and some timeless Western ideas of masculinity.

Virtuosity we've covered—great if you've got it, nothing wrong with using a calculator. For most of our alternists, if you go back to Malcolm Gladwell's notion that it takes ten thousand hours to master a skill, that time was split between experimenting with other instruments, working in other fields, and just generally straining against the idea that it was all one could do to practice scales over and over, especially since the alternative guitarists tended to reject the solo, which is where those scales most directly applied. ("The blues tradition established the importance of the solo player," Millard added.) As opposed to solos these players favor textures, parts: Television and Sonic Youth depend on the interplay between two guitars, with neither being the "lead," while Johnny Marr and Bob Mould cherish rhythm playing above all else. Moving on, Millard's notion of the "heroic dimension" doesn't translate, either, in part because the alternative sphere is more scene-oriented, econo-jamming, to the degree that someone like Robert Quine can start out as merely an unabashed fan of the Velvet Underground and end up playing with its principal malcontent, Lou Reed. ("Fame-wise, they were hardly on a Stones/Beatles level," Quine told the *I-94 Bar*. "That's unfortunate, but it made it not so difficult to meet them, hang around with them.") Finally, there's the idea that even the most "heroic" of indie guitarists, J Mascis, would invariably follow his Hendrixian outbursts with pleading, self-doubting vocals only marginally more masculine than Lou Barlow in full wool. It was always a part of Mascis's "power" that undercutting the usual guitar-god swagger was this constant unease.

This brings us to what is likely the most fundamental element of the mainstream guitar tradition: the blues, a source that led many a player to reliable pentatonic boxes and shuffle structures, to an aesthetic of "tasteful" chops, to images of the individual genius, recurring lyrical motifs, and, for many British and American appropriators, problems with authenticity. An avoidance of the blues is likely the most tangible way the alternists depart from mainstream rock convention. That's not to say that they never touched on them (our exemplar Quine evoked blues elements as much as anyone), but on the harsh side, Johnny Marr told *Guitarist* that the blues is "the sound of people not thinking, at best." Ultimately, I think Michael Rother speaks for the lot of these alternative guitarists when he explains in his interview that this break was simply necessary to staking out a new path. "The first step was to avoid all the elements of rock and pop music, like playing blues notes, playing solos," Rother says of his own development. "Even the idea of being a virtuoso, that was something I wanted to leave behind." Free jazz and minimalism (and classical, in Rother's case) helped provide a vocabulary for these alternists that wasn't blues-based, and because those forms weren't guitar-based either, anything borrowed from them involved an element of creative transposition. "If you're trying to play jazz in the language of jazz, it's a bad thing if you don't know it," says Zoot Horn Rollo. "If you're inspired by jazz but you're not using that language, it's pretty cool because it's not so cliché-laden. And that's what we did." Of course, Zoot and Captain Beefheart's Magic Band are the closest thing in this tradition to a blues outfit—you could say they were a blues band, albeit the rarest of cutting-edge ones—but as Zoot puts it, they were ultimately "a bigger amalgam" of styles and attitudes. Now a guitar teacher, he asks his students, "Do you want to learn the clichés of the blues language, or do you want to be anti-cliché and have your own voice? You've got to choose." That seems the essential question.

All of these are ways the so-called alternative lineage departs from the so-called mainstream one: solo becomes part; lead becomes rhythm; hero becomes deserter; riff turns to drone; twelve-bar becomes twelve-tone; the measuring stick for "talent" is splintered; even the usual Gibson Les Paul with its beefy humbuckers is ditched for the offset Fender Jazzmaster and Jaguar along with their twangy siblings, the Telecaster and Strat. But the truest marks of this alternative strain are often slipperier, entwined with the gestures of the mainstream tradition even as they subvert them. In *Ranters & Crowd Pleasers*, Greil Marcus looked at Public Image Ltd. and found that "PiL's sound is at once the rejection of a form and an attempt to follow certain implications hidden within that form to their necessary conclusions. PiL's music may contradict rock 'n' roll as it is generally understood, but without rock 'n' roll it would make no sense whatsoever, and it makes a great deal of sense." This helps explain why if you listen to an old live tape of the Velvet Underground you hear folk rock songs and long free-form jams with extended guitar meanderings; in some ways, the Velvets weren't that different from other bands of their day after all. Perhaps you will detect some difference, though, in the lurid content of "Heroin" or the flatline tone of "Venus in Furs" or the never-quite-grooving form of "Sister Ray"—just enough that, as with the Stooges and garage rock, a shift is made into something else.

Terms such as "mainstream" and "alternative" are especially hard to capture given that, on top of their subjective nature, they only have meaning in opposition to each other. I can try to define "mainstream" as music that does not challenge the existing codes—be they stylistic, aesthetic, or even political—music that, often because of this, can be embraced by a mass audience. I can try to define "alternative" as music that does challenge such codes and that, often because of this, confuses or provokes a mass audience. The difference between an alternative guitarist and a mainstream one can be like that between a hit song and an outtake—unmistakable on the one hand yet untraceable on the other. But if I had to boil this distinction down to one characteristic, it would be the alternative tradition's palpable sense of *questioning* and *resisting*, especially how the guitarist situates himself or herself in relation to the image of the hero, codes such as the blues, and the expectations of the rock audience.

As I suggest above, my purpose here is not to bury one group but to praise another. But if there is a problem with mainstream rock and the culture it's connected to, it's not that they situate one type of music as good. Rather, it's that the standards they set suggest that other types of music—the work documented in this book, for example—are *bad*. And that by extension the life such music reflects, a world of alternative tastes, ideas, and behaviors, is unworthy. It's like what Quine said about the Velvet Underground, thinking they were terrible at first; that's the insidious part, that even a musical mind like his could get so turned around he didn't recognize cold New York love at first sight. Sure, it makes a good story, the notion that this underground loner didn't break through until his mid-thirties, but it's not as charming when you really think about how he struggled through all those years, not just as a musician but, I suspect, as a human being. (Quine was never an upbeat soul, and heartbroken by the death of his wife, he committed suicide in 2004.) I recall that as a kid I was permanently scarred by seeing Iggy Pop on TV, realizing at the age of eight how sad and broken-down I already was. As I watched him squirm out of a cheap suit like some junkie Houdini, I wondered, "Wow, all these walls I see, this guy actually broke through them . . . but will I?" In Iggy I was thrilled to find someone going against the grain, who seemed to perceive the grain the same as I did. But still, to my young mind he seemed intentionally bad—he seemed *wrong*—and I didn't have the nerve to see the purpose in that.

So many times over the years I thought of my anecdotal tale as one of mislocation—being in the wrong place at the wrong time, being exposed to the right things under the wrong circumstances and the wrong ones too often. Yet that is the story most rock listeners have, because outside of a relatively small circle, the musicians in this book are still known only in that shadowy manner, as disconnected, disenfranchised outliers who don't quite fit into the usual lineup of guitar gods, who may come across as "weird" or "not good enough," "missing something" or "not ambitious" or, like Iggy once seemed to me, "bad." This is the most redeeming thing I can say about lumping together this book's free-ranging interviewees: that by doing so it's easier to see how they were not failed, flawed, wannabe insiders, but in fact effective outsiders who carried on their own sophisticated call and response. Despite their unquestionable ability to operate independently, they did in fact constitute a counter-tradition of rock guitar, one that still lurks in the shadows of the popular heroic pantheon, with its own language and sensibility.

Some readers might wonder why there's been so much talk in this introduction about *duende* and free jazz when we could've been obsessing over Fender Twins and Big Muffs. While it's true that gear choices help distinguish this group, it's things like being on a search that really unite them. The goal of presenting an innovative sonic concept, the resolve of being lifers in this underground conspiracy, these also make our guitarists what they are. When someone ties these things together, the results can be powerful: a personal vision, presented in high-risk fashion, driven not by anger or resignation but by the tension of one turning into the other. The best music these guitarists make captures this transformation, and in the *very* best both the personal and the aesthetic metamorphoses are fused. Of his experiments in making Public Image Ltd.'s landmark *Metal Box*, Keith Levene says herein:

> I wasn't sure if it was good or bollocks. I didn't even fucking know. I was thinking, "Should I go back into Eddie Van Halen mode or should I go back into Joe Walsh mode?" If I was thinking too much in a rehearsal I might start playing that stuff, but it just sounded so alien, and then I realized, "Wow, if that sounds alien then basically what's alien is the boat everyone's just got off. *That* sounds out of place." So I just went with my instincts and I dubbed myself. I subtracted and subtracted anything that was like Jimi Hendrix.

When someone walks you out on this tightrope, there's the excitement of looking at a piece of abstract art for the first time, realizing as you're trying to take in the craft that something is also happening to you emotionally. It's not just formal and it's not only expressive—it's both at once. This is the difference between the way an innovator reaches you and the way a traditionalist does, the difference between someone looking ahead and someone looking back. "Really I was just treading out into this world of mine which was very difficult to access," Levene confesses. When the interviewees reach that point, they surpass what Miles Davis called great musicians and become something even richer: true artists in the medium of guitar-based rock.

When I think back, I realize that old Iggy Pop performance I saw really was bad. It was a dark period in his career; he was lip-synching, I think; there was a forgettable touring band behind him; it was kind of weak all around. But as Iggy told an alarmed Dutch TV reporter around that time, "For something like this, I wouldn't rehearse. . . . I just come in and do it. And sometimes it's fun. I think if it's tense it's maybe because I have to make it tense." This reflects the most primary of all powers for artists truly working from the outside in, that being the force of simple "documentation," as Lydia Lunch calls it in her interview. Irrespective of what song is being played or how "on" the performer is that night, the simple act of hitting Record does a lot of the work itself—provided that the subject is searching hard enough, moving fast enough, to make any snapshot interesting. As Lydia says:

> Part of my sadism onstage, especially in spoken word, is when I know I've just riffed on a passage, on a sentence, on five sentences in a row, and one image is sticking out, and I don't know which one but there's one image that's sticking in your mind and you're stuck there, and I'm going forward, and that's where I get off. You know? *That's where I get off.*

So, then, the artist's pleasure comes in staying a step ahead of an audience that might not keep showing up otherwise, for they are on their own search for performers who can keep provoking them. To me that makes a certain sense, as it makes sense that Ms. Lunch would have the last word in all this because . . . well, I think people like her ultimately will have the last word. Some artists strive for success, others for survival. Some guitarists long to be heroes, others only to smuggle something illicit across the border. Like her collaborators Robert Quine, Rowland S. Howard, and Lee Ranaldo, Lydia Lunch belongs to a particular subset for whom survival is success, who become antiheroes through their virtuoso visions.

①

. . . IF YOU DUG IT

LENNY KAYE

PHOTO BY ARIEL HAMEON; COURTESY OF THE PHOTOGRAPHER

"From the other end of the hallway a rhythm was generatin' . . ." —Patti Smith

"This is the story of a transition period in American rock and roll, of a changeling era," Lenny Kaye wrote, "only noticeable in retrospect by the vast series of innovations it would eventually spawn." Of course, this was in the liner notes to *Nuggets*, his 1972 collection of garage rock "artyfacts." With this double-album time capsule, Kaye put his finger on a pulse that had been beating across the tail-finned, Farfisa-meets-fuzz provinces, a wooly resistance bashed out in anthems such as the Standells' "Dirty Water" and 13th Floor Elevators' "You're Gonna Miss Me."

If *Nuggets* was "the original sin" of rock, as Kaye once claimed to *Rolling Stone*, its tenets were the Ten Commandments: thou shalt not indulge in lyrical poesy; thou shalt not covet thy neighbor's chops; thou shalt hold no chord progression higher than the I-IV-V. The impact of *Nuggets* on the technique-challenged punks was obvious, yet even bands like the brainy Television returned to its ethos, the deep structures of three minutes by two chords or two minutes by three chords. Of this, Lenny Kaye as guitarist of the Patti Smith Group was a perfect example: a master of the short-attention blast who, on the flip side, specialized in sound fields that drifted into free verse.

Born in 1946 in New York City, Lenny Kaye got a taste of garage life in the 1960s playing the New Jersey frat circuit. As "Link Cromwell" he recorded a minor hit in 1966, but after finishing a history degree at Rutgers he headed back to the city to pursue another interest, rock writing. Just as he would find himself within the CBGB whirlwind a few years later, Kaye mixed during the early 1970s with Sandy Pearlman, Richard Meltzer, all the great new-journalism shit-slingers, matching them for merit if not audacity. "My role as a critic was more as a cheerleader," he laughs. "I look at my *Rolling Stone* reviews and I'm just wavin' the flag for the J. Geils Band." Success as a journalist was attainable for Kaye, but he never completely let go of his other aspirations. "One reason I became a writer was because I couldn't put together a band that could reflect my beliefs," he said outside CBGB in 1979. "When Patti and I joined forces, it was the beginning of a way to fulfill whatever musical aims I had."

Part Bowery poet, playwriting crow, and friend of Mapplethorpe, the equally multitasking Smith was a logical counterpart for Kaye. The duo first got together for a reading in February 1971: as Patti rapped, "This readin' is dedicated to *crime*," Kaye scrubbed along on repetitive guitar, keeping things simple but hitting all the right notes. The audience received them as a new kind of cabaret/rock hybrid, but it would be more than two years before their second gig. Slowly they brought in pianist Richard Sohl, drummer Jay Dee Daugherty, and bassist/guitarist Ivan Kral—"It happened on such a gradual basis that we didn't realize that we had a band until we actually had a band," Kaye said in 1979. "Which, in retrospect, was where we were aiming at, unconsciously." By June 1974 the band that would become the Patti Smith Group took along Tom Verlaine as they recorded their first single, "Hey Joe"/"Piss Factory," which was packed with the ideas they'd explore over four albums beginning with 1975's masterpiece *Horses*. With their piano, their poetry, their freehand guitar, equal parts chamber whisper and rave-up, songs like "Land" reflected the band's unusual evolution: rock 'n' roll, yes, but tested part by part, rebuilt and renewed as "Rock'n'Rimbaud."

For much of the 1980s and '90s, Patti focused on family life in Detroit with guitarist Fred "Sonic" Smith of the MC5. Lenny busied himself by playing (gigs with Jim Carroll and 1984's solo *I've Got a Right*), writing (innumerable articles, books including the coauthored *Waylon* with Jennings in 1996), and producing (artists including Suzanne Vega and Soul Asylum), striking a balance he's maintained since. Patti returned with 1988's *Dream of Life* with Sonic on guitar, and then, after his regrettable passing in 1994, she was back with Lenny as of 1996's *Gone Again*. Billed as Patti and Friends, the band picked up where they had left off, trolling the cutout bins of rock history—which by then included their own nuggets, such as the classic "Rock n Roll Nigger."

DAVID TODD: I wanted to ask about cover songs, since the Patti Smith Group has always done them and recently did a whole album of them (*Twelve*, 2007). Was there anything in particular behind your choices, whether it was the songs you picked or the reasons you played so many over the years?

LENNY KAYE: Well, especially early, a lot of stuff was part of these kind of segues: Patti would do a poem and then we would have a [cover] song illustrate it. I believe "Gloria" started out like that. We had bought a bass from Richard Hell for forty dollars, a little Danelectro, in thoughts of maybe she would play a note on it when we hit the E chord, you know. We played that at the start of her poem "Oath," which goes "Christ died for somebody's sins but not mine." So then from there it was, "Let's do 'Gloria,' that will be fun." "In excelsis deo," you know what I mean? We put the two together. Sometimes [with cover songs], especially the ones that have a circular chordal pattern that just keeps repeating, we would use them as fields and see where they went. "Land of a Thousand Dances," for instance. Once we got past the song and started cycling the chords, Patti would improvise over it and it would grow into what it would grow into.

Sometimes you wind up spinning the songs so that they become yours. A lot of them on the *Twelve* album, especially Jimi Hendrix's "Are You Experienced?," have grown. You start expanding upon them and find a whole new way of approaching them. Then they become a space in the same way that John Coltrane would use "My Favorite Things."

DT: I heard one of your live versions of "Are You Experienced?" and halfway through I forgot what it was. The Nirvana song too.

LK: Oh yeah. Actually, "Smells Like Teen Spirit," that one Patti wanted to approach really differently, kind of as an acoustic hoedown. When we recorded it, we got a bunch of banjo players and mandolin players and just set 'em up in Electric Lady [Studios] and said, "Let's see what happens."

Sometimes we just do 'em for a night. Usually when we play our Bowery [Ballroom] shows we do a special [cover], you know. We've done "Kashmir"—I mean, we've done 150 to 200 covers over our life according to one of the fan sites. The other night at the Tibet House benefit, because it was the fiftieth anniversary of the passing of Buddy Holly and Ritchie Valens and Big Bopper, we did a little medley and I got to sing, "Hello, baby, this is the Big Bopper speaking." And to think that I was a twelve-year-old kid living in Brooklyn when I heard the news on the radio, and fifty years later I'm singing the songs at Carnegie Hall. I thought, "That's a nice little circle completed."

DT: Were those '50s rockers as important to you as the doo-wop of that time?

LK: I grew up to it, you know. I was young enough, or old enough depending on how you look at it, to hear Little Richard's "Tutti Frutti" as the first song I remember hearing on the radio. I always think of my life as growing up with rock 'n' roll, and it was. I was able to mirror all the changes. When the music went into its glorious adolescence in the mid-'60s, I was a glorious adolescent. And when it became self-conscious, not in a bad way necessarily but when I became aware of certain elements that needed to be revived in the '70s, I—within the parameters of what they call now punk rock—was old enough to have a memory of what was and what could be. And now that the music is in its baroque period, I feel like I'm pretty similar.

DT: I was thinking about that before, that not many people who heard the music of the '50s and experienced the '60s firsthand would have made the transition into the punk era.

LK: Well, I think you have to evolve musically. I mean, obviously you respond to the music of your youth the most. I still can put on a doo-wop record and be transported in a way that I don't know I would if I hadn't lived through that time. But the fact is that music is ever-evolving at a rapid rate. The difference between the texture and tools of sound that we have now and that we had in the '60s is remarkable, and yet the power of the song can transcend that. You know, it's nice to reinvent a song or to bring it into its future, but a great song is a great song. When I hear a great song on the radio, even if it's done by some wacky sixteen-year-old Disney artist, if it's got a good hook it's gonna pull me in.

DT: Is that always what you're looking for? I take it there are times you want something more experimental.

LK: My attraction with music is to something that tries to step outside the predictabilities of it. There are genres, blues for instance, that I find very formal, and I appreciate a great blues player, but what I look for is someone who takes it out of the *ordinaire*. You know, some people like to play covers and get all the moves in them correct. I like covers where you kind of learn the song and then interpret it through your own musicality. I'll learn the chords for most of our covers, but the guitar lick, unless it's a total classic, I'll just put in my own string theory.

You know, I don't like musics that are pure. I like when they mongrelize. To me it's more fun to take a jazz thing and take a punk rock thing and spin 'em together; that's in a sense what we were always doing with Patti. And we loved a classic three-minute single, we loved the hook, the sense of affirmation that comes with call and response, and yet we always wanted the chance to deconstruct that song so that it became pure noise. And I think if you look at our body of work, we have songs that are classic three-minute verse, verse, chorus, bridge, and we have songs that can go anywhere, like "Radio Ethiopia." And to have that kind of breadth is important to avoiding definition.

The best thing I ever learned was on the back of an album by a group called the Red Crayola in the '60s. There was a little quote that said "Definitions define limit," and I always remembered that, because I'm not a blues player and I'm not a jazz player and I'm not even a rock player in the sense that I can do those Chuck Berry licks. I like to grab from all of 'em, to have the freedom to do a beautiful '50s slow dance and then over the course of a song or two be atop the amplifier wrestling out feedback and going into the place where all musics become the same and you're not bound. To me the greatest parts of free jazz are where you've been released from any formal thing and you're just playing sound upon sound in that kind of mystical way.

I like surprise, and I like to be taken to someplace that I haven't been before. I like uniquity, if that is a word.

DT: Is that what you were looking for with *Nuggets*?

LK: I didn't really know what I was doing when I did the first *Nuggets*. I was just gathering a bunch of bands that seemed to fit conceptually. I could try to figure out how they fit, but in looking at it there are many things that probably wouldn't have gone on that album had I been more conceptually aware, and I think it would have made it a lesser record. Because what's really enchanting to me is that there's nothing generic about it. It's not just a fuzz tone, just a yowling lead singer. It's all kinds of musics; all the bands seem to be moving toward an open-endedness that I found exhilarating. And I think what makes that record unique is that I'm questing as much as the bands.

One of the things I like about '60s garage rock is that it doesn't fit into the definitions that we think of now as "garage" rock. That word didn't even exist. If you look at my original *Nuggets* album, the music is all over the place.

DT: Although it was a kind of oldies album, it seems like *Nuggets* came out when it was most needed.

LK: I think it did. If it had come out a few years earlier it would've seemed dated, and if it had come out later it would've seemed like it was riding a wave. Don't forget I was a rock writer, and these were concerns of rock writers at the time, who were a little more proactive than today. You know, you definitely had a point of view, like the *Cahiers du cinéma* critics like Jean-Luc Godard or [François] Truffaut. You wanted rock 'n' roll to respect certain virtues that you felt were important, especially as the music started getting further from those virtues. And as I said, we did like the expansion of things in rock, but then it started to get professionally dull, and you start realizing that some of the reasons why you were attracted to the music—its energy, its confrontational sensibility, its sense of empowerment and excitement—were getting lost. I think even the liner notes of *Nuggets* allude to it, that these virtues were being forgotten as people ascended a certain ladder of professionalism. You wanted the grass roots to keep regenerating, and there was a lot of chat in the rock press about the groups that you saluted—the Flamin' Groovies, the Stooges, the MC5—bands that you felt were continuing a certain high-energy, youthful tradition of noise and illumination. So I was aware of that, and in some sense I was waving a banner for these rock 'n' roll assets that people were forgetting about. And so *Nuggets* did come along at a good time.

The original album sold hardly any copies, but everybody who got one responded to the . . . I don't know what the word is . . . the sense that this was important. This was a way in which the music could [go]. And I think in some ways it did provide a certain sensibility that punk rock would go to.

DT: I have a couple more questions about *Nuggets* if you don't mind.

LK: I can talk about *Nuggets* forever. *Nuggets* is part of my greatest hits, and I'm very grateful because it helped define certain aspects of how I wanted my music to be.

DT: That was one question, how close you thought your music was to that lineage.

LK: Even though with Patti we're not really a garage band, there are elements that I like to keep alive. I like the sense of adventure, the sense of being a part of the stream of rock 'n' roll. I think that is a great privilege.

DT: On a musical level, were there riffs you picked up from the bands of the *Nuggets* era, a catalog of some kind?

LK: I guess it's more to me the catalog of songs that you could play than riffs, you know. I mean, if you know a few Chuck Berry licks and "Satisfaction" you would have them, but mostly I kinda strummed along to the songs and let them point the way. I can only speak for myself, but I was never good at learning riffs as opposed to interpreting them in a way that I could play them, so in a way I was forced to find my own path.

You know, there are things as a guitarist that I did well. I had a strong rhythm hand and in that sense appreciated someone like Pete Townshend. I could not really aspire to be Jeff Beck because that kind of facility, aside from being outside the ken of most humans, was not my thing. But I did like to see the music through my own eye, through what I could play and back up.

DT: When it comes to your playing, did you find your approach change when you started performing with Patti?

LK: Actually, it was right in my pocket when we started, because I wasn't a lead guitarist at all. Like I said, I was essentially a rhythm guitarist, so it was natural for me to just pump along behind her and ride her dynamics. I mean, even from our first reading, Patti had a very musical way of performing. She would almost sing her poems, so if you could find the chords to fit behind them they would become songs. And you just had to make sure she kept moving, and you would get louder when she would rise. We played a lot with dynamics, Richard [Sohl] and I. The possibilities we had were louder/softer/faster/slower, essentially, 'cause we were playing very simple chords and rotating progressions. And it suited my style at the time. I would learn more as the songs got more complex, but we were very much in synch with what I could play and what Patti required as a singer-slash-raconteur.

Patti and I had one other thing in our back pocket, which was the free-form sound of jazz. When we got into an improvisation we would start sharding the sound so it became less musical and more just sound. And as a guitarist I had feedback; I had the clattering of the reverb in the amp; I had the way the guitar could make sound that wasn't musical by scraping my pick along it. I had sound manipulation that was not specifically musical, though it could be regarded as that. And we would employ that as the songs became more abstract.

I think sometimes that because I was so haphazardly trained, it allowed me space to go in that direction. Because I'm not able to read music per se, or to take apart a chord and see all its substitutions, it forced me to find my own way, to create a style that is unique to me, which if it's somewhat limiting in some ways, it's also very expansive, because there are places I can go to that are not bound by a sense of what should be done. Sometimes it means I hit a really great clinker in the middle of trying to find something, and sometimes it leads me to a note that I would never have thought to place in any context and yet it's the exact right semitone.

DT: You're looking at me as if that doesn't make sense. I think it does.

LK: I don't know if it does, but you know . . . [laughs]

DT: How much have gear choices played into your work? Are you a gear person, so to speak?

LK: Well, I can be a geek as well as anybody. That's part of the fun of guitar playing. I can expound upon the beauty of the Magnatone for hours and spend time in vintage guitar shops. I like the subculture; I like the difference in guitars and the sense that they each have their own personalities.

DT: You tend toward the Stratocaster, right?

LK: Yeah. The Strat has a couple things that I like. One, I find its body shape to be very sensual. It's like the most beautiful of guitars, and it's a little bit lighter, and I like the sway bar action—I'm a big sway bar fan—so it's always seemed like home to me. I've tried Les Pauls and I had a small enjoyment of the SG family. I like the SG as a look; that's from the John Cipollina universe. But Strats seem to do it.

To be honest, there's a joke in the band that no matter what I pick up and what I put it through, I always sound like myself. I guess that's either good or bad, depending.

DT: Certainly that clean tone suits you.

LK: Yeah, I like a tone that's clean but has some roughage around it, you know.

DT: Articulated, too.

LK: I do have an articulated tone. I like to hear each string; I'm not one of the Marshall "blur" guys, you know. But I do like a kind of . . . I guess "cleanliness with a tail" would be a nice way of putting it.

You know, now I have a Strat I play live that just has the middle pickup. They've taken out the other two pickups since I never used them. I just have a volume knob and the middle pickup, and that's it. The Unicaster, we call it.

DT: The Unicaster?

LK: Yeah. They got a pick guard, they just cut out one middle slot, and it's just this one knob and the pickup. You know, even though it took me a while to get used to it visually, I must admit I don't really miss anything.

Actually, now that I don't have the extra pickups, sometimes I wish I could dial in something a little bit different, but the truth is, live, I never move from the middle pickup.

DT: Before we get too far away from it, I had one other question about *Nuggets*. I don't know if anyone can answer this, but I was wondering what you think makes a song like "Pushin' Too Hard," which seems to be right up there in your pantheon, so good. Is that something you think about?

LK: Well, I think about it all the time, especially since I spent a year singing "Pushin' Too Hard" during my little "giving Patti a rest" slot. I mean, they're great songs. They capture what I love about the two-and-a-half minute single, which is it gets to the point really quickly and it enervates you and leaves you remembering it. But, you know, you can dissect these things. Last night I was driving home and Sly and the Family Stone's "Dance to the Music" came on, and I hadn't heard it for a long time. So I listened for things that I don't normally listen to, and I was amazed at, once you start deconstructing it, the things in there, the little hooks like the guitar and the bass doing a similar lick at one point. And you don't realize it. The same thing with "Pushin' Too Hard": there's an electric piano solo in it that you don't think of as being garage rock, but it captures the spirit of the time. It just pumps. I mean, geez, we just played it and it's two chords, it's truly two chords, and it allows for a lot of elaboration.

DT: If you go from a *Nuggets*-era song to one that came after it, what do you think is the difference between, say, "Gloria" and "I Wanna Be Your Dog"?

LK: Not much. I mean, both of them are very immediate to play. "Gloria" is more celebratory. "I Wanna Be Your Dog" is perhaps more ironic, especially with that line "I'll lay right down in my favorite place." That's totally great. But they're extremely accessible. You know, I always call "Gloria" the national anthem of punk rock, because anytime I'm asked to sit in I can say, "Well, let's play 'Gloria'—E, D, and A." And whatever beat the drummer comes up with and whatever bass part, we can play it. To me, "Gloria" is the greatest of 'em all, and it has that spelling thing ["G-L-O-R-I-A"]. It's a great crowd sing-alonger. It's got a great sense of release, and when it hunkers down on those chords, you can do anything. You can take a solo; you can spout out about the night. It just lends itself to everything. And it's almost the same chords as "Land." For us, those two are like our bookends of the *Horses* album.

   "I Wanna Be Your Dog," that's another one that is just so simple, and it's not that easy to write a simple song. The Ramones certainly did it—"I Wanna Be Sedated" or "Beat on the Brat." And like the songs on *Nuggets*, everybody knows them. It's amazing. It's so ironic that all the Ramones are not here to enjoy this, because they would be headlining stadiums now. It's the final irony of punk rock.

I think a lot of the bands that we're talking about were essentially underground bands, you know. The Stooges were an underground band; they were popular but only among a certain cognoscenti of people who believed in a heightened version of rock 'n' roll. And I remember when the Ramones first went out and opened for Johnny Winter at some place in Connecticut, leaving the hive of CBGB, they were bottled off the stage. Or Suicide, another [underground group]. These were all very unique worlds that didn't seem to fit.

DT: Is there a line you can draw between the bands that were *Nuggets*-era and the ones that were underground or proto-punk?

LK: I don't know. I mean, if the last cut on *Nuggets* was from 1968 and the Stooges came out in 1969, the Stooges weren't influenced by those bands—they were the evolvement of them. Especially at a time when the music seemed to split: some of the *Nuggets*-era groups would go off into the long improvs, the rock as art, the jazz and classical influx that became popular. The Stooges almost went backwards. It's like if you have garage rock standing center, the Stooges went left when most of the music went right, and so there was a split. And you could make cases for either direction. I love the Grateful Dead or Quicksilver Messenger Service, and when they would go on a twenty-minute excursion, I'd be there. But sometimes you want something short and sharp, and that's the other thing. It's like the New York Dolls going to see bands at Madison Square Garden and wishing the drum solo could be over, wanting to get things back to how they were. These are the tensions within the music, how complex you make it or how simple you make it.

I think you need all of these different ways in which to do it. But sometimes you just want to go, *pfft*, "Let's just make a statement like *this*," you know? And with the Stooges, at a time when [other] music was becoming weighty, you hear something elemental—that's the word I always use with them, *elemental*, like, "Let's bring it down to just what it is"—and parse it through not this hippie sense of infinite love but the reality of most people's trailer-park lives.

You could feel that there needed to be a reaction to all these poeti-cal garlands of lyrics that were being proffered at that time. I think the Stooges just took out all the big words, and I think the music needed it, and the Stooges did it in a way that another group that might have wanted to couldn't, because they had in Iggy someone who could enact that on stage. In Ron [Asheton] you had someone who would enact that with his guitar. I mean, it's amazing to me, listening to those records, just how central Ron's guitar accessorizing is for Iggy. There was definitely a sense of mental edgi-ness that the Stooges embraced.

And how conscious was it? I don't know how conscious anybody is of what they do. We didn't sit down with Patti to say, "Well, we're going to mold poetry and rock," we just went into the rehearsal room and jammed out on stuff and watched it grow live. We would get a series of chords and as we played 'em live, we would hit moments where we'd make a move, and the next time we played [those chords] we'd make the same move, and then the song would kind of arrange itself in a weird way. Especially something like "Free Money," we all would interact through improvisation, and in remem-bering that improvisation it became part of the arrangement.

DT: What about when you got to something like your own "Rock n Roll Nig-ger"? That's pretty "Gloria"-esque in musical terms, isn't it?

LK: Same chords. [*laughs*] You know, those great three chords.

DT: To me, that's one where the lyrics are even further down that line from "Gloria" to "I Wanna Be Your Dog," but the music still has an elemental feel to it.

LK: It's totally like that. I know that there are moves in it from "Highway Star" [by] Deep Purple, and "Paranoid" by Black Sabbath—it's got some of the twitch of that. But, I mean, same chords. You could go from "Gloria" to "Land" to it. In fact, sometimes we do.

DT: Do you think with "Rock n Roll Nigger" you made another crossover from garage to proto-punk to something else?

LK: Oh yeah. That's our punk rock song. It's a hardcore song, and we meant for it to wave a flag and to make a point that art must be redefined. That's what that song is about. And perhaps placing it in a racial context is some-what insensitive and somewhat daring and somewhat shocking in the way that punk rock is supposed to be. But I've been proud to sing it all over the world. And defend it. Because that word does have very barbed connotations.

But you know, "Rock n Roll Nigger" was another one that grew like topseed, truly like topseed out of improvisation, because it used to be just a little phrase that we would stick in the middle of "Radio Ethiopia," and then it became a song and developed its parts and its little outside section. But we didn't sit around and plan it; I can't tell you just how unconscious the process was when we started working on it.

DT: It's interesting how important intuition is to you when you're also such a historian.

LK: I'm a big fan of intuition because that to me is what my strength is. I'm not the greatest technician and I certainly have holes in my ideas of music theory. Sometimes it takes me a long time to figure out how to do something very simple, and when I want to translate what I hear in my head, I have to sit down and count the frets and . . . whatever my process is. But my great strength as a musician has been to feel the music in my insides, to be able to move it from intuition onto the neck, which is something that's surprising for someone who's also a writer and likes the side of the brain that is analytical and intellectual. A lot of writers—and I don't say this against any of my fellow writers, but when they make music there's a self-consciousness to it, and my great strength, and I don't know how I do it, has been the ability to short-circuit that. When I play music, I don't approach it analytically. I can feel it. That's what melds Patti and me together, or when I play with anybody—that I'm not coming from thinking about it, I'm coming from feeling it.

DT: You've said it takes a long time to learn how to play the guitar, that it's not necessarily a matter of training but of gradually learning. I was wondering, after forty-five years, where do you feel like you stand as a guitarist now?

LK: You know, it's funny—every time you feel like you've gotten as accomplished as you're gonna get, I find there is a leap ahead. In the mid-'90s when Patti came back, I realized that instead of just kind of plateauing and maybe learning a new lick or a new chord every now and then, I was suddenly starting to see the fretboard in an entirely new set of relationships, and I was not only getting better but getting markedly better, not only my awareness but also my ability to play what I heard. My confidence was similarly moving up, and now I find that I can go into situations with the weight of my years of playing and feel like I fit, you know. I can do what it is I do.

A few months ago I played at a Les Paul tribute at the [Rock and Roll] Hall of Fame with virtuoso guitar players like James Burton and Lonnie Mack, Dennis Coffey, Duane Eddy. And I felt like, "This is who I am, this is what I do," and I put myself in that situation and I just let it fly. I figured, "I'm not them, but hey, they're not me," and that's a great feeling of accomplishment. And I know that whenever I go out I can play something that comes from me, I feel like I have these years to use as a kind of emotional support to do what it is I do, and I feel comfortable with who I am as a musician.

DT: You have every reason to be confident, but still, that Les Paul gig sounds daunting.

LK: [*laughs*] At the end of that thing I was standing next to one of the guitar players from the Ventures—the *Ventures*—and there are like twenty guitarists lined up and everyone was playing [a different] version of the lick, and I'm thinking, "Well, what the hell am I doing?" So I just played almost like a horn thing, I'm going "*bop bop, bop bop*," and the guy from the Ventures looks over at me and starts playing something; I'd go "*bop, bop*" and he'd go "*adooom, doom, doom*," and we'd get into a little horn section thing, and I thought, "Yeah, the thing about guitar is that the simplest things can be the best things." You listen to what Steve Cropper is playing on Stax records— these are not hard licks, he's just putting 'em in the perfect place, and that's something I always remember. Sure, there are guys who can go out there and play the most incredible tapestries of soloings, but sometimes in the studio what you need is just the right *snick* over the snare drum and maybe a little *wooohooo* and then, you know, you're the genius.

Sometimes I think that combination of not just showing off your knowledge but having the knowledge and being able to slide around it is a good thing. Because, like I said, I'm not a revivalist. I'm not interested in purity or the great garage thing. I like music with feeling. And if I feel it, you know, it will infuse anything.

DT: I can see why there are times you want to put that feeling first, as opposed to the analytical, writer side of your approach, but are there other times when you don't want to keep them apart?

LK: You know, all of these things feed into who you are as a multipersonality. If you look at anybody who has had a lifetime career . . . I went with Patti to see an exhibit of the artist Cy Twombly in Berlin a few years ago. Here's a guy who's been doing his art for sixty, seventy years, and you notice that there's a period of five or ten years in his early life, then there's nothing, then he comes back and there's a different style happening. Then there's nothing, then he comes back and there's a style that's different but evocative of his early work. And I think as an artist you just can't keep doing the same thing. I love the fact that when I feel tapped out musically I can go downstairs and write for two or three months and move my writing along and then come back to the music and forget some of the habits that I'd gotten myself into and see the fretboard in a different way. I've renewed myself. And I think that's important if you're going to be in this for life.

I'm glad that with Patti we didn't have some huge success and I spent the rest of my life trying to recreate it at state fairs. I like the fact that I'm spread over several mediums, because there's always something rising when something else is falling. It keeps you moving forward, and that's really what it's about.

I feel that you do the work that's in front of you, and hopefully there's good work in front of you and you enjoy it, and my whole raison d'être is to continue. I have a survivalist instinct and I've done every conceivable job in the music business, and I can find joy in writing reviews or playing pedal steel with the Lonesome Prairie Dogs or playing with Patti at a festival for fifty thousand people, because to me it's all an expression of one's creative instincts. And if you can spend your life in those creative instincts and keep on understanding yourself through the mirror of your art, you're having a good life.

THE INDIVIDUALIST

RICHARD THOMPSON

PHOTO BY RON SLEZNAK; COURTESY OF BEESWEB

"All music is a knife-edge!" —Richard Thompson

At first, British folk rock virtuoso Richard Thompson seemed an unlikely choice to compose the soundtrack for *Grizzly Man*, a 2005 documentary by film fiend Werner Herzog. Sure, Thompson (born in London, 1949) had been reliably brilliant for about forty years by that point as a guitar player and singer-songwriter, so the safe guess would've been that he could do anything. But there was always something eminently *sane* about him, something too down-to-earth for the pop market, much less the maddest of New German auteurs. When Herzog attacked him for coming in a half-note behind the splice, I wondered whether Thompson would pull off his *Henry the Human Fly* mask and respond or simply chuckle it off, step aside for a few moments of Islamic prayer, then stun with another air, jig, or reel.

Watching *In the Edges*, a doc-within-a-doc on the scoring session, I was relieved to find Herzog's and Thompson's parallel paths to the extreme merging—all ego meeting no ego, outside the realm of medium ego where inspiration dies. When Herzog finally launches into one of his legendary skin-thinnings—"It's too melodious," he Bavariates; "this is the law of the Earth!"—Thompson barely shoots him a glance. He simply gazes forward and improvises with disturbing grace, while Herzog comes to the conclusion that this is as good as it gets. At this point the genius of Herzog's casting hit me, because Thompson is no different than the other visionaries the director has been chasing with his camera all along. Like Fitzcarraldo, Thompson has been dragging his ship across dry land ever since he joined Fairport Convention in 1967 at the stutter-shy age of eighteen. Having gone decades without mainstream recognition, he has the stamina of the most fervent antihero, except instead of frothing mania he's possessed by a quiet irreproachability. "At some point, I figured that I had no talent as a commercial artist, so there was no point trying," Thompson admits. "That's very liberating."

Certainly, there appears much to be gained from a proper overview of Thompson's career, which includes recording five albums with Fairport Convention (late 1960s) and one solo (1972), before hooking up with then-wife Linda for six (1974–82), then embarking on a sustained solo period (1983–present), performing both alone and as the leader of bands big and small. On the other hand, a list of details may not bring the uninitiated any closer to who the real Richard Thompson is. For some, he's the folkie who visits Fairport's annual Cropredy Festival to run through singalongs of "Meet on the Ledge," the first of his many great downers. For some he's the lead player who extends bitters like "Calvary Cross" into ten-minute meditations on electricity. He's half of Loud & Rich, a fourth of French Frith

Kaiser Thompson, the fingerstyle master of seemingly every alternate tuning ever documented in the British Isles. He's the lyricist who pounds out casually genius couplets like "Did they run their fingers up and down your shabby dress? / Did they find some tender moment there in your caress?"

All of this can't tell you as much as one moment of sustain in the "Main Title" of *Grizzly Man* alone. Though not one of Thompson's recognized major works, this instrumental has to be among his most revelatory. Freed from his usual story-driven song, what's left of Thompson is pure, riveting guitarism: snarling and soaring on his aqua Ferrington over a slow shuffle, he digs deep with string bends, capturing the full vistas of Herzog's imagery: the rock faces, the ice caps and the silvertips lumbering beneath them, the joy and isolation of a bear-baiting protagonist. "Scotland is about on the same latitude [as Alaska]," Thompson deflects when asked how he connected so well to the scenery. That captures his polite wit but undersells the command that emerges from his playing, the way his free-form lines seem worn into stone. Herzog puts it better when he tells his collaborator, "I needed the raw soul of you, and I think you understood what I meant."

I ask Thompson why "Main Title" was imported to *Grizzly Man* from his 1981 album *Strict Tempo!*, where it was the only new tune among a set of traditionals. "It was used as a temporary track during the editing process, and seemed to fit well," he replies. "As to why it fit—that's more difficult." But I'm not sure it is. I think the answer lies in the song's original title, "The Knife-Edge." Because works like this take us with him and let us see who he is when he's there. As a guitarist and writer, Thompson has immense capacity, as if Bob Dylan could have not only written "All Along the Watchtower" but also performed Jimi Hendrix's version of it himself. But when Thompson puts the song aside and simply plays, his virtuosity becomes an abstraction like that of the great experimenters.

DAVID TODD: I've heard you say that you "hate rock," but can you talk about how you felt about rock music when you were starting out, and perhaps how you feel now?

RICHARD THOMPSON: When I was starting out, rock was Buddy Holly and Elvis and Gene Vincent, and it was really a kind of folk music, close to its roots and fairly unpretentious . . . and then it was the '60s, melodic pop moving into experimentation . . . and then it was the '70s, when rock became Rock, and that's probably the strain of music I dislike, or if I like it, it's in spite of its pretentiousness, bombast, and self-importance. If I listen to rock now, it's usually the rootsier end of it.

DT: The Who seem to be a band you liked.

RT: The Who were a great club band, before they went "stadium." Pete [Townshend] was writing perfect three-minute pop songs, they had great visual ideas borrowed from pop art, and the destructive stuff happening, which came probably from similar ideas in classical music.

DT: That destructive stuff is often what I think of first with them, their performance style in general. Were you ever tempted to adopt a more aggressive presentation like that?

RT: I would never seek to copy the Who's style.

DT: Not that you'd copy them, but it seems like rock music has always had a confrontational side. Do you think that coming from the folk world you took that on at all?

RT: Rock is sometimes lyrically confrontational, and if you come from folk music it is sometimes musically confrontational. But in many senses that style became clichéd very quickly after the Who and Iron Butterfly and a few others had done it. It became ludicrous. The smart people were not leaning toward heavy metal after 1966.

DT: A lot of people, smart and not, were leaning toward the blues at that time. That seems like another problem area for you.

RT: Authenticity is a huge factor in music, and you hear so much bad white blues and soul. I always felt I could never play black music well enough, but that it was OK to be influenced by it, as long as I provided a strong base for my music rooted in my own tradition.

For me, the most interesting stuff to come out of the British blues boom was the original compositions. The Yardbirds playing "Mannish Boy" I think is pathetic, but I find "For Your Love" interesting and original, as it mixes ideas from Tin Pan Alley and European classical tradition with blues.

DT: More than just the music, you seem to have never become enchanted with the whole counterculture of the time.

RT: I could just never share the clichés. Woodstock seemed faintly ridiculous, *Easy Rider* absurdly dated even when new. I felt more affinity with the surrealists or John Cage.

If you're going to be a writer of any kind, you have to be alienated from your own generation, and from society as a whole, or you'll never have enough perspective. I try to be an independent thinker, and I encourage that in my kids—and of course independent thinkers find each other, sooner or later. I dressed a bit hippie in the '60s in order to meet girls, but inside I was pure alien.

DT: Did these aversions have much to do with your guitar style as it developed, or was that coming more from things you liked?

RT: You learn from your influences, and then try to find your own voice. I always thought it a good idea to listen and learn from other instruments just to bring some different ideas to the table. For me, there were a lot of pianists like Earl Hines, Mary Lou Williams, and McCoy Tyner, traditional players like Billy Pigg and John Doherty—Northumbrian pipes and fiddle, respectively—and horn players like Lester Young and Louis Armstrong. The idea is to find something new by trying to play something workable on another instrument but near impossible on your own. By pursuing that, sometimes you get to stretch a bit further.

It's a balancing act between treading the path less traveled and building your own recognizable style.

DT: I've asked a few other people what they thought of Hendrix, just as a barometer of where they were coming from. Hendrix actually sat in with Fairport Convention, but in general how did you relate to him?

RT: We mentioned authenticity, and there was something totally real about Jimi and his music that terrified other guitarists like Pete and Jeff [Beck] and Eric [Clapton]. No one since has embodied the music of the guitar in quite the same way, and no one has been as simultaneously melodic and dissonant. He was like a pop/blues Coltrane.

Music can be a path of personal or spiritual exploration, and some would say it has to be one or the other, or both. I'd see Hendrix and Coltrane going for much the same thing, but in seriously different musical worlds, and with greatly contrasting harmonic knowledge.

DT: Among guitarists, Django Reinhardt may have had the biggest impact on you. What's so compelling about his playing?

RT: Its essence is shifting and elusive, which is why it is so attractive. Its apparent virtues are virtuosity, melodic invention, phrasing, drive, swing, and a large "etcetera." Django moved the guitar forward from Eddy Lang and others; he was really the first great guitar soloist in jazz, who knocked down the door for others to follow. Django and Charlie Christian are the foundation for everything.

At the same time I love early jazz, I try to learn from all eras. I've always loved Coltrane and Ornette, and I've listened to Stockhausen, Schoenberg, and Stravinsky since I was at school. Most of the time, as a songwriter trying to communicate with an audience, the more melodic influences will be the most apparent.

DT: I assume that's where a lot of the folk music you heard growing up affected you, the Scottish and English forms. Especially in terms of songwriting elements . . .

RT: . . . verse structure, use of imagery, melody, symbolism, succinctness. A song like "Vincent Black Lightning" uses a whole bunch of elements learned from that tradition: the conversation between the protagonists that conveys most of the action, definitely the shape of the verses and meter, also the slightly archaic or "special" language that links it to other songs in the tradition. A Dylan song like "I Am a Lonesome Hobo" does the same thing, also with great economy of language.

DT: What was it about Scottish and English music that you wanted to revisit in Fairport Convention? Why was that so important?

RT: There was a gap in the tradition, as we saw it. That music was, for the most part, no longer being handed down the way it had been before the gramophone, TV, and cinema—the British do tend to pooh-pooh their own tradition, and treat it as "novelty." We wanted to restore its position closer to popular music, and then create a new popular music, as composers, based on that tradition—English, Irish, and Scottish.

At the same time, we wanted to play a form of music at which we could excel, and which would be ours. The power of all that is such that I continue in pretty much the same direction.

DT: What changes to that direction do you think you've made? I read that you decided to go solo because Fairport "got pigeonholed."

RT: I don't know what I was talking about [when I said that], but I do think that the music was becoming too pastoral in mood.

DT: You wanted to get away from that with *Henry the Human Fly* (1972)?

RT: It was more about inventing a language of contemporary song. Because I was entering such new ground, and there were so few rules, I needed to spend some time experimenting. *Henry* was just an exploration of the possibilities of the genre.

I felt I needed to do it alone, and the sound was driven by the songs, rather than by saying, "This has to be folk rock!" I was pulling songs out of the air, and using whatever was on hand to record and arrange them. Much the same could be said of the next album.

DT: In some ways, you have more genuine folk elements in your "folk rock" than others for whom the term has been used. I wondered if there were parts of the old traditions you noticed working better for rock audiences than others.

RT: You could say that the audience is more ready for the Celtic end of the tradition rather than the English end. Our modern taste also resists or possibly precludes some subject matter—we like it more urban, less pastoral, are probably less preoccupied with the supernatural, and our attitude to the love song has become more cynical.

   A ballad is a story song, and traditionally it used a lot of verses, but in olden times people had fewer distractions and could sit for an hour to hear a tale about Robin Hood's heroics. People still seem to be able to absorb the ballad form—my two most requested songs are ballads, and many rap songs and Jamaican rap songs are telling stories in much the same way. In modern popular music, you hear three-verse ballads told in a more cinematic way: first-person narrative, jumping right into the middle of the action with no preamble, and jumping out again before the end [of the storyline], really just describing a few events, and leaving the imagination of the audience to fill in the rest.

DT: The storytelling aspect of the ballad, that reminds me of something you said about having the rule "complex lyric, simple tune; complex tune, simple lyric." Why is that so important?

RT: Otherwise respectable musicians sometimes think they need to set Shakespeare's sonnets to music, or some equally pretentious quest, and the results are usually a disaster. That's what can happen when complex meets complex. A band like Squeeze manages to get away with a fair degree of complexity on both sides, and I'm not quite sure how they do that. For my taste, Joni Mitchell sometimes crosses that line. When Dylan is singing about "electricity howling through her cheekbones," he is generally whining along on one note.

DT: Speaking of the Bard—Shakespeare or Dylan—you're in the contingent who suspect that "William Shakespeare" was an alias for someone else. One argument for this is that he lacked the education to write about nobility and all the other things covered in the plays.

I was curious as to how you thought that might apply in the case of a songwriter. Is worldliness important or is it more of an innate ability—are Hank Williams and Leonard Cohen really that different?

RT: I think there is room for everything. Hank was a lover of poetry, and obviously educated himself along those lines. Lenny is a huge fan of Hank, and started out in a country band, as well as being academically trained. He knows how to keep a song simple, at least superficially. Somehow we pick up the bits and pieces we need along the way.

If one were to teach a songwriting course, one might set the polar opposites as examples: "Today, we listen to Hank Williams, and then we go away and write a simple, direct song, straight from the heart." Three chords only allowed. "Next day, we listen to Rodgers and Hart, Noel Coward, Gilbert and Sullivan, and we go away and write a sophisticated song, full of observations, cynicisms, world-weariness," what have you. Then you know how wide the playing field is, and you can pick your own patch to dig.

I've always been able to see the world through other people's eyes, but I don't think I got good as a writer until I was about forty and had a bit of experience of life. But, then, everyone's curve is different.

DT: Is writing in a more confessional way something you developed over the years?

RT: I'm not as confessional as Loudon [Wainwright, the other half of Loud & Rich], or Joni, or Lenny, but do it sometimes. I probably start more with fantasy—I sit down, for pleasure usually, and try to tell a story. In retrospect, the stories are always about me, to a greater or lesser extent. I'm always in there somewhere, if only as the moralist.

DT: "The moralist" is an interesting role to play. Wouldn't that involve judging somehow, though?

RT: Perhaps "moralist" is too strong. It's more laying out a landscape, allowing characters to act and interact, and then leaving the listener to make conclusions. The morality of the author is inevitably expressed, though, if only through a moral vacuum. I don't think anyone could write anything without [a sense of] morality—or lack of it, which is also a kind of morality—showing through somewhere, even on the lightest and fluffiest of pop songs.

DT: How do you connect emotionally when singing a ballad, or for that matter any type of song? Does the emotion come from what you're feeling in the moment or does it come from the lyrics, or does it shift?

RT: It has to be in the song first of all, although I've heard some singers pull amazing things from pretty flimsy material. And the performance has to be right for the song—overemoting is the worst thing you can do. You hear great R&B singers sing a Joni Mitchell song and get the emotion totally wrong.

They say of Shakespeare that it's all built in; all you have to do is deliver the lines and not bump into the furniture. Every song has an emotional core, and you have to try to locate that. With a David Bowie song that core is hard to find, and he would be a tough artist to cover. With a country song it's easy, and the trick is to not go overboard into maudlin territory. Sometimes singers find things in a song that the composer was unaware of—"My Funny Valentine" first appeared in a musical and was a shadow of the extraordinary song interpreted by Sinatra and Chet Baker. Sometimes a singer gets so much from a song that he or she "owns" it, and makes any other version redundant.

DT: When you were writing for your music-theater performance piece *Cabaret of Souls* (2009), did that involve another layer of distance?

RT: *Cabaret of Souls* called for a different, more theatrical style of writing than what I usually do. Each character had to be recognizable to the audience as a type, so I suppose there is less of "me" in these songs. I'm being more satirical, and looking for the audience to respond to familiar human traits and failings.

DT: Did you find yourself drawing from the musical world songwise? Brecht and Weill, maybe?

RT: The biggest influences were probably Brecht and Weill and Gilbert and Sullivan, with a strong influence from traditional mummers plays and passion plays. Probably the biggest influence was the British pantomime tradition, but musically *Cabaret of Souls* covers a lot of ground, from folk music to Stravinsky to twelve-tone.

DT: It's interesting that you mention all these sources, because from a distance you can appear to be more of a traditionalist. Like when you were playing with French Frith Kaiser Thompson, did you feel like the most naturalistic of the group?

RT: I was the most rootsy of the chaps, I suppose. But I have dissonant leanings.

DT: Do you mean that in a philosophical sense?

RT: No, a musical one. I express those influences in the music.

DT: Did playing with them allow you to get into those areas more openly?

RT: It was a broadening experience, and it did mean playing a whole bunch of things that would not have occurred to me on my own. "Killerman Gold Posse" would not have appeared on a record of mine. I used more guitar tones as well—at one point, Henry [Kaiser] and I are imitating each others' solo styles and sounds.

I don't know if I did fit in with them, but it was fun to try.

DT: Ultimately, you're able to integrate so much into your playing without calling attention to it. All the historical songs on your *1000 Years of Popular Music* (2003) seemed to fit right in.

RT: I think it's just that I have a playing style, and in dragging various forms of music to the guitar, it all ends up sounding like something of mine. A song like "So Ben Mi Ca Bon Tempo" is a guitar transcription of the score for four crumhorns. It happens to fit quite nicely at the bottom end of the guitar, otherwise I might have had to pick a different tune.

DT: That goes back to what you were saying about importing things from other instruments, I suppose. You did roughly the same thing with *Strict Tempo!*, didn't you?

RT: I was just looking to do some guitar versions of traditional songs. We were between labels, and rather than release a record of songs that might have compromised any upcoming deal, the idea of doing instrumentals was more of a tangent.

DT: The "traditional" part is what I find interesting. Some of those songs are from one tradition and some are from another. I'm not sure if the next guy would combine "Do It for My Sake" and "Rockin' in Rhythm."

RT: "Do it For My Sake" came from O'Neill's *Waifs and Strays of Gaelic Melody*. I remembered [Duke Ellington's] "Rockin' in Rhythm" from my dad's record collection.

DT: There you go. OK, one last question: I meant to ask more about the guitar, but instead we've focused on songwriting. Do you see any separation between those areas or are they both coming from the same place?

RT: It's all the same—the song is the focus for all activity.

③

DON'S SECRET

ZOOT HORN ROLLO (BILL HARKLEROAD)

The threshold question when it comes to Captain Beefheart and the Magic Band—at least from the guitar perspective—is how the music actually came about, how the Captain's whistlings were converted into melodic arrows that punctured the late 1960s as if fired by a subversive angeloid. That's because albums such as *Trout Mask Replica* (1969), arguably the most singular piece of pop resistance of the day, were composed of equal parts excruciating rehearsal and phoned-in accidents, half Beefheart insight and half grunt sweat. Now, it's hard to discredit the great Captain himself; born Don Van Vliet in 1941, the guy was forty years ahead of his time, could howl like a wolf in the moonlight, turned the blues into Noh theater, and played a great air trumpet. But as good as Van Vliet dreamed it up, he was beholden musically to the interpretations of band members like lanky guitarist Zoot Horn Rollo, born Bill Harkleroad in 1949. Over his five albums as Van Vliet's primary foil, Zoot hatched a new warped expressionism, an anti-jamming that became one of the bases of the alt-guitar tradition.

"I was definitely a street blues player before I joined the Beefheart band," Zoot told *Guitar* in 1995. "But almost everything changed." That happens when you're rehearsing sixteen hours a day under your boss's "kind whip," staring at your equally strung-out bandmates with hostage eyeballs. By the time they recorded *Trout Mask*, Zoot's Delta stylings were abstract and antagonistic, launching "Moonlight on Vermont" with acidic slide, pricking "Dali's Car" on strings that seemed unnaturally brittle. ("Often I was literally torturing the guitar with these metal fingerpicks," Zoot recalled in that same interview with Danny Eccleston. "I was aware of wanting my Telecaster or ES-330 to sound like, uh, shrapnel!") On the equally potent *Lick My Decals Off, Baby* (1970), his Telecaster swerves through a proto–math rock decathalon of riffs, spirals, and even grooves, riding hard strokes down melodic drainpipes. Like their angular precursors, *Lick*'s title track and "Doctor Dark" encapsulate the mix of hard bop, hard blues, and hard art only the Magic Band delivered.

"[Captain Beefheart] was a very creative force—but his creativity wasn't so clear cut as far as being very musical," Zoot reflected in an interview with Justin Sherrill. "It was more the mentality of a sculptor using sound and people as the tools. From there we had to turn it into music—something playable." In this authorship model, frontman and sideman were locked in mutual dependence, although as Zoot keenly notes, only one received credit. ("He took claim for every line that came out of my fingers," he said in *DISCoveries*.) Despite this tension, or perhaps because of it, the pairing led to inspired moments such as "When It Blows Its Stacks" (from 1972's *The Spotlight Kid*), wherein Zoot follows a lecherous vocal with an absolutely stinging solo, or "Big Eyed Beans from Venus" (*Clear Spot*, also 1972), in which Beefheart stops time for Zoot's legendary long lunar note. That is to say, when the Beefheart band was working, it was working, a fact that even Zoot, who can get grumpy on the subject, admits. "Good or bad," he conceded to *diskant*, "there is nothing like it."

Following the tame *Unconditionally Guaranteed* in 1974, Zoot and company finally quit en masse, leaving Van Vliet to replace them with

"Tragic Band" scabs. Not surprising, neither faction would be the same. The Captain had his moments musically but eventually retired to pursue a painting career, while Zoot and bandmates Rockette Morton and Ed Marimba released two albums in the mid-1970s, as Mallard. Zoot relocated to Oregon, where he worked as a guitar teacher, collaborated with drummer John "Drumbo" French, and published a memoir. Despite all the baggage, Bill Harkleroad has yet to forsake his alter-ego entirely. His lone solo album, *We Saw a Bozo Under the Sea* (2001), is a tasteful set of "sonic movies," mellower and less frantic than past work but unmistakably Zoot Horn Rollo.

DAVID TODD: What were you listening to before joining the Magic Band?

ZOOT HORN ROLLO: Being in L.A., I grew up listening to Wolfman Jack. I started with surf music, and then the vocal stuff started happening from England. Then the Beefheart band started playing, and they were doing blues stuff, so by '64 I became pretty strongly into the blues. Into the Beefheart band, I was getting jazzier, listening to Coltrane. So, basically, jazz and blues, and not Led Zeppelin or things like that.

DT: The Magic Band seemed to restrict their sources to blues and jazz.

ZHR: Very much so. We were listening to Albert Ayler and the later Coltrane years, Mingus, Pharoah Sanders, Ornette Coleman. That was the real schooling of the band for me. I was just a nineteen-year-old kid and I'd listened to a few things that were straight-ahead jazz, but I didn't have the understanding to get deep into it. And so a great part of the education was hearing Thelonious Monk, and Muddy Waters also—I put Muddy Waters in with that group because he was pretty sophisticated—and other blues guys like Son House, Robert Johnson, Bukka White.

DT: There are a lot of examples of how blues can be adapted into rock, but what about jazz?

ZHR: There were rhythmic things we did that were definitely out of the jazz language. Harmonically, no, and that's what made it interesting. If you're trying to play jazz in the language of jazz, it's a bad thing if you don't know it. If you're inspired by jazz but you're not using that language, it's pretty cool, because it's not so cliché-laden. And that's what we did.

DT: On top of technique, it seems like the band was more interested in a jazz profile than a rock style.

ZHR: Definitely not the rock bands. That was how I was before I even got there. And then as I got there it was even more reinforced. I mean, when you're listening to a band that was a blues band moving into more experimental stuff, and it's your favorite band and then you end up in it . . . right? My influence was the band itself before I got there. And they were much bluesier then, but there were elements of where they were going. Even in *Safe as Milk* it started moving away.

DT: Were there any rock guitarists you liked? Hendrix?

ZHR: Hendrix influenced me early on, because [his style] was such a break. I liked the freedom of what he was playing, and because I wasn't studying jazz and things like that, his vocabulary seemed big. As I look back at it now, it was very small. But the thing is, he was very creative and he probably would've been one of the few people to actually challenge [those limitations], because he was just touching on moving forward with [Buddy] Miles at the end. So he was an influence for sure; when I was seventeen, eighteen, I learned every lick he'd played.

Of course, I had learned Beatles songs, the basic bar-chord mentality and blues licks. Being a teacher now, if I look back at myself, I see a bunch of riffs that are unconnected. The parts are just whatever you played in that song instead of part of the vocabulary for all songs. I didn't have that awareness then. And then in the Beefheart band there was no thinking like that, because there were only memorized parts and the voicings had nothing to do with guitar voicings or even piano voicings. They came from a guy [Van Vliet] who didn't know anything banging on a piano. Anything of harmonic structure.

DT: It's an interesting source, at least.

ZHR: Don't get me wrong, I'm not saying he didn't construct great music. But he did not use theory, you know what I mean?

DT: In your book, you mention that when you were putting songs together, the music was often more dependent on rhythm than on melody or even on a key or set of notes. Is that because of what you were just talking about, those cases where you were working from the rhythm of Don Van Vliet's piano lines?

ZHR: Exactly right.

DT: And there were some more melodic parts that were based on the whistling?

ZHR: Right. Where it came from was totally dictated by whether it was a piano-based thing or something else. Those types of rhythmic structures— "Neon Meate Dream of a Octafish" or whatever, where you're pounding out these rhythms—came out of a piano mentality, and then when the things were whistled, those were the lines that were more nursery-rhymey, because there were a lot of little nursery rhymes in there too. So, in other words, the piano parts were dense and angular, the whistling parts were more melodic and nursery rhymey, and there were also the blues licks. Those were the three styles that I saw, at least in the era you're talking about.

DT: The *Trout Mask* era?

ZHR: Yeah. If he was whistling, it was either going to come out as a blues lick or as a sweet little C major melody thing. I mean, he did these corny melodies sometimes.

DT: If you look at conventional singer-songwriters, they write the songs, they play the songs. But with Captain Beefheart everything was refracted through the musicians. Do you think that that was part of the unconventionality of the band?

ZHR: Yes, and I think he was aware of that. There was a very artistic aspect to his beating on a piano, like Jackson Pollack throwing paint. He knew in an overview sense what he was doing, but he was too lazy to get in there and learn the music and control it to the degree that he could claim to. There was a big laziness factor in there.

DT: You think Captain Beefheart was walking a line between positioning himself as a genius and being a little lazy?

ZHR: All of it. He was smart enough to do that. I mean, about twenty years ago, after the Beefheart band, I saw a picture of Albert Einstein and I remembered when Don went out and bought a wardrobe that was the exact same look. I didn't know then that was the look that he was going after, but obviously he'd seen the picture, right? "It's a cool look; I'm going to adopt it." [*laughs*] He was aware of how to market himself in that way.

DT: I hear you on that. Still, as I was preparing for this I was focusing on the guitar parts, but so often I was struck by his singing or his lyrics. Do you think there were times when he delivered?

ZHR: Do I think he delivered inspired things? Constantly! Yeah, I'm not saying he didn't do that. I'm just saying—being part of the machinery that he was using to do so—that in the process he just took a little too much credit. Here's an example. And what a weird one to bring up: Michael Jackson, right? He's sitting there in the studio and he's telling this ripping bass player, "Bass player, can you do this? *Uh uh uh uh uh uh.*" And the bass player turns it into something great. Now, who wrote the tune? You know what I'm saying? That's the line I'm talking about. It's easy to walk into a room full of great players: "Hey, you guys, let's do this and do that." They're going to create great music because of the skills that they brought there.

It's a two-sided coin. I think he was brilliant; I think he was an incredibly creative person. But he created this machinery . . . he wouldn't let us play things that were jazzy because he knew we weren't good enough to play in a Coltrane-y way. He knew that he had to create some type of setting, and as we were working on these things we had to stay in this nebulous area that's not blues, it's not harmonic, it's not anything. So he had that overview, but he wouldn't have known something he'd written if he heard it played backwards. He wouldn't have recognized it.

DT: Did you have faith in Beefheart's overview, as you call it?

ZHR: Yes. I recognized the power of it. It was transforming to me. I couldn't even listen to other bands, they were just too simple, too dodo. But there was so much other emotional crap mixed with it that I was blinded by it. The experience was just so brutal.

The truth of the matter is that there is no simple answer to questions like those because of the overpowering effect of the brainwashing environment of that band. There were positive things? Yes! My answer is yes! It was very stimulating creativity. His stuff, his vision—and his mind was just on fire all the time. Unless it wasn't. So I learned from it. But it's hard to say I even learned from it because it was just so painful.

DT: At least the idea of transformation could be a good thing.

ZHR: Of course it was. I was in the process of trying to learn these parts and wondering, "Where does this go?" And after a few months of that, you've made the change. You are the music and you start hearing it and living it. So there was this incredible transformation in what I felt. But, I mean, in hindsight, if I knew how gruesome it would be, I would never have done it. The things that I learned—the pulling me out of "Billy Boy," the normal little L.A. guy that'll work for the post office—changed my life forever. Meeting Ornette Coleman. Meeting people who were working very hard in artistic ways. Those were great, wonderful things. And the musical part of it, too. But it was hell to live it.

DT: You were totally cooped up in that house.

ZHR: Yeah! It was very Manson-like.

DT: Hopefully not too much.

ZHR: No, we didn't go murder people. But inside the house we beat the shit out of each other, so it was very Manson-like.

DT: You briefly lived in a commune before that, right?

ZHR: Yeah, I went from one Timothy Leary–based LSD guru situation to another control freak. Somewhere along the line I had to take more accountability for myself. It took quite a while.

DT: Going back to the music itself, I wanted to ask about the physical aspects of playing in that style. Did you have to be conscious at all times?

ZHR: Of course.

DT: Was that an effect you were trying to have on the audience too?

ZHR: I don't think that anyone in the band was doing that. We were becoming this molded, great thing in our minds and we didn't give a shit about the audience, period. We're going to go out there and give you a haircut with this music and that's it.

DT: Giving the audience a haircut seems pointed enough.

ZHR: Yeah, but I'm saying those things were one-word thoughts, not sentences-and-paragraph thoughts, you know?

DT: You just felt it.

ZHR: Yeah, and I'm still that way. Especially when you go in and clear a place like we did. You have to think that way for survival. To tell you the truth, when you're that age you're trying to get laid, so there was that aspect too. In the bigger picture, it became more survivalistic: "I want to get laid, I want to get paid."

DT: . . . And?

ZHR: It didn't happen. [*laughs*]

DT: It seems like there must've been some break from convention you were conscious of, especially with things like the time signatures.

ZHR: Yeah, but none of us were traditional rock players even before we were in the Beefheart band. We were playing blues-based things, but it wasn't that traditional rock thinking. So there really was no traditional rock mentality in the band beforehand, during, or after. How could we have that consciousness if it'd never been in there anywhere?

DT: That makes sense. I guess what I'm getting at is why the band took the form of rock music at all if everyone leaned in other directions. Was that just by default?

ZHR: No, the thing is . . . first of all, you're playing music. That's it. No label. It's noise. It's organized sound in some way. Because that time was the heyday of the hippie period and there were all kinds of music going on, and different types of music were starting to become part of the rock world. So I don't think there was a consciousness of any [particular] type of music. It was simply, "This is the sound we're making; here it is." Now, we were on the extreme end of that, for sure. But I don't think that there was anything conscious other than maybe not being any of the "other." That's it. Just, "We're not a jazz band. We're certainly not a rock band. We're just white with long hair." And how do you get marketed? Do you sign a record deal? Are jazz labels going to sign us? No. You know, we were never a pop rock band. It just got sold through that vehicle.

DT: That's what I meant, whether rock was the best vehicle for you even with all its baggage. Like how were you being booked?

ZHR: As a rock act.

DT: So what did rock audiences think?

ZHR: "What the hell are those guys doing? I'm leaving!" [*laughs*] That's what they thought in the early times. And if it was a bill where there were six bands they'd put up with us until Frank Zappa came out as a headliner. Later on it was different, because we were opening for Jethro Tull—those were huge gigs, and sometimes it worked. But we were playing a much more user-friendly music by then.

DT: What relationship did the band have to the hippie ethos of the '60s?

ZHR: I think we were an antithesis to it early on. That's why we didn't go to Woodstock. "Why go out there in the fray with all those hippies? We aren't hippies, we're maharishi meditators. We're high-minded, selfish artist pricks." [*laughs*] That's what we were trying to be, so we were the antithesis of it at that point. Although, we had long hair and fit in by a look that was newish at the time, and there were certain things like the environment, ecology, that were a huge amount of what Don's lyrics were about. But we definitely weren't like, "Let's go to the love-in and be part of the hippie crew." We were trying to be artists.

DT: Did you think that the hippie culture would hinder you?

ZHR: Mmm-hmm.

DT: Were you cynical toward that—or cynical overall, is that a word you're comfortable with?

ZHR: Yes. Very much so. We were low-minded punks doing blues dribble. And I hate that, to be honest. I hate that I was thinking like that. I wasn't any better than the guys I was condemning: "Oh, you're just doing the same old riffs. Jesus, wake up, buddy." That's where we were at. We were very cynical of the music scene: "God, you guys suck." And then seeing them score the chicks was unfortunate. [*laughs*] You know, as a nineteen-year-old you're going, "Well, I want that side, but I want to think of myself as an artist too instead of just this reproducer of the same old shit."

DT: In addition to the ecology you mentioned, were there other '60s ideas that seeped in?

ZHR: Oh yeah, yeah, there definitely were, more for the band guys than Don. Don was psychedelicized for sure, but his artistic mentality had started even before that. You can read anything about [Don and Frank Zappa's time together in] high school—they were studying things. They were already apart. So Don, I think, had that '60s generation never existed, that path would have been there for him anyway. For us? No. We needed the explosion to blow us out of our predestined routines. It took that mentality to break us apart.

DT: Do you think that was also the only way the audience could make sense of the band, as a product of the times?

ZHR: They did [make sense of it that way]. I don't know if they needed to. But I'm guessing so. With YouTube here, I'll look up John Cage and he's on some weird talk show from 1959 and these people are laughing at this guy, you know, and I'm thinking, "This guy's got a lot of balls," because he's got to know that they don't have a clue. And they might lynch him any minute. So I think we had security in that time period that we didn't get lynched. People left and threw things at us, but they didn't shoot us. [*laughs*]

DT: In your book, you use the phrase "art attitude" in reference to Captain Beefheart, which seemed very Beat Generation to me.

ZHR: Definitely. And that's what I meant, that [Van Vliet] was already there before the hippie generation. So he's coming from the Beat Generation, right? That's definitely where the be-bop poetry and that attitude come from. That was way more of our mind-set than the hippie thing.

DT: With all the sources and styles we've been talking about, what do you think was at the center of the band's music?

ZHR: Are you talking sonically?

DT: Yes, or in terms of feel. You have all these elements like blues and jazz, the '60s and the Beats. Do you have a sense of what was most important?

ZHR: I don't know. All I can do is throw out intrinsic parts that would be sources from other things. The aggressive, over-the-top nature of the performances was core for sure. I'm leaving lyrics out now, and any of the vocal things, because that's a whole other side. Basically, just an over-the-top aggressive performance style with a huge amount of Howlin' Wolf and John Coltrane.

DT: Were you trying to merge these things, or was it a juxtaposition . . . ?

ZHR: We just did it. The elements were there because that was how we played and how we felt about music. You're not going to hear any rip-offs from the Beach Boys in the tunes we did. Our music had a lot of power and angst in it, but with a lot of humor from the lyrics side—that's where some of the nursery-rhymey parts would show up, which were so out of context, so "juxtaposition" would be a great term to describe the intent behind things like that. But the effect wasn't that conscious. We weren't conscious. We did it. We worked hard. We made sounds.

DT: Maybe a better way of going about that question would be to look at a song or two; perhaps you could talk about how they reflect the elements you were working with. Like "My Human Gets Me Blues," was that representative of the *Trout Mask* sound?

ZHR: Well, it definitely was, but listen to the rhythm there—it's jazz. *Bom, bam . . . bomp.* That's a horn section, right? All of that is just jazz riffs. But do you mean, technique-wise what was going on?

DT: I just mean, if you consider that song as reflective of the *Trout Mask* style, where would some of its parts come from, or what would they be?

ZHR: Multirhythms. A lot of three against four. In that one we were all kind of on the same thing, right? It had a swing groove that we stayed with, and then it broke apart. Tunes written before *Trout Mask*—that would be like "Sugar 'n Spikes" and "Moonlight on Vermont"—had rockish rhythmic structures through the whole thing. But "My Human Gets Me Blues," "Steal Softly Thru Snow," any other hard ones like that, or tunes that were of that newer batch of music for *Trout Mask*, they would always be in the shape of the improvised part. Not conscious "This is in five," "This is in seven"; the time signature was just based on the shape of the part and how it played out. There was never a conscious effort to line things up to where they all stayed in four; if it came out that way, it happened that way. It's almost like, roll the dice and see how it comes out. So the construction was very loose on that end, OK?

And the happenstance is part of the charm for me. Besides, the multikey, polyrhythm things that were going on, when they finally did come together, it was a relief, you know. You'd be on the outside rhythmically—you've got three against four, almost where there was no real time at all, there's polyrhythm and then there's this arrhythmic memorizing of the overall shape of your part—and then we'd come together at this point, and we'd go off again. So that would be very typical of those tunes at that time. It was not written down or lined up in any way. It was just how they kind of came out. You just threw 'em on the ground and played 'em.

DT: That's like what you said earlier about piano voicings, where the time signature comes from the original improvised line.

ZHR: Well, that's how a jazz player does it now, too. I mean, if you start thinking, "How am I going to write in seventeen?" it's like college jazz or something.

DT: That actually explains a lot about how you got into these unconventional modes.

ZHR: Really simple. It's a lot simpler than you might think.

DT: So for a lot of this stuff, you can talk about it theoretically after the fact, but at the time it was pretty unconscious.

ZHR: Absolutely. But the unconscious part isn't total abandonment. There was an awareness that that process would create something unique. That [Don Van Vliet] was very much in control of.

DT: Looking back, do you consider *Trout Mask* the band's main statement? Or would you include *Lick My Decals Off*?

ZHR: What I'll say is that *Decals* and *Trout Mask* were of the same mentality, so I consider both of those to be very strong. It used to be I liked *Decals* better, but I won't say that anymore. They're both historical landmarks for me. They were huge undertakings and therefore they loomed large in my life. The next one [*The Spotlight Kid*] is when it kind of went down to the simple style. And there are some elements there that are cool. We were a blues band by the time we got to *Clear Spot*.

DT: When you say you were a blues band, how literally do you mean that?

ZHR: Not literally at all. To me, blues is a sound and a feeling, not a twelve-bar form and a Jimmy Reed riff—he might have done thirteen bars, you never knew. The vocal lines changed from sea chanteys to more of a minor pentatonic, therefore . . . blues.

DT: That change allowed Captain Beefheart to highlight his singing, at least. Was that a worthwhile trade-off at all?

ZHR: [*laughs*] Here, I'll describe the whole vocal thing. Start from "A" and go to the end of the line. In the beginning, he didn't ever practice; he didn't know what he was going to do vocally. On *Trout Mask*, he went in and did vocals without even hearing the tunes in his headphones. Part of that was the effect he was going for and part was his basic paranoia. When he was singing, he'd turn into this little kid who was freaked out. And that really dictated what he did. So then *Decals* . . . more of the same. Then [his accusation] was that we ruined his music; he needed to sing slower. So then we did *The Spotlight Kid*, where it's like we were in *Night of the Living Dead* the tempos were so slow. It was like we'd died so that he could get all those lyrics in. You listen to the mix and it's all vocal. He wiped the band out because his ego needed to go back to his blues roots.

Across the board, what the man could do in a room standing there singing never was recorded, period. Interviews, live gigs, I would say the best you ever saw of him was sixty to seventy percent. What he could do when he was relaxed would have scared you to death. He could sit there and whistle be-bop like crazy, could imitate Teresa Brewer and Howlin' Wolf and was just amazing at it. As soon as the light was on, his voice would get tight, he'd start blaming people—"the room isn't right, it's the wrong color"—every time. We're talking about a very intelligent person with a huge paranoia when he was put on the spot. What a weird job to take on, to be the front of a band when you're that paranoid.

DT: What amazes me is how his singing doesn't sound that much like borrowed blues, especially when you compare it to, say, Mick Jagger. Even if Beefheart was never captured at his best, why do you think he sounded so different than those other guys?

ZHR: Because they sucked. [*laughs*] I mean, listen to Howlin' Wolf, listen to Muddy Waters, listen to the guys he learned his chops from as a twenty, twenty-one-year-old man, even younger. Mick Jagger wishes he could have done that. Mick did a lot with his squirrelly little voice, more power to him. But Don had the chops. The guy could really sing.

DT: Relative to most groups, the Magic Band has an enormous legacy. What do you think people get right in retrospect?

ZHR: First of all, I have to say that you're dealing with a band from 1968—now that's over forty years ago, right? And over that time there was an evolution in the attitude of music, the effect of other bands, whether it was

Iggy Pop or the Clash. So the mind-set has changed. Listeners are way more sophisticated now. And so the legacy is kind of the interpretation of a more intelligent younger person listening to this stuff and having a whole different idea of what it was than the people who were around in the '60s when we were doing it. I mean, it was very different then. I think for Zappa even to put *Trout Mask* out—which wasn't that gutsy because he was fringe anyway—but for somebody to put it out in the rock world gave it a bigger space and let it hit a wider audience than maybe it should have. I won't say "should," but nobody's going to get that chance again. And because of that, it's indefinable what the legacy is.

People are more specialized now, you know? That's why someone like Bill Frisell excites me as a guitar player. It's like, "What's he going to do this time?" You don't know if you're going to hear Civil War themes or atonal electronics. And that's hard to do, and it's really cool. Most people are specialists. We were a bigger amalgam.

Doing the Work

Wayne Kramer

PHOTO BY GREGORY DAURER, COURTESY OF THE PHOTOGRAPHER

The MC5, managed by White Panther poet John Sinclair and napalmed into the zeitgeist via the fuck-bombing "Kick Out the Jams," didn't define the 1960s so much as initiate their redefinition. Aggressive, guitar-gunning, the Five were down with the revolution even if the revolution wasn't down with them, maybe because, as their appearance at the 1968 Democratic National Shitstorm suggests, they were the one band that actually wanted to *revolt*. Despite the cloud of turmoil hanging over their eight years together—the split with Sinclair as he went off to serve ten years on the slimmest of marijuana charges, the various other personal crises and media assaults—this mightiest of Detroit muscle bands believed that they could change things with their music. And they were only partly wrong, for while they may not have changed "things," they did signal a new direction in rock. Sure, these boys from the modest suburb of Lincoln Park weren't real street terrorists like the NYC Motherfuckers, who destroyed their gear, or real gangsters like the Michigan mafiosi who sold Wayne Kramer the cocaine that led to his 1975 bust. But they were real.

MC stood for Motor City and 5 came from the Dave Clark Five, and while you'd need some Sun Ra, Chuck Berry, and Funk Brothers in there, their sound could be described as maximum R&B animated by drag-strip adrenaline. Their three albums—*Kick Out the Jams* (1969), *Back in the USA* (1970), and *High Time* (1971)—alternate tight rockers like "Gotta Keep Movin'" and space travels like "Starship," leaning more toward free jazz than psychedelia, more toward backbeat than West Coast noodling. Two of the five were Kramer (born 1948) and Fred "Sonic" Smith, childhood friends who started as rhythm and lead but melded into one twelve-stringed compound. If there is a guitar heaven, the pair will get in on "Kick Out the Jams" alone. But they were also behind the Yardbirds–meets–Albert Ayler "Black to Comm" and the speed-boogying "American Ruse" and the simmering "Miss X" and the hatcheting "Poison." Across the board their music had what Kramer calls *drive*—"this forward power," as he put it to Fred Goodman in *The Mansion on the Hill*—and that made the MC5 an anomaly in a period of hippie digression. Yet musical treason is a matter of dates, and though the Five faded out ignominiously at the end of 1972, their avant-Diddley style clicked with the next wave a few years later, when along with their "little brother band," the Stooges, the MC5 became the blueprint for punk.

Post-Five, Sonic Smith went on to play thinking-man's classic rock with his Rendezvous Band but otherwise lay low with wife Patti Smith. Still, his Mosrite tones ring out long after his untimely death in 1994. Following his release from Lexington Federal Prison, Wayne headed to New York City, where he wrote a musical, *The Last Words of Dutch Schultz*, and formed Gang War with Johnny Thunders. He later relocated to California and recorded a series of solo albums beginning with *The Hard Stuff* (1995) that redirected his red, white, and blue Stratocaster into singer-songwriter territory reminiscent of Steve Earle or Tom Waits. From there on out, Wayne was more productive than ever before, recording with Brian James, touring with the other Five survivors as DKT-MC5, scoring the 2008 documentary *Narcotic Farm*, even venturing back into prison to share his rare brand of wisdom—street smarts + intellectual curiosity + poetic grit—in talks on addiction and reform. The MC5 had been overstuffed with musical aspirations, J. C. Crawford brimstone, "Zenta" calendars, too many elements to pull off in so short a time, but in the adult Wayne Kramer these elements come together naturally. Brother Wayne still has that drive, only now it's under control.

DAVID TODD: Although the MC5 formed in the heart of the garage-band era, you seemed serious about being more than that from the start.

WAYNE KRAMER: I think we were, yeah. You know, after having played all the neighborhood parties and all the Elk and Moose halls, we reached a crisis point. The traditional direction in those days was that you go into the clubs. But the problem—for me, for [singer] Rob [Tyner], and for Fred—was that to play the clubs you had to play Top 10. We had another rhythm section at the time and they loved the idea. And, you know, it was everything I was shooting for too, until I started to see that there were greater possibilities. Because the reality was that playing five sets a night and having to play Top 10 kept you from putting time into writing your own songs, from skipping the bars and playing concert halls. This was the era of the first wave of the British bands, and we were getting jobs opening for the Rolling Stones and the Dave Clark Five 'cause we were this hot-shit local band. And I'm saying, "I would rather be the Dave Clark Five than Jamie Coe and the Gigolos," who were the greatest Detroit bar band there was. So the rhythm section quit, and [bassist] Michael [Davis] and [drummer] Dennis ["Machine Gun" Thompson] came into the band.

DT: I read that your first drummer didn't even want to play "Black to Comm."

WK: He thought it was just noise. And he had good reason to believe that, because when we would play it we would empty the room. And he would get angry, angry, angry, and then finally when he would start playing he'd be beating his drums to death, and we'd say, "This has got great spirit to it now!"

[*laughs*] But, yeah, that was a quantum leap, that we were going to develop our own sound and identity, and that it would by necessity have to be serious. And at the same time, that's when the ballroom idea came to Detroit, and of course that was our perfect environment, because it presented the music as a dance concert. We could play the kind of music we wanted and put on our own show.

DT: Being hired as the Grande Ballroom's house band must've sped things along.

WK: I think so. It was the high point, because of the sense of possibility. We could rehearse in the venue and plan our concerts—plan our theatrical spectaculars [*laughs*]—get our clothes together, work on how to cut down the time between songs, everything. Listen, in the early days of the Grande, Sly and the Family Stone came through. And we played with them for three nights, two sets a night. And they opened and closed every set with "Dance to the Music." [*laughs*] But we got to watch . . . I mean, that was a fucking incredible band. They could really play and they danced, and that's what we were talking about.

DT: That's an interesting band to mention, because they're so far from the usual rock groups of the day.

WK: Well, I personally felt a lot of those ["usual"] bands were lame. A lot of it was pretentious; it sounded thin to me, watery. It was like, "Go back to wherever you came from. Don't bother us with this." In a way, we created that audience at the Grande. We drilled it into their heads that they were the greatest rock audience in the world. They became famous on the touring circuit: if the Detroit audience loved you, you had a career. Humble Pie came through, people loved them. The Who. But other bands, not so much.

DT: It wasn't just the stage show you liked about Sly and the Family Stone. Wasn't there was a lot of R&B in your sound?

WK: Yeah. Growing up in Detroit, the music on the radio included James Brown and hard-core soul and southern R&B, the blues—all that stuff

existed in Detroit in a way it didn't exist anywhere else. It was like growing up in New Orleans; it seeps into you. And bands would come from San
Francisco and the rhythm sections would be weak, and the bass players
would be playing a simplified version of what the guitar player was playing.
That ain't the bass player's job. The bass player's job is to play the *bass line*,
which could be something completely different, the way [James] Jamerson
played or [Bob] Babbett, my idols. I was always trying to figure out what
Jamerson played: "How does he get an A-note in an F-chord?" [*laughs*] His
shit was so sophisticated.

Of course, as [John] Sinclair exposed me to free jazz, then I could make
the complete leap from the instrumental bands and Chuck Berry to Albert
Ayler and Archie Shepp. I could hear the connection and I could approximate it on the guitar.

DT: What was that connection as you saw it?

WK: Well, I'd come up on Chuck Berry and the Ventures and the British first
wave, and then I started to hear what was happening in free jazz and it was
the next logical step. I could hear it in what Jeff Beck or what Pete Townshend was doing; I'd say, "See, they're going away from notes on a staff into
pure sound." Just like [John Coltrane] was doing. After "Giant Steps," Trane
just kept on going, you know, to a level above most musicians on earth.
"Giant Steps" goes through every key—well, what else can you do? Then you
gotta let it all go. And that resonated with me. And on the guitar, I found
that if I played my best Chuck Berry solo as fast as I could, with as much
velocity—if you just moved what he was doing over an inch—it started to
turn into those sheets of sound that Trane was playing. You just have to start
modulating and you're into something new.

DT: Did you derive much from any of the traditional '60s rock guitarists?

WK: Maybe you can't hear it, but I really was into Pete Townshend. That
rhythm, the way chords are set up—it's funny, that's something he got from
Motown. He was trying to reproduce Martha & the Vandellas!

I thought the Who were just a spectacular band. They had come
through America and they played a teeny club in Ann Arbor—I mean, there

might've been fifty kids there—and I stood right in the front, and it was a low stage, and it was like, "Damn! They could really play." [*laughs*] Same thing with the Yardbirds with Jeff Beck, they came through on their first tour and they played at Green's Pavilion, which was a roller rink out in the country. And Jimmy Page was in the band, but he played bass. And it was the same thing, you know, like this set the bar for what I was trying to do.

DT: Were you interested in the Rolling Stones as much as bands like the Who?

WK: There were aspects of both that I was attracted to. Every now and then the Stones would put out a single that had a sound that was extreme—you know, like "Have You Seen Your Mother, Baby, Standing in the Shadow?"— that I identified more with. Every now and then they would do something that was so odd, I thought, "That's the direction." And then Pete Townshend's idea of autodestructive art, where he would take this incredibly expensive guitar and smash it, just fucked me up. I didn't know what to make of that. [*laughs*] And then I would hear Jeff Beck and I thought, "Well, this is all fitting together to me. Tie that in with Sun Ra, and I know where I fit."

DT: One of the MC5's terms for itself was "avant-rock."

WK: Yeah. I mean, Tyner wanted to change the name of the band to Avant-Rock. He was voted down. [*laughs*]

DT: Even though "Black to Comm" was written early on, it seemed to put together a lot of that complete sound.

WK: It did, yeah. It was like the portal into a whole different approach where we weren't playing chords anymore and we weren't playing structure. All of a sudden we would just have a motif, and that motif we would improvise into new motifs. You know, Fred and I played together so long that we achieved an ego loss where I could listen and adjust to what he was doing, and he would do the same to me. Pretty soon neither of us was playing solo or rhythm, and we went places that we wouldn't have gone by ourselves. Because the band was fundamentally guitar-driven, we controlled the flow of the music and then the rhythm section would try to catch up. And Tyner brilliantly positioned himself as the front to this thing, so he's up there improvising vocally and being a focus of attention. It was a completely synergistic unit.

DT: I guess the idea with the first album, *Kick Out the Jams*, was to record the band live since everything was clicking so fast. I know you weren't that happy with the album yourself.

WK: Well, that just reflects my immaturity. [*laughs*] You know, it's an old resentment, based on the fact that Elektra Records told us that if we didn't like the recording, we could record it again. And I said I didn't like it, and everybody around me said, "Oh, no, it's great. We're going with it." And, you know, I gotta get over that, but I'll tell you, it was not a great MC5 gig. Some nights the band was just unbeatable, and that wasn't one of those nights. It was a B+. I mean, there was so much pressure: "You're going to be remembered forever for this." And we're human, and maybe we were all reaching beyond our grasp, and we miss sometimes. We did our best, but when I listened to it I said, "I've got better tapes from some gig that we did six months ago." [*laughs*] But I didn't get my way. I guess that's what it amounts to.

DT: What about your second album, *Back in the USA*—did you still have that same avant sensibility then, even if the record features a back-to-basics style?

WK: You know, I can't really talk for anybody else. I was so bruised by the reaction to *Kick Out the Jams* that I wanted to make a tight rock record, a rock 'n' roll record. Maybe I . . . well, not maybe, I pushed the band really hard in this direction. We brought in Jon Landau to produce it, and Jon and I talked for hours and hours about what needed to be done. Had he not been in the picture, who knows what kind of record we would've made? But he was, and . . . yeah, I don't think we ever turned our back on our avant-garde ideas and that part of us, but we certainly did focus on the more traditional aspects. Although, you know, some of the music on *Back in the USA* is more stretched out than on *Kick Out the Jams.* "Human Being Lawnmower," it's like a little concerto. Nothing repeats in it. I mean, some of those arrangements are pretty tricky. So we were still pretty adventurous. Even in our conservativeness, we were more stretched out than most bands of the era.

DT: Are you more comfortable with how *Back in the USA* turned out relative to *Kick Out the Jams?*

WK: I'm probably hypercritical of both. I didn't feel like we really hit our stride until the third album. By that time we were comfortable enough with the recording process and what we represented as a band, who we were as players and songwriters. But that was unfortunate because we had already burned everybody around us and nobody gave a shit about that album. Everybody just wanted the MC5 to go away at that point.

DT: We've been talking about how the band's sound was formed, but something I was thinking about is how much of the coverage of the MC5 is not about the music, it's about the politics or the media attention or the odd brand of success you had where it was fraught with all these undertones. I'm building up to a big question here, just warning you, but I was curious, when you think back to those days, is it the music that you tend to remember or do you think of other things first?

WK: You're right, that is a broad stroke.

DT: I can break it down a little.

WK: It'd be better, yeah. Let's unpack that. [*laughs*]

DT: For instance the band was pulled into such a media storm and maybe never got to separate itself from the hype and just play. Nowadays you see the MC5 logo all over the place and people write about the band as a political phenomenon or as an influence . . . so I was wondering how you look back at it yourself.

WK: Well, with the advantage of looking back—and believe me, my understanding of everything is not crystal-clear—I don't think my experience in the MC5 is all that unique, in terms of the personal, social, cultural aspects of what it means to be in a band and to achieve some recognition at an early age, and then to see it all go away. To find out that talent isn't enough to create a good life out of. [*laughs*] Because I had some talent, and my talent got me somewhere, and then when the going got tough—as it will—I didn't have anything to hold me up, and I really crashed hard.

DT: You mean when the band broke up?

WK: Yeah. My only friends were the guys in the band, and once they were gone I had no support system, I had no family, I had no ethics, no philosophical base to stand on, and when we say crash and burn, it's not inaccurate. Look at me, I ended up in federal prison and acquired drug addiction and alcoholism, but I don't think that's all that unusual. I think certain people are driven to play music out of a desperate need for attention, and that sense of ambition, that almost mystical attraction, can be a positive thing, but it can also be dangerous ground.

DT: That's part of what I was asking before about the goals of the group, the seriousness you had—it seems like some of that wasn't just musical.

WK: You know, I wasn't conscious of it in my younger life; it was just who I was. I was somehow driven to have a band. But that ambition, you know, it's tempting to be revisionist and tidy it all up as something more romantic than it is. I think the truth is somewhere in between . . . I had some damage in my youth, as a boy, so I thought playing the guitar was going to fix me. That's on the psychological side. And then, you know, I've told this story about how being in the MC5 was a way to not end up in the factory, and there's some of that too. If you grew up in Detroit, your options were limited, and in my particular family, my mother's dream was that I would finish high school. College was never discussed. So music became a reasonable option for me.

I only know this stuff in retrospect, after years of trying to figure out who the hell I am. But I don't know if that's so different from anybody else. I talk to musicians all the time and we all seem to come from those dark places. The music represents a way to be somebody, and I think that's natural. You know, much good in the world comes from musicians, whatever their motivations are. Music tells our stories, tells us that we're not alone. I listen to James Brown and he's singing my song. [*laughs*] I listen to Sun Ra or any music that I connect to, and it's in the connection where its real benefit is.

DT: After the MC5, have you found other ways to connect besides the guitar?

WK: I have, and I think that's the process of growing up. You know, this idea that "I'm going to be a big star" is childish. It's a fantasy. Because if you're troubled and you think that having a hit record is going to deliver you to a good life, it won't. Not only will it not make you better; it'll make you worse. What I've done—at least what I'm trying to do—is to at least move in the direction of maturity. And that has a lot to do with things that aren't necessarily my work, but who I am and how I connect with other human beings in my relationships. And out of that can come things like collaborating with people on projects where my ego goes down in the hierarchy. You know, making music for television and films—many musicians can't do that, because ultimately they're there to serve the director. It's actually his vision and they're just there to help. But I think it's good to take a back seat most of the time.

DT: Another part of that big picture with the MC5 was the media. You always hear that the media is so massive now, but you guys were put through the wringer as much as anybody today.

WK: It was very rough. Part of it was because of my ignorance, all of our ignorance. I used to think we lived in a meritocracy, that you got a story in the newspaper because you were special. I didn't know you got a story in the newspaper because your press agent worked it. Elektra would fly journalists out to Detroit and they would interview the band, and then they'd go back and write this story in *Newsweek* about this hard-core rock band that was going to change the world. And I would read this stuff and go, "See! I told you so!" never once realizing this was bought and paid for. [*laughs*] I mean, did we have the goods? Yeah, but that's not what I'm talking about. I'm talking about how we ended up in this crossfire.

In the context of the '60s, many journalists were suspicious of our leftist ranting and raving. To them we felt like something invented in an office, like love beads. So we would get that kind of criticism, and it was hard for me to reconcile. And the low point was Lester Bangs's review of *Kick Out the Jams*, where Lester said, "*Whoa*, these guys can't even tune their guitars," which went into my heart like a dagger. I was on acid when I read it; put me on a bummer that lasted for decades. [*laughs*]

But I saw my career going down the drain. I was the goat. First I was the hero, then I was the goat. And nobody could explain this to me. [John] Sinclair, I don't think he understood it any better than I did; the guys in the band understood it less. And so it was troubling to be this political football being kicked back and forth, to get hammered by a leftist journalist who wants to talk critical theory and Marxism—what did we know? All we knew is the world's fucked up, we're for the people, and we wanna rock the fuck out. I wasn't educated; I didn't read any political tracts until I was in my forties! [*laughs*]

So maybe that experience was unique for the MC5 and for me.

DT: Did it matter that neither of the two media centers was behind you?

WK: Oh yeah. That's certainly a component. You know, we wore it as a badge of honor. We knew that we were ridiculed because we were from Detroit, and nothing cool can come out of the industrial Midwest. But part of our inability to build on our start was that we didn't have a Bill Graham like San Francisco did, we didn't have the guys that ran the nightclubs in New York City—that was Graham on both ends, actually—we were flying by the seat of our pants.

DT: Something I found fascinating was your trip to New York City in 1968, when you were ambushed by a group called the Motherfuckers outside Graham's Fillmore East.

WK: We landed in the middle of a conflict with this group, the Lower East Side Motherfuckers, part of the International Werewolf Conspiracy. [*laughs*] Because of our stance we would attract these things. We had problems in San Francisco, Seattle, Boston. The end result being that the MC5 was effectively blacklisted from the touring circuit.

You know, I have to take responsibility for part of it, because we did those things, we had the Motherfuckers come up and harangue the police. But I sometimes wonder if there was more to it than that. I mean, when I read that G. Gordon Liddy declared he would use the power of the federal government against us, I wonder: did he call [Elektra Records'] Jac Holzman and say, "Fire this goddamn band or we're gonna audit you?" I'm just speculating.

DT: It's not that implausible.

WK: Well, we know through the Freedom of Information Act that they were tapping our phones, they were trying to slide undercover operatives in on us. They did it to every antiwar organization in the country—SDS, the Black Panthers.

DT: Maybe I'm skeptical, but I find the Freedom of Information Act suspect. Do you buy that they're giving you all the files?

WK: They're all redacted. Some of them are pages that are all blacked out. It's kind of a joke, really.

DT: Was there a file with your name on it or the band's?

WK: Both.

DT: What was it like to look at those?

WK: I'll tell you, after the MC5 broke up, in the '70s when I was spiraling downward, I was arrested for being part of a drug conspiracy. I asked this federal agent, "How did you guys get onto me? I'm not really a kingpin." And he said, "Kramer, we've got shit on you going back to the '60s."

DT: That also might've had something to do with being in a smaller market. It was easier to stand out in Detroit—for John Sinclair, too.

WK: That's true, yeah. Sinclair became the focus and the scapegoat. The symbol.

DT: I read up on Sinclair, because I wasn't sure what he did besides just talk, really. Maybe I underestimated that, because I realized the kind of talking he did was political in itself.

WK: Absolutely. Well, he was a poet. That was the beginning of his troubles. He liked to smoke pot, and a policeman busted him, and he wrote a poem about the policeman, "The Poem for Warner Stringfellow." And the policeman got pissed and busted him two more times.

You know, John was very much a product of the day. The day I met him he was just released from the Detroit House of Corrections, where he'd served six months on a marijuana conviction. So this was hovering over him all along. And it's things like that, when people are faced with injustice—and nine and a half to ten years for two marijuana joints is not justice—that radicalize folks. That polarize.

DT: Was being in prison another experience—this sounds ridiculous because obviously it would be—that was radicalizing for you?

WK: Well, it was, and sometimes I've reflected on the experience and tried to sort out what happened to me and why it happened to me. And, yeah, you start to see that things aren't always the way they appear, that there are forces you have to reckon with that are not obvious. It's like, growing up you have this Pollyanna-ish view of the world, and as time goes on your naïveté gets stripped away. So then you've got to figure out a way to make peace with the world in more realistic terms. Sure, I had great resentment against the federal prison system and the DEA, but that resentment had to be refocused on things that were harder for me to see.

You know, this is an area of activism for me, that the injustice surrounding drug laws is unconscionable. I've tried to identify the core in this issue, and the best I can come up with is that is there seems to be this lack of reality about people getting high. There's this sense of, "We've got to do something about these people who take drugs and drink too much," but the truth is people have taken drugs and drunk too much from the beginning. It's a human condition; it's not a legal condition, it's not a moral or ethical condition. Which isn't to say that if people have trouble managing their drug use we shouldn't help them—there are treatments that can succeed—but the idea that you should lock them up, that they're not good citizens, is hard for me to get my arms around. If you go back in history, where does that come from? We know in American history where it comes from, but before that?

So I connect all that up to me ending up going to prison [laughs] and more than that, and more important, the million people who are in prison in America today for nonviolent drug offenses. You know, I just spoke at a prison here in California, and those guys in there are me. They're not gangsters; they're not criminals. Yet you're sending them to crime school. There's a great potential for them to become criminals once they're locked up, but as it is, they're just people.

DT: You'll get no argument from me on any of that, Wayne, but I think to your credit you're also willing to look at your role in things, in your own case at least.

WK: Of course. I have to. I mean, I'm not a victim. I think everybody needs some sense of integrity, and for me, taking responsibility for my own actions is part of how I've been able to build a grown-up who can live in the world. I have to be realistic and own up to my part in the good and the bad.

I never understood this back when it was happening, but it's not enough to criticize. You have to offer a plan of your own that's better. That's what we were trying to do with the MC5 and the White Panther Party—we were pretty amateurish but that's where we were coming from—and I think everything I do today is from that point of view. I mean, the trouble I had in the MC5 was that I couldn't articulate my feelings. I could play the guitar and I could connect what I was trying to do with Archie Shepp, and then connect our music to what LeRoi Jones or Malcolm X was talking about, I could make all these connections but I couldn't talk about them very well. Maybe I've improved that to some degree.

DT: Are you still a work in progress?

WK: Well, yeah. I haven't pulled over and parked. I guess we're coming back around to this idea of ambition, and I actually feel like I'm just getting started, you know. My career as a film and TV composer, I'm only about five years into it, so I've got another five thousand hours to learn how to be proficient. I've got to learn the language of the orchestra, the woodwinds and the violins, what it means if somebody says *pizzicato* or *marcato*. And I've been studying the great American songwriters, Gershwin and Cole Porter, trying to deconstruct the language they were using, the chord changes, how sophisticated their melodies and lyrics were. So I'm really trying to continue to move forward. I feel like I'm just nowhere near done. That's why I'm grateful that I'm alive, I'm enthusiastic about every day. I know that my time is finite, but it's enough time. It's exactly enough time if you're using it as best you can.

⑤

RIFF APPEAL

JAMES WILLIAMSON

PHOTO BY HEATHER HARRIS

"But there was a record called *Raw Power*." —Iggy Pop, 2009

he guitar playing of Iggy and the Stooges' James Williamson has been called slashing, jagged, deviant, skullish, proto-punk, even proto-thrash, so many times that all those words have nearly lost their meaning. To me it sounds *smart*. There was always more to Williamson than the need to gut you, take your dope, and leave your hotel room stained with his shadow. There was a radiant positive/negative force, the absinthe that seeped out of "Gimme Danger" just after the (yes) stinging, furious chords of "Search and Destroy." It was never a surprise to this listener that Williamson wound up vice president of technology standards at Sony Electronics, because that focus was always evident in his work. (Had his counterpart Iggy Pop decided to play it straight, he could've taken a similar route, possibly as a debauched anthropology professor, teaching shirtless of course.) The strength of the *Raw Power*-era Stooges—i.e., the 1972–74 version with Williamson, as opposed to the beloved 1967–71 Ron Asheton–driven prototype—was this mental toughness, which translated into James's visceral riffs and leads and Iggy's howling "chookums."

Born in Texas in 1949, Williamson arrived on the Stooges scene in 1971, a few years into their object lesson in how paradigm-shifting brilliance doesn't pay enough to scrape by on. With Asheton on guitar, their 1969 debut had injected pop art into greaser numbness via the classic "I Wanna Be Your Dog"; the next year's *Fun House* was a howl from the deeper skronk of "L.A. Blues." In 1970 the Stooges made national TV playing the Cincinnati Pop Festival: Iggy walked on the audience's hands, his chest smeared with peanut butter, the group's rare combination of grace and pugilism on full display. And yet within months they were languishing in their house in Ann Arbor, still two years away from the first of David Bowie's attempts at their (or at least Iggy's) salvation. Enter James Williamson with "You Don't Want My Name," a swinging parody of "Cool Jerk" that, as Iggy recounted to Paul Trynka, "perfectly suited where I was going." Iggy pulled the young "thug" aboard for the band's second collapse—the two-guitar Stooges' suicide by record company—then kept him on for the full failure-topping grandeur of crash number three. In the process, Williamson created a style so abrasive that it spawned the legend of Straight James as some kind of demonic heroin overlord ("I was just what they call a 'chipper,'" he explained genially to *Paraphilia*).

Needing only his Gibson Les Paul and Vox AC-30 amp, Williamson achieved a perfect signature: roaring, unsentimental, full of the natural distortion that was in his fingers. He played rockabilly in "Shake Appeal," linear boogie in "Raw Power"; his music was more conventional than it may have appeared, replacing Ron Asheton's soulful alienation with a pummeling antagonism that was just as polarizing. (Asheton devotees,

join me in being thankful that both versions of the band even existed—or
see the introduction.) Perhaps more than anyone else in this book, James
wanted to be a Jeff Beck traditionalist, but in the act of translation something changed. Just as Iggy carved a more ironic face for the 1970s out
of his Jagger and Morrison masks, James wound up with something less
tasteful than his heroes but more aggressively new, a sound lunging into
the moment with a menace that was exhilarating. His "Penetration" was
spooky and severe; "Cock In My Pocket" lecherous; "Scene of the Crime"
jab-stepping; "Your Pretty Face Is Going to Hell" grotesque; "Rubber Legs"
frenzied. Instead of looking toward Ornette and Coltrane, Williamson
found a way to get *out there* simply by cranking up the tone on his satyri-
con Chuck Berry routines.

The fact that within the Stooges, Williamson displaced Asheton from
guitar to bass didn't help James's image much, especially the way the tale was
told in Legs McNeil and Gillian McCain's *Please Kill Me*. Ron was always the
more endearing of the two, James the less vulnerable, as each of their styles
became a template for much of the alternative music that followed. But I
wouldn't say Williamson had it easy. Following 1973's *Raw Power*, there was
enough left in his Stooges tank to fill the *Metallic K.O.* bootleg (1976)—a
document of their final gig in all its legendary, bottle-breaking glory—and
the *Kill City* demos (1977) and then some. But for Williamson, doomed
to being both aesthetically extreme and personally reasonable, five years of
frustration was enough. By the time Iggy got to Berlin and started his *Idiot*
(1977), James wasn't even playing anymore, and with the exception of a few
riffs while producing the Ig's *New Values* (1979), it would take thirty-five
years before he'd come back.

To hear Williamson tell it, his second-wave Stooges were effectively
knocked out of commission on February 4, 1974, by a biker at some dive
called the Rock & Roll Farm in the wilds of Wayne, Michigan, mere nights
before their doomed finale in Detroit. Even so, the group tore a psychic
wound in the rock world that owed much to his striking playing.

DAVID TODD: Recently, tapes with both you and Ron Asheton on guitar were
released [*You Want My Action*, 2009], from the brief period in 1971 before
that version of the band broke up.

JAMES WILLIAMSON: We created a whole album that was turned down. Bill Harvey and the Elektra [Records] guys came to our house in Ann Arbor to hear the material, and they were appalled. You could see the shock on their faces.

DT: How did you deal with a response like that?

JW: It's hard to say. How are you supposed to feel? You've got to remember that we never were popular at the time. It's like there was always this inner group of people who thought we were ultra hip and cool, but then the mainstream people hated us, and those included the record companies. We felt like, "How are you supposed to make this go?"

DT: You were pragmatic about it?

JW: No, we thought they were stupid. They were square.

DT: In terms of finding an audience, it seems like the Stooges were more of a national band than a regional band that broke out.

JW: I would say you're absolutely right. The Stooges became popular much more readily outside of Detroit than in Detroit. Actually, it was a lot of New Yorkers who first recognized the Stooges, probably due to [original manager] Danny Fields and Iggy's relationship with Nico and all those inside people. But especially in those days, I would say that we were only well known on both coasts and in London.

DT: Maybe I'm asking this because of the path you took, but when the 1971 Stooges broke up, did you think you would have a career as a professional musician?

JW: No, I didn't think anything. That was the only skill I had, and, really, after the band broke up the first time, I had zero prospects. It was a bleak existence facing me, and I think that was probably true of all of us. Then Iggy fortuitously took a trip to New York and ran into Bowie, and Bowie's manager put together a record deal for us—well, for him—and he wanted me to come along. Iggy called me up one day, and the next thing you know we're in London. It was lucky.

DT: Do you think that 1971 band could have worked?

JW: I don't know. The big difference in the new lineup [after the 1971 breakup] was that Ron moved over to bass, which is where I thought he fit the best, especially as the rhythm section with his brother [drummer Scott Asheton], because they were in lock-step.

I've always thought Ron was a good guitar player, but the thing is that as a two-guitar band, he played a certain way and it was not the same as I played. Ron was a kind of lilting player, a soloing kind of guy, and what I liked was . . . well, it was what you got. So if I was playing my songs, it was hard for me to do it with him. And that's what my interest was, playing my songs.

See, the thing about me is that I have always written my own music. So from day one we started playing some of my songs and going forward. And so, yeah, I didn't have any interest in playing any particular style they had before.

DT: I understand, although I've heard Iggy talk about that transition with more zeal. He said that you and he "knew we could do something better."

JW: Yeah, I don't think that is totally accurate. What happened in my mind—and obviously the thoughts I have are quite different from Iggy's, and sometimes I feel like his are more revisionist than mine, but anyway, let's just leave that alone—was that I just wanted to play music. If there was a vision, it was that we came over to London at the time of T-Rex and all that stuff going on, and we hadn't seen anything like it since the Beatles. In London, T-Rex were huge, and we wanted some of that. But we sure had a funny way of going about getting it.

DT: You mean in terms of blending in?

JW: Yeah. It was totally alien to us over there. You had never seen more of a bunch of Beverly Hillbillies than us going to London with all these really high-styling guys—you know, Bowie was truly playing the pop star role. I guess Iggy and the Ashetons had traveled more than I had by then because they had toured for a few years, but we were a sight to behold.

You've got to remember, we were young, we were in a strange country, and we didn't know what the hell we were doing. But we were doing it. We were making it up as we went along.

DT: *Raw Power* is often seen an antidote to the progressive rock of 1973. What did you think about releasing it in that climate?

JW: Well, that is what we thought about it. We didn't like that climate. We had our distinct taste in music and that wasn't it. We thought the album sounded terrific when we made it, frankly, and then we had to bring it over to L.A. to have it remixed because nobody else liked it. And when we finally got the first pressings of it, I remember, we were up at our house in Los Angeles and I had my girlfriend over, and you could tell the first time she heard it, she *hated* this stuff. Because it really did sound different and that's pretty much the way it went.

I can only speak for myself, but I think what we did was perfect. It's just that nobody liked it.

DT: Even your manager at the time, Bowie's manager, didn't like it.

JW: You mean Tony DeFries? Well, I think it was simply that he couldn't understand us. You know, David Bowie is a very tuney, poppy kind of guy, and he made sense to DeFries, right? DeFries could make a pop star out of him and David would play along, and we weren't like that.

DeFries had a gig set up for us in London, and we were so different they practically called the police. *They* were appalled. They had never seen anything like it.

DT: That period in London was when you and Iggy wrote a lot of your best-known material. As a listener, I always wondered how in tune you were.

JW: At one point we were really close—actually, the two of us were very stream-of-consciousness together. I could come up with a riff and we'd usually work out the chorus and the verses right there. With lyrics, he makes them up as he goes, and that's kind of the way I write songs too, but I do it a little more labor intensively, because I've got to work through a lot of different changes until I like what I'm doing.

DT: Were there times when you'd bring in a song and he would write something close to what you envisioned for it?

JW: Always, yeah. That was across the board. Even on *New Values* with "Don't Look Down."

DT: Could you talk about the writing of "Search and Destroy"? It's become this kind of manifesto for the band.

JW: Yeah, I know. It's really gotten to be well known. I always liked it, and still do.
    I remember when I wrote it. I wrote almost all the songs on that album in my room in our house in London on a Gibson B25 natural. I would just sit there and write the riffs, and when I came up with something I liked I would take it over to Iggy. At that time he had actually moved out of the house and was living at this little hotel. We'd go over there and work stuff out, and we took that one and once I started playing the electric on it, then we wrote the changes for it and it was done.

DT: Did that riff stand out to you as a good one?

JW: Yeah. Well, that's the way it always was. I would just play them until I liked them. If I could stand playing it more than once, then it had a chance of being a song.

DT: The opening solo on "Search and Destroy" is also pretty iconic. Did you work that out in advance?

JW: No. In fact, I almost never did that. No, all those were improvisational solos done over lots of different takes. Some would come out better than others, and once you play something enough times, it starts to take a pattern. So some of the things, like the solo on that one, I think, had reached that point, so I didn't get too sloppy on them.

DT: The second song on *Raw Power* is "Gimme Danger." You don't mind talking about a few of these?

JW: No, I love talking about it.

DT: That was a different style, not based on power chords like many of the other ones. What does that open with?

JW: I think it's a D minor 7. That first chord.

DT: Did you work a lot with things like that?

JW: Sometimes. I liked to do that because I came from playing a lot of acoustic guitar early on, and I still love the acoustic guitar. There are a few songs on there like that. But it's just all music to me, and some has different moods to it. Each song was unique. Every one was worked up uniquely.

DT: I don't want to make you go through all of them, but what do you think of, say, "I Need Somebody" now?

JW: I think it sounds OK. That's a more standard construction of a song. In their own way I like them all. Oddly, I think "Shake Appeal," for example, is to me one that I was never terribly proud of, but actually in listening to it, it's kind of neat now. It's kinda cool. I was in my Gene Vincent period, definitely, on that one.

DT: How about Iggy's vocal effects on *Raw Power*, all the growling and things like that?

JW: A lot of them I asked him to do, because the howling, all those things, we used to call them chookums. That's kind of a trademark of his. Yeah, it was very good.

DT: As a songwriter, it must have been freeing to work with someone like that.

JW: It's also difficult to . . . let's just say it's easier if you can do everything yourself, but I couldn't, and so I had to work with somebody else. He was the easiest guy I could find.

DT: Who else could sing over "Shake Appeal"?

JW: Well, that was the beauty of it, that he could relate to my music and come up with stuff effortlessly. I mean, think about the way I play—most people can't sing to that. I was always relieved when he could make a lyric and a melody out of these riffs, especially the ones I liked. I don't know who else could've done that.

Although I will say that his style and the style of the band forced me to write certain types of music that I wouldn't necessarily have done if given a blank page, if you will. The tunes were written for the Stooges; they had to be things that Iggy could sing and they had to be rocking.

DT: Even though you were in tune interpersonally, it seems like Iggy was perceived as more relatable, and you were seen as the darker personality.

JW: Yeah, I get that a lot. I've always been interested in the perceptions people have of me versus the reality, and I guess part of [the reason for their perceptions] is that I wasn't a particularly verbal person, especially in those days. A lot of people project on me things that aren't true, but that's because I don't do anything to change their opinion. I'm essentially a shy person, and some of that is just me being nervous.

DT: I mentioned that because I've heard you talk about expressing yourself emotionally as a guitarist, but your playing was often received as aggressive or even unemotional. Do you think people heard your playing as you had hoped?

JW: I have no idea. I've heard a lot of descriptions, and the way my guitar playing is described is usually "slashing," "metal," or that whole "power guitar" thing, and I guess I never really saw that. I knew what I liked, and that's all there was to it for me.

DT: Part of it might be that your playing wasn't lyrical.

JW: Yeah, I agree with that. Maybe something like "Gimme Danger" is a little more lyrical or at least has an interesting set of chord changes, but, yeah, by no means could you call it lyrical as a style.

DT: Despite your reputation as a lead machine, do you think of yourself as a songwriter first and foremost?

JW: At that time I used to think of myself as a really hot soloist, but in hindsight I was a much better songwriter. I prefer that characterization because I feel that's the contribution I made, and I can still do that now. It still comes naturally for me.

DT: Are there songwriting influences you're conscious of?

JW: It's hard to say. I don't know how you distinguish between people you listen to and people who influence you. I used to listen to a lot of folk music and a lot of blues, a lot of the '60s rock. For that matter, a lot of Motown and R&B. The Stones were a big influence. The Yardbirds. The Kinks. Really, most of the British bands. I think the Beatles influenced everybody. But I would say the biggest influence I had other than the Stones was Dylan. Dylan was my idol when I was growing up; he symbolized the whole antisocial, counterculture philosophy of the '60s. At one point he was godlike.

DT: How '60s did you ever get?

JW: I was never a hippie—I was a little too young—but I could have been one if I had been born a few years earlier.

You know, with Dylan—of course, subsequently in all the stuff that's been written about him you start seeing a different Dylan, and in that movie

[Todd Haynes's *I'm Not There*, 2007] you see a lot of different Dylans—but the thing about him was that he wrote the most amazing songs. Really, I can't think of anybody other than the Beatles whose songwriting was sustainable like that. Even the Stones, it's off and on.

DT: With the Stooges, a lot of the discussion of influence involves the group's legacy as opposed to its precursors. And as we were saying before, Iggy might be more comfortable with seeing the band as proto-punk or anything along those lines.

JW: Well, I don't care about that. You can call it anything you want. I never had any conception of punk, and being pre-something-I-didn't-know-the-meaning-of didn't make sense to me. I think the Stooges were an authentic music. I try to think of labels like "indigenous urban music" or something like that. If people understand that, it's OK with me.

DT: Would you prefer to do away with labels?

JW: I don't think music's any different than art in the sense that good art is always hard to get your arms around. That's the beauty of it. Myself, I was always attracted toward different stuff; I liked everything from John Cage to folk music. I was really interested in minimalism and would like to have made a statement like that. I mean, with our music I wanted to make it stylized in some way, and I think we did that. I don't know if it was stylized in a popular way, but the thing I am proud of is that people still feel that it's contemporary. It still sounds like somebody could have done it this year. And the other thing I like is that I hear a lot of guys in these bands today and a lot of them do sound a little like me. So I've obviously had some impact on their playing, and that's flattering.

DT: A lot of the bands that borrowed from the Stooges watered down what you were doing as opposed to exaggerating it.

JW: Yeah, I think that's true. In fact, it was interesting for me to see the success of some of those bands. I had already put the guitar down by then, but when the Sex Pistols came around, they had lifted a lot of stuff. But you're right, they sort of toned it down, and it worked for them.

DT: What kind of feedback were you getting when you were still in the band? Did you hear from other guitarists?

JW: No, because I didn't know that many. I knew Johnny Thunders—I think he liked the way I played—and I'd hear from some of the people in the Bowie camp, but they were kind of kiss-ass people, so I didn't take that as meaning anything. A lot of guys thought we were good, but it was always this cult following. There weren't a lot of compliments being shared.

As I was saying, I could hear the influence over the years, but without being in the music business it didn't mean a lot to me. Although, even as early as *New Values* . . . I mean, the reason Iggy called me up to [produce] that album was the fact that he was getting so much feedback from *Kill City* getting released. So it started taking off then.

DT: Were you ever tempted to get back into playing during that period?

JW: No, I wasn't. I played the one song on *New Values*, and Iggy wanted me to play on [his 1980 follow-up] *Soldier* but I didn't. I guess the stock comment I have is that he wanted me to catch the rock dream again but I never did. And there were a number of factors behind that, not the least of which was that my relationship with Iggy was not as strong as it once was. That probably was the overarching thing. But I just didn't have my heart in it anymore.

DT: After hearing about all the indignities the band endured, I can understand why. Plus, I know you did a lot of exhaustive touring after *Raw Power*, long runs in places like Atlanta.

JW: We did some good shows in Atlanta. They're kind of a rocking town, so they liked us, because we were jumping on tables and having a good time.

DT: Did you have to establish an audience there?

JW: Yeah, they didn't know us. I guess some people had heard the records, but I think they got into us because they could drink a lot and it was a wild scene.

DT: Obviously the Stooges weren't a shock band like Alice Cooper, but was there an aspect of that bringing people to the shows?

JW: Oh yeah, that was a big component. But the thing about us that was different from those other acts was that they were *acts*; there is nothing really shocking about Alice Cooper. He's got a big set and he made it a safe-shocking thing like Halloween, you know, and we weren't that way at all. For us every night was different and real stuff would happen and not all of it was good. It was more of an experience; it wasn't a show as such. I mean, we would play different songs not on a nightly basis but on a weekly or biweekly basis. We'd get new sets because we got tired of the same ones. So even being in the band, it was quite an experience to see these shows, because it was definitely improvisational.

DT: You were always in the moment.

JW: Definitely. Yeah, without a doubt. But that's hard to do. It was hard on us, and ultimately I think we had this false sense of security, because we continued to do that unchallenged for many years. And the night we played the Rock & Roll Farm when that biker stepped up and coldcocked Iggy, that was the night it all changed, because then we became vulnerable.

DT: That was something I had a question about, because I've heard you say that before.

JW: Yeah, it's true. If you think about what we did, it was an illusion. I mean, this is a big, bad world out there, and for some little guy with bleach-blond hair to be taking his shirt off and jumping out in the crowd and freaking people out was not a realistic scenario, you know? But we did it, and actually I think it changed the interaction between the audience and the performer, which was groundbreaking. But that night brought the reality back into the picture, which was that this *was* a little bleach-blond guy with his shirt off, right?

DT: I guess I was surprised that you still believed in that effect after all you'd been through.

JW: Yeah, it's funny how that works, but, I mean, nobody made us think any different.

DT: We were talking about the band being suited to a national stage, and it always struck me as regrettable that you were even dragged into that confrontation. I couldn't see Mick Jagger getting beat up—which could've happened, I suppose, at Altamont—but especially not in some roadhouse.

JW: Yeah. No, that thing was a mistake. Our manager at the time was in New York and he just booked us at every place he could. He didn't even know where these places were. So we had no idea what we were getting into. It was just a little dump with a lot of bikers.

DT: It seemed like the wrong person was deciding your future.

JW: Yeah. But that was the last straw. The band was barely limping back to the barn when that happened, and then [five nights later] you have the *Metallic K.O.* performance, and everybody at that point was broke, tired, fed up, you know? After that, the band really didn't want to play anymore.

DT: For what it's worth, I always thought the Stooges were more together than people gave them credit for, or at least were capable of being so.

JW: Yeah, I felt like I was clear on what I wanted to accomplish. Actually, the Stooges were not at all un-together most of the time. The problem the band had, and it happened over and over again, is that Iggy has this conundrum where he will achieve and then he'll sabotage, and then he'll achieve and then he'll sabotage. And he did that three times while I was around him, and three times was enough for me.

That was the bad part. When he got into those modes, the band really suffered, because you can't keep it together if everyone isn't pulling their weight. That last tour, it's well-documented, was pitiful many times. There were shows where the road crew had to throw him up on stage, literally, and he couldn't stand up. It was just not good. If you're going to get paid, you've got to be a little professional. You've got be able to *walk*.

DT: As with the Elektra version of the group, do you think the breakup of the *Raw Power* version was inevitable?

JW: I think so, yeah. I mean, there was nowhere to take it. Our deal expired with Columbia and we couldn't break through with getting another one. We did some demos—at first we tried John Cale who was out in L.A., and then we had Elton John, but I don't think he ever saw it as commercially viable, which it wasn't. Of course, the next phase started when Iggy and I started new material for what became *Kill City*. And of course Iggy was in terrible shape by then. The only thing that held that together was our desire to get a record deal. It was really a desperate effort by all of us to keep it together.

DT: Around the time of *Kill City* you were phasing into producing. Did you think that would be a better way of staying in the business?

JW: Yeah, I thought so, but the truth was that I couldn't produce people I didn't like any more than I could play with people I didn't like. So it was not a good job for me. [*laughs*]

DT: So then in the late '70s you went back to school in engineering, which led you into the computer industry . . .

JW: Actually, there was a question you asked by e-mail about that I was intrigued with. You asked about creativity in the business world as opposed to the music world, and I think it's true that I've met some of the most creative people I have ever known in the business world, and they don't get credit for it, because it's a very buttoned-up environment. But it's a necessity to be creative in the business world, because it's such a competitive environment. I've also met some of the biggest egotists in my life there. There are some huge egos; they make the ones in the music business look relatively small.

I especially thought that the early years of the PC, when I first got involved, were more like the music business than the music business was in those days. The excitement of creating new things, and even now with this second wave, Google and those companies, it's really exciting.

DT: Was it hard for you to transition into that lifestyle?

JW: Well, no. My wife domesticated me years ago. [*laughs*] I mean, at first it was hard, because I wasn't used to getting up and going to work every day, you know? But you get used to that, and after I did that for so long it was actually the other stuff that was odd for me. I went to an Iggy concert about fifteen years ago and I swear to God I thought, "I couldn't do this anymore."

DT: So you went all the way over.

JW: Yeah. I put the guitar down and walked away.

DT: What kept you from picking it up again for so long?

JW: Well, I never felt like I needed to pick it up. For one thing, I got married and started having children, so I started an entirely different life on top of my career. And I feel like I'm richer for that, but the other thing is, I just didn't have any desire to go back. I didn't have the need to play music anymore. It was only recently the guitar found me again.

DT: In his book on Iggy, Paul Trynka mentions that by around 1975 you'd concluded that you weren't going to make it as a guitarist. I don't know if that's an exact quote but . . .

JW: Yeah, I think that sums it up.

DT: Looking back, isn't there a preponderance of evidence you did make it?

JW: Yes, but I never thought of it that way. It was very flattering and every-thing, but . . . [*laughs*]

DT: Along those same lines, you once said, "I can't accept this mythology surrounding the Stooges. We were just guys playing rock 'n' roll." Have you come to view the music as having a more lasting importance?

JW: Well, it's always flattering to think of yourself as larger than life, but I don't. I think that is all we were doing, and I think that's the beauty of it—we didn't have any illusions. There was no artifice about it. There was only a bunch of broke guys out there playing rock 'n' roll because we liked it. And I think that's the strength of it. So, you know, it's like James Dean dying: he became much bigger after he died than when he was alive, and sometimes when things aren't there anymore, people project onto them. I mean, it was good, but I don't know if I'd put it quite as mythological.

DT: I agree that mythologizing yourself would not be good, but personally the Stooges were one of the few rock illusions I found worth buying into. Even you, going back to that story you were recalling just a few minutes ago about the guy punching out Iggy, there were times you bought into that yourself.

JW: Right.

DT: So I just thought that along with seeing the impact of your guitar play-ing, you might've become more aware of the effect of the band as a whole.

JW: People have made me aware, let's put it that way.

DT: And that's a good thing, knowing you pushed things along?

JW: [*laughs*] It was a good band. There's no doubt about it.

DT: So you're back to playing now. Is that cyclical, or are there some things straight life can't give you?

JW: Well, I do think that the arts are satisfying in ways that are not as easily found in the business world. I think the arts have a human element that is lacking in the business world, because the product in the business world is money. But the thing about the arts is that if the product of the art becomes money, then it becomes a business too. And what I didn't like about the music business was the business of music, you know? And I never did change the way I saw that, and that's why in getting back to the guitar I just want to do it for my own enjoyment. That's the part that I liked the most.

DT: It's funny, because I never thought the Stooges got to the point of being a business, to where the band was a job and not a total-immersion experience they put their whole lives into.

JW: No, no. All we ever did was total immersion. We never became a professional band, exactly. Thank God.

⑥

FORST EXPOSURE

MICHAEL ROTHER

"There wasn't a pre-phrased concept," Michael Rother once told *Perfect Sound Forever* about Neu!, the *kosmische* accident he started in 1971 with his partner/nemesis, the dearly departed Klaus Dinger. But then again, he also told the fanzine *Face Out* that "Neu! was a concept." Only in a band like this are those statements not contradictory. Visionary yet with no fixed premise, Rother and Dinger had only the sensation of constant motion to unify them (it sure wasn't camaraderie—the pair never spoke). At its most tangible, this drive appeared in the form of Dinger's "Apache" drumming, the hammer beats he played on tracks such as "Für Immer," all eleven pulsating minutes of it. On guitar, Rother's evolutions were metaphysical, and they had to do with evading expectation rather than plowing through cliché. "I always had the rule that my own work shouldn't possibly be influenced," he said in that same *PSF* piece. That meant it all had to go—the blues, power chords, jazz. With Dinger laying down motorik monorails, Rother was free to airbrush colors and moods all over the skies of the band's home city, Düsseldorf.

Rother (born in Hamburg in 1950) met Dinger in a flute-metal iteration of Kraftwerk, in which both spent a half year in 1971. Splintering off as a duo, they opened their 1972 debut with percussive, almost classic-rock upstrokes that start repeating and then just *keep going*, as Rother puts it, like a "strong machine driving to the horizon." The template for one of their main modes—extended un-riffing atop a rhythm that's part organic, part mechanical—"Hallogallo" was the ideal platform for Dinger's relentless energy and Rother's trancelike wandering. Recording fast and loose (and cheap, for Neu! was always broke), the combo was fortunate to find a sympathetic producer in Conny Plank, who instead of seeking to blend their incompatibilities wisely pursued the sparks resulting from them. As their collaboration went on, there were times when the fooling around sounded like just that—the second half of *Neu! 2* (1973) was taken upon its release as a Dadaist put-on of the highest order—but it also led to even newer extremes such as the B-side of their finale, *Neu! 75*, in which Dinger spews punk vitriol while chugging on rhythm guitar. If "Neu! was the epitome" of so-called Krautrock, as Julian Cope claimed in his book *Krautrocksampler*, it's because it may have been the most difficult of those mercurial German bands to pin down.

Neu! 2 and *75* were separated by the first album from Harmonia, a supergroup Rother formed with Hans-Joachim Roedelius and Dieter Moebius of Cluster. Relative to Neu!, Harmonia was ambient, electronic, and even more obscure; their primary releases, *Musik Von Harmonia* (1974) and *Deluxe* (1975), attracted the attention of David Bowie and Brian Eno but few others. Rother sensed a new path opening for him with these collaborators, but the X factor was a visit to their retreat in the quiet town of Forst, off in the Weserbergland, an ancient stone house with full recording capabilities where Rother still resides. In the solo work that followed, he ventured further into these meditative landscapes, eventually turning to the Fairlight

Music Computer as his reliance on the guitar waned. Rother's 2004 album *Remember (The Great Adventure)* was the tenth in an individual career that's been much more commercially successful than his groundbreaking groups.

David Todd: The German bands of the early '70s were all so individualistic. Where do you think that came from?

Michael Rother: I think it was a feeling that was in the air in the '60s. It had to do with the general situation with postwar Germany, with the many political changes happening. With the Nazi past of Germany, there was so much to repair, and it was a sort of vacuum for change. I think it was quite a natural behavior of many German people to embrace something new. And I think out of that certain artists became aware of the necessity of developing their own identities. After the war, especially in Germany, the Anglo-American culture was embraced. There was hardly anything going on besides what came over the Atlantic or from England. So there were many reasons to think about what had to be changed.

You know, my brother is ten years older, and when I was young, he listened to rock 'n' roll, and that is still deep in my system. And I grew up trying to be just as close to my heroes as I could, by copying the guitar players of the times, like Eric Clapton, George Harrison, Jeff Beck, and Jimi Hendrix. And at the end of the '60s, the political changes were at their peak in Germany, and I think that there was a sort of virus of change that reached many artists. And the results, what people actually did with that feeling of trying to find their identities, were also very different from one person to another, and so I tried to be different from the people who wanted to be different. [*laughs*]

So that was actually the beginning of my voyage, in the musical sense, of trying to find my own handwriting.

DT: Did you have to remove those American and British styles from your subconscious?

MR: Yeah. That was a very difficult process, because one of the main systems I had learned was the blues, from Jimi Hendrix and Eric Clapton. And it became clear to me that this wasn't my culture, this wasn't what I could express as my own signature.

The first step was to avoid all the elements of rock and pop music, like playing blues notes, playing solos. All of that. Even the idea of being a virtuoso, that was something I wanted to leave behind. What I needed to do was reduce all these clichés, to avoid them by concentrating on only one note, one harmony, which is something you can hear on the first Neu! album. And I did this gradually, step by step, as if you were finding yourself in a strange country and trying to find your bearings. I was very careful, and I remember at the beginning being unsure whether even one additional harmony was necessary. If you know the first Neu! album, there's the track "Weissensee." All of the other tracks are only on one level, with one harmony, and "Weissensee" has a second harmony that, for me, had the idea of breathing in and out, like an up-and-down movement. But I was very cautious, and I remember thinking hard about that being right at all.

So that was the beginning, trying to forget all the idioms of rock and pop music.

DT: If you weren't aspiring to be a virtuoso, what were you aspiring to?

MR: I think the focus shifted from trying to impress people by moving around the guitar neck like a wizard playing a thousand notes per minute. [*laughs*] That felt ridiculous. Instead, the focus shifted to a feeling like being the conductor of an orchestra, of concentrating on the whole picture of the music. That was the goal, to replace the idea of being a great guitarist with making great music, of course.

DT: As you were going through this phase, were there other musicians you saw doing this?

MR: Hmm. Once I developed that idea of trying to be different, I think that it's logical to say that there weren't any heroes anymore. They had to be removed, and instead it was just the long way of trying to be your own hero.

Like I mentioned, I had grown up with all the heroes, and I still respected their music. Of course, Jimi Hendrix, he will forever remain an inspiration. But he was the best Jimi Hendrix that will ever be. There's no need for Michael Rother to try to become a second Jimi Hendrix. That's something that I realized as a late teenager.

DT: What was going on for you at that time?

MR: Well, for a while I was working as a conscientious objector in a hospital, and I was really wondering what to do next, because I wasn't happy with my music and I hadn't found any musicians who were on the same path. And I stumbled by chance into the people of Kraftwerk. I hadn't heard of them, but I ended up jamming with Ralf Hütter and that was the beginning of something new. Because he had the same feeling that I had. It was very simple: we just jammed and were so clear that we didn't need to talk. It was something I hadn't experienced before.

Shortly after that jam, the other band members invited me to join them. Hütter left the band for eight months or so, and we went on tour as Kraftwerk with Florian Scheider and Klaus Dinger.

Everything new started at that time. In Germany we have this expression "hour zero," the new start.

DT: You've said that all your bands relied on the chemistry among the personnel. How did you stay open to that?

MR: I think the reason was that each member of each band was as important as the others. Each one had his own strong ideas about music, and it was always a sort of struggle right from the beginning. And if you take one member away from any lineup, the result would be different. It had to be different. And that was the case, actually.

DT: It was never the usual situation with a guitarist and singer . . .

MR: . . . and they just replace the bass player with a new guy and nobody notices a difference? That wasn't the case with us, yes. All of the people with whom I've collaborated were artists who also inspired me, and of course it was a bidirectional inspiration, I guess.

DT: It seems like you and Klaus inspired each other, so to speak, to come up with things very quickly.

MR: Well with Klaus Dinger, I've said it many times, we're so very different. We're just two extremes of temperament, character, etc. And it's very difficult for me . . . you know Klaus died recently, so it's not so easy to talk about him. But he was a very difficult character, and I have to say we never were friends. We met in the studio, made music together—and we both knew we didn't have to talk about that; it was clear we complemented each other. With the help, of course, of Conny Plank, who must always be remembered. If you talk about the albums, you should bear in mind that without Conny Plank the albums maybe would never have happened. He was very creative—and, also, with a combination like ours, a strong guy like him was important as a mediator. He was someone who helped us move forward, instead of just saying yes-no, plus-and-minus.

In Harmonia, the three angles were a bit different, but still equally different personalities. It was just fortunate that I met those people, because working with them I was able to develop my ideas about music, and I'm sure that without the collaboration in Harmonia, my solo work would have sounded quite different. And also the third Neu! album, it was valuable to have worked with the two Cluster guys before that.

DT: It seems like you experienced both extremes of being fairly unfriendly with your bandmate in Neu! and very friendly with your bandmates, even living communally, with Harmonia.

MR: [*laughs*] It's not that easy, actually. You know, we chose that name, Harmonia, as a sort of joke, even. Because right from the beginning, it was clear that we were very different characters, and just like with Klaus Dinger, we knew we could do interesting music together, fascinating music that helped us individually. You know, it was always about your own feelings first. First of all you had to be convinced yourself.

I was equally convinced of my work with Klaus Dinger as I was with Harmonia, but Neu! certainly had different problems. With Neu!, we tried to do some live concerts in '72, but as a duo that wasn't possible. And we tried to find some musicians to help us and we just couldn't get anybody who excited us, who could help me create more of the sound of what I had done in the studio. With Harmonia, that was different. We had three people and electronic drums, and so Harmonia was capable of creating music on the spot that was convincing. And of course the personal aspects were quite different also.

It wasn't always paradise with Harmonia either, because in the beginning we played spontaneous music, no real fixed ideas, maybe like, "Oh, that's the song where you start with the drum machine," or "That's the one with the black keys." [*laughs*] And so sometimes we ended up nowhere. But having that much freedom also makes it possible to end up in really exciting places, with music you couldn't think of theoretically if you tried to compose it. For instance, "Ohrwurm," on the first Harmonia album, was recorded live. But I think the song is five minutes long and the concert we did was probably two hours. And I think the five minutes of "Ohrwurm" is the most intense music I've been involved in, but the remaining one hour and fifty-five minutes must've been quite a challenge for the people. You know, we were searching, searching, and getting nowhere. But that was the idea.

DT: Along with these interpersonal elements, chance and circumstance seem important to these bands, at least when working in the studio with Neu!

MR: Oh, sure. We didn't have any money, and we didn't have a record contract when we did the first Neu! album. I think we recorded the first album in four nights, and then we had a few days when we did the mixing. And in those four nights, we just had to move forward all the time. There was no chance to contemplate and try to improve the recordings. I think we were very fortunate in the end, especially with the first Neu! album—I mean, the second Neu! album was also a very difficult situation, but the first Neu! album could've crashed completely. I think there was always the danger with Neu! of crashing. We didn't have money to work in detail, so we had to just throw in some colors and see what happened.

I remember the recording of "Hallogallo." We didn't theorize before we went in, we just laid down the basic pattern, playing together for twelve minutes, maybe. And from then on it was just trying to add some colors, and that's when I suddenly had this feedback in the studio. That was very fortunate, because it helped create these long notes, these long clouds flying over the beat. That was something that surprised me. And the way we worked—I mean, Conny just had the idea, "OK, I'll turn around the tape, make it run backwards," and then I played a few more guitars, and then he turned it around again. We were jumping from one stone to the next. And in the end we just managed to fill an album, and maybe the fact that we didn't have time to improve made it so special. I mean, "Hallogallo" has a very fragile sound. I love it to this day. When we did the second Neu! album, we tried to do a sort of super-"Hallogallo" on the first track, "Für Immer," but we got lost there in a way, and that led to some problems you may have heard about: we only had one week in the studio, and on the beginning of the last night, we just had material for one side.

DT: That was probably the most extreme circumstance-driven decision you made, to do several different remixes of "Neuschnee 78" and "Super 16" as side two of *Neu! 2*.

MR: Well, we had the single [of those two songs] and the record company just didn't promote it. We wanted to present those two tracks on the album because they had been wasted. But that was only seven minutes; that's not exactly a whole side. And Klaus started kicking the turntable, and then . . . it was a crazy night. I mean, Klaus started all that. And I knew I didn't have any other options, but I also felt, "We aren't going to get away with this." [*laughs*] I mean, I liked some of the sound experiments, because I did sound experiments at the time at home, but I was completely sure that people weren't ready for that. And back then, the reception was very bad, especially to the second side. We took a lot of abuse for that.

DT: Now it's seen as innovative.

MR: Yeah, nowadays it's different. Maybe it's hard to imagine what the audience, especially in Germany, was used to. I can show you, I have those reviews and it's quite funny to read them.

DT: In general, did you think much about the audience?

MR: I think we were quite optimistic, because we had these concerts as Kraftwerk together and we both knew how we could excite the people. I mean, even then people were going crazy sometimes with the kind of drive we developed. And even though the Neu! drive was different from what we did with Florian, we were optimistic that people would like to hear it.

I think the main thing is that there were no compromises, really—we weren't willing to make any. I remember we had just finished recording the first Neu! album and there was a guy from a record label in the studio, and he listened to "Hallogallo" and he said, "Ah! You can't do it that way! Look at that stupid drum sound! You must listen to English drums!" [*laughs*] But there was no way we would have allowed anybody from a record company to discuss anything with us. We were very self-assured, self-confident. We just presented the music and that was what you got.

DT: Not many artists can refer to themselves as uncompromising and optimistic in the same breath.

MR: Yeah. But whenever I loved the music—and I was fortunate that I loved all of the projects that I worked on—I wasn't always right with that optimism. I was equally convinced of Harmonia, and that really crashed into the next wall. I mean, nobody wanted to hear Harmonia back then. And later on when I recorded my first solo album, I was again equally convinced, but then I heard that the distribution company ordered 150 copies for all of Germany. [*laughs*] I lost all hope. I knew in that moment, "Nothing's going to happen, nobody will find the music in the record shops." And then of course the album took off.

I'm just trying to say that I knew I needed this belief and it was always there, and looking back to when we started with Neu!, the optimism was there, and the love for the music was there, and the conviction that it was worth it. But what the audience does is something completely different, and that's up to factors you can't control. Sometimes you have to wait for thirty years, like has happened with Harmonia. I'm not sure if you've noticed all the attention Harmonia's been getting. It's amazing. Nothing similar happened back then. Nothing. Even Neu! was more popular back then.

DT: Do you still have the same belief in all your past projects? There are still a lot of echoes of Neu! in your solo work.

MR: Oh, definitely. Maybe even more these days than in earlier times. Of course, the focus shifts, you know, in spirals: when I look back, I know that I more or less come back not to the same point, but I pick up the ideas that I once was very fond of and then I confront them with what I'm thinking today, and also confront the old technology with new technology—that's always exciting. I still have all the old gear, and if you look at what I use these days, you have gadgets from 1968 next to gadgets out of the store right now. That changes the possibility of sound-creating.

But you were asking about the feeling for Neu!, or that idea of flying to the horizon. I know that's a picture I'm using, but the idea was really to rush forward; it was a fast movement without anything being in the way. Unlimited forward movement. And that of course has appeal and it's very close to my heart these days, definitely.

DT: Where do you stand with the guitar these days?

MR: As I say, you move in spirals, and sometimes I don't feel like playing guitar. There was only one track with real guitar, live guitar, on my last album, but I'm happy that there was one track, because these days I feel very close to playing it. Maybe I'll move away from the guitar again sometime in the future, but I very much love playing the guitar now, with all the gear possible.

DT: Ultimately, do you think of yourself as a guitarist?

MR: It's the instrument that, in a technical sense, I play the best. And of course—it sounds maybe a bit like showing off—I created some sort of style on the guitar that I never hear anywhere else. I know that the guitar has a quality I love.

I am a guitar player, but the difference in my music is the addition of all the manipulations, of what I can do with all the sounds I create. It's not trying to impress people by moving my fingers around the fretboard; it's about the results coming out of the speakers. And there are many contributions, many different aspects that all add up to that sound. It's not only playing the guitar.

DT: Do you think you could express yourself completely on the guitar if you had to?

MR: [*laughs*] But what does that mean, express completely? There's always only one thing you can focus on at a time. There are many colors in the soul, and you can only express one or maybe a mixture of some emotions at some times. But *completely*? I wouldn't sign that.

⑦

INFINITE DELAY

RICHARD PINHAS

PHOTO BY LYNN S.K.; COURTESY OF CUNEIFORM RECORDS

French alternist Richard Pinhas provides a continental lens through which British blues and science fiction come into focus. In his prescient way, Pinhas "responded" to experimenters such as Kraftwerk and Robert Fripp despite having yet to discover them when he founded Heldon in Paris in the early 1970s. From those early days into an extended solo career, Pinhas refined his formula of Moog loops, detached drums, and highly conscious guitar, establishing himself among the founders of electronic rock. Yet Pinhas (born 1951) is far from a technophile relying on software in place of personality. "The important thing is that the musician understands how to compose his own music and knows how best to express this music—whether electronically or not," he told *Electronics and Music Maker* in 1982. "You have to be a musician before you can be an electronic musician." Similarly, viewing Pinhas only in the context of his study with philosopher Gilles Deleuze overlooks the emotion buzzing through his anti-oedipal compositions. "Music helps me understand some philosophical concepts just as concepts help me to make my music," he asserted more recently to *Express Night Out*. He may have lectured at the Sorbonne, but that doesn't reduce his affinity for the raw noise of Wolf Eyes.

With Heldon, Pinhas had no electronic rock tradition to draw from, so he made up his own, moving quickly from Tangerine Dream–scapes to Faustian postindustrial suites. Having named the band after a city in Norman Spinrad's novel *The Iron Dream*, Pinhas perhaps crystallized Heldon's futurism with *Interface* (1976), but that could be an effect of the bug-eyed spaceman on the cover. The album's sequence of "Les soucoupes volantes vertes," "Le retour des soucoupes volantes," and "Le fils des soucoupes volantes" reflects Pinhas's "process of process," or philosophy of doing and repeating as ends unto themselves. "I've spent all my life trying to do all I could against this fucking system by sending out pieces of wildness," Pinhas effused to *Prism Escape* in 2004, in a more hyperbolic mood than I found him. "Making the strongest music ever possible in its inner intensity would be the ideal." Pinhas's intensity manifests in the dissonant "Zind destruction" and the gritty "Méchamment rock" from Heldon's 1975 album *It's Always Rock 'N' Roll*, or the fourteen-minute prog metal attack that opens 1979's *Stand By*.

Given that Richard Pinhas essentially *was* Heldon, there wasn't much concern that his late-1970s solo break would diminish their essence. Yet over the last thirty years, Pinhas has edged closer to ambient or trance, even free jazz. "They have different names for my music in each country," he laughs. "I don't care about this. Are you a post-rock guitarist or . . . ? I'm just a guitarist." As such, Pinhas uses tracks like "Tranzition" (2004) to achieve a dream-lag effect; his sustained meditations on *Metatron* (2006) are disrupted only by sampled bits of spoken word from writers such as Maurice Dantec, Bret

Easton Ellis, and Philip K. Dick. What holds these voices together is what holds the rest of the songs together—i.e., Pinhas, who lurks behind them like a DJ spinning paperbacks. In its best moments, his guitar becomes pure consciousness, unwinding beneath layers of harmonizing, what the BBC described as "music that's in flux and stasis at the same time."

DAVID TODD: How is your music informed by the philosophy you've studied?

RICHARD PINHAS: The relationship with the guitar is very direct for me, immediate. I like to play with empathy, feelings. I'm not transcendental at all. But in the conception of the music, that's a completely different thing. As a composer, there is a serious relationship—and I mean this after thirty-five years of thinking about this—between a lot of philosophical concepts and their applications in the kind of music I do. I think that for all repetitive music—[Steve] Reich, [Philip] Glass, even people like Robert Fripp—there are some main concepts that are also main concepts in the history of philosophy. As an example, there is the concept of time, the concept of repetition, of difference—the concept of process as something phenomenological, an immanent way of playing and composing.

As you know, the immanent philosophy came first for me. At the time I was doing my Ph.D., everything was focused on the concept of repetition, of time, and that went right with the repetitive music that I was doing in, let's say, the year '72. And then I spent one year teaching philosophy, and then I stopped, because I thought it was not possible to do both seriously. But I still enjoy coming back to philosophy every day, so philosophy is pertinent in my comportment and in the composition of music. So I hope I answered your question.

DT: I think so. The ideas apply more with composing than with playing, which you approach intuitively?

RP: Yes, of course. When I'm doing a solo, I'm not thinking about the concept of it. I hope to be spontaneous enough that I can express what I want, because music is not word, it's something very different. So you need a lot of technique, but if you don't have the rest, it's not very important. You can do music without technique, but you can't do music without feeling. Without soul. But it's better to have both, and arrive at the point where you have enough technique to do what you have in your head. I just need to have the technique to express myself.

But that doesn't mean that I don't practice. I play every day, and I even like to do scales. Because I've lived with this for nearly forty years now, and if I don't play every day, I feel like dying. But if I don't read, I feel like dying too.

DT: Did you study music at all during your philosophy years?

RP: No. At that time, in France, you didn't have teachers. Rock 'n' roll was just coming, so there was no video, no books. I think that's why a lot of guitarists of that era, guitarists who are fifty and up now, have a special way of playing, each one. They can't play like you would see in a school . . . this row, this row, hold your pick in a certain way. And my way of playing guitar became a kind of process joined to the act of composing.

DT: What was the music scene like in Paris when you were starting out?

RP: In Paris, because of the Rolling Stones, Hendrix, Miles Davis, it was like everywhere else.

DT: What about French music?

RP: Oh, there was nothing. In France, the only interesting thing you had was Magma. Magma started in '70, just two, three, years before Heldon. But I can say that Magma was very interesting.

DT: Did you see a way that you could fit into what was going on?

RP: To be honest, no. The thing is, at this time, the main vector was politics, because it was just after the year '68. The political struggles were the main force, so the question was how the music could fit into the political field. I mean, I was very involved in the leftist movement at this time, and we had the feeling that music could change the economic system. In fact, it could not. In fact, after thirty years we see that it could not at all. [*laughs*] But music can change people in their ways of thinking and hoping, so it can always be a vehicle.

I'm still very anarchist, really. Very anarchist.

DT: Is that a good thing?

RP: I don't know if it's good or not. It's just a thing.

DT: You've said before that music must be revolutionary.

RP: I think so. Of course, the only thing that changes is the meaning of "revolutionary," because we've learned that revolution in the Marxist sense is not viable anymore. But, in fact, the art itself and the music itself still have revolutionary potential, at least in the minds of the people, on their feelings and on their ways of living their lives. I hope so.

DT: So you put that expectation on yourself?

RP: Of course.

DT: Were there times when you made decisions to make your music more or less revolutionary, so to speak, more or less conventional?

RP: No, not [more or less] conventional, but each time you have to think in a different way to make an innovation. It's like in science: you have to find each time a new way to go, so it's more and more complex. A new formula, new form, new materials—it's a process of innovation, and the process of innovation in art is something very revolutionary. It can be. It's not always, but it can be.

DT: What were you listening to in those early years?

RP: I was very influenced at that time by classical music—Stockhausen, things like this—and by Jimi Hendrix. The Jimi Hendrix concert I saw was amazing. As a guitarist, I was mainly in the British blues tree that produced Jimmy Page, Jeff Beck, and Eric Clapton. I also discovered Miles Davis and a very different use of the synthesizer, so I went into the looping stuff too, and I discovered people like Philip Glass, Steve Reich. And so I went off with the guitar on these strange things, because mainly those things were happening with keyboard and I had to do something with guitar. The thing is that I didn't want synthesizer music; I wanted to have a real instrument like the guitar, because I played guitar, and with real drums. So that was the difference from the German groups. I had a mix of electronic stuff and real rock instruments.

DT: Did you know the German groups then?

RP: At first, no. I discovered them after my fourth or fifth record, through journalists who made me look into them. It was strange for me.

DT: People kept comparing you to them?

RP: Yeah. But when Kraftwerk came to Paris, I met them. They wanted to see me and I was very honored. To be honest, of the German groups, the one I preferred was Kraftwerk. They made something very different.

DT: It seems like the music world has changed over the years in a way that puts Heldon in a better light, especially mixing guitar and electronic elements.

RP: It's common now; it was not that common at the time.

DT: The younger bands you've worked with, like Wolf Eyes, seem to appreciate what you did.

RP: I'm just interested in working with these guys. I was very . . . not ashamed, but surprised by the way they told me that Heldon affected them very much.

DT: Why did that surprise you?

RP: Because when people who are ten times more well known than you say, "Your music influenced me a lot," it's always surprising. I've not such an ego that I think I've done so much, you know. But I realize that after thirty years, Heldon was more important than I thought in the interim.

DT: Were there a lot of ups and downs for you over the years?

RP: Oh, of course. I have had periods where I didn't do anything. I can wait for months and if I don't feel the necessity to do the thing, I don't do it. And it's happened for me that for five, six years—I didn't make music at all. In the '80s, I thought that the process was finished for me. It was impossible for me to make music at that time; I had no ideas of new things. I was really afraid.

DT: The '80s were good years to lay low.

RP: Yeah. I remarked at that time, Kraftwerk wasn't doing anything, Eno was doing very small things, and I realized that as an honest musician I was having a long nonproductive period. The other ones were just repeating the same things, but I don't have the need to repeat myself. I prefer not to do anything than to repeat the same thing, you know?

DT: Eventually, you came back.

RP: Yeah. It was a change to come back. You know, when you stop for four or five years, generally, in ninety-nine percent of these cases, you'd stop [for good]. It was a great chance to come back and to have the energy to play, and something new to say.

DT: What prompted that?

RP: It was the grunge music, these people like Nirvana. Even if I don't make music like Nirvana, they were of real importance, because the best thing you could hear in the 1980s was Michael Jackson. It was like a tornado, the '80s, you had to put your head down during those years. You didn't know how long it would last, and six, seven years later, it changed.

DT: Going back a little, the other musician I wanted to ask you about was Robert Fripp. What's your relationship with him?

RP: I know him. We've had a friendly relationship, until recently. Yeah, and I always recognize his influence, that's all. I love very much the music he does, more for the first years of King Crimson, between '70 and '74, and the so-called Frippertronics, before Fripp and Eno released their records.

At one time, when King Crimson were giving concerts in Europe, before starting they were playing some tapes of unknown music. That was the music of Frippertronics, and that was very influential on me. I recognize it now. It was a big influence when I was younger, yes.

DT: Didn't you develop a looping system, not necessarily a version of Frippertronics, but something similar?

RP: Later, yes. In the '90s, I developed a kind of looping system, like everybody did. I mean, it was a very cheap system, very practical to take on stage. Because the Robert Fripp one was very complex. And for the last ten years I've played on the Eventide system I have. We had a lot of discussions about this, Robert and me.

DT: What was the concept for your looping system? I thought you used a term like "evolving" for the patterns.

RP: Evolving? I don't know, but they're changing, yeah. They are processing.

DT: How does that come about?

RP: It's a question of the way you attack the strings of the guitar, and which preset you use in the process. The main indication is how you attack the guitar with a pick and a volume knob and a pedal, if I'm going into process. Then I've got algorithms: one to do the sound, and another one to create action on the loops. So I can decide if it's a hundred-percent action or a ten-percent action or whatever. But there are two very different things. One thing is to work on the songs. And another thing is to control the looping system just as I wish.

DT: So parts go into the loop and then . . .

RP: I let them go, for what kind of harmony, repetition I need, and which type of song I want. I try to have complete control on this. Of course, there are a lot of advantages to this system, but you have to remember that if you make only one mistake, it can run forever, you know, with the repetition.

DT: When you are composing, do you begin with things like experiments with your Eventide system or do you tend to work thematically?

RP: The thing is, I have an idea in my head and I want to make it real. That's always been the only thing for me. So this goes by stages: you have an album and the tracks and all the different sequences of the tracks. And at each level the idea has to be getting more concrete. So the main thing of the composition process is to give life, and to give reality to each level I've got in mind.

Let's say for one album I have an idea of the general stuff I want. It's like a border, and into this border I fit the music that I want to do. So I will focus on the time aspect at one time, and on the perspective at another. I try to have something like a guide and respect the boundaries of this guide.

Sometimes it can be real work to get inside the border something that is not naturally inside. So a part of the work is to fit it in. For example, for my last album I tried to make a very special connection between some Magma musicians, some musicians from Wolf Eyes, Merzbow, and my guitar. And everybody said, "What's the relationship?" And I said, "That's just the problem, I hear something and I want to make it." So I went to record the drums with my engineer, only two tracks. We just had an *idea* of the drums we were putting down. And after hearing those two tracks, he said, "Ah! I was not thinking about this at all!" Because they were fitting. And even my own engineer, who knows me very well, was surprised.

I'm evolving, processing, but I haven't changed my approach. There's my love of the music, and there's the way I do it. Of course, there are things that thirty years ago would have been very hard to do but are very easy to do today with technology. But it's always the same things.

DT: When you are working out your guitar parts, what techniques do you use? I assume it's not a lot of chord changes.

RP: No, I hate that. For the guitar, you mean? No.

I play a lot with computer effects on the guitar; I love to work very deep inside with the effects that can give you this type of expression. I mean mainly the Eventide Harmonizer, but not in the harmonizer mode. It lets you work on time squeeze, time shift, a lot of things like this. If you get down inside it, you have a very open platform. And I can spend days with this.

DT: Is that where "the process of the process" comes in?

RP: Yeah. The process of the process, that means it's endless, and you'll always have to work on this thing that you worked on the day before, to try to make the form more perfected, to get something different and more developed.

I think it's a given that you have to have a reason. A plan. And the music succeeds on the realization of the process of this plan. But, of course, the material is also important. More important than the notes themselves or the lengths of the notes, the thing I try to find with the music is a feeling. In one way, it's a very technical and complex process, and in another way—and maybe more important—it's about the feeling. And they are antithetical; they are paradoxical. But, in fact, that's the way I see it. And to realize both aspects, it's very difficult, because logic is very opposite to feelings.

To succeed with a composition, it has to be immediately emotional. Even if it's complex, even if it's classical, the emotion has to be there. And it's my problem as the composer to try to make it immediately emotional for the people who hear it, even if it's with computers. The public's perception has to be exactly as it [would be] with only a guitar plugged into an amp.

DT: As the composer, do you feel like you're ever able to put your finger on the emotion of a song?

RP: I say this because I'm a guitar player: I don't know, in reality. I don't have a definite idea about that.

DT: I like how for one of those you're a composer and for the other you're a guitarist. So do you consider yourself a guitarist above other designations?

RP: It depends on how you define a guitarist. If it's Jeff Beck, it's odd, because that's a high comparison. Generally, the most important things are writing, reading, playing, and composing, and composing is perhaps where I can give the most as myself. So I prefer that you look at me as a composer first.

But I like the idea of being a guitarist. I preferred it to teaching philosophy. I had that choice, and I decided when I was twenty-two what to do with my life.

DT: You said earlier that you come from the Clapton tradition in terms of guitar.

RP: Oh yeah. Of course, I come from the blues tradition.

DT: How do you see yourself as fitting into that?

RP: At the very lowest level. [*laughs*]

DT: But you're not in that tradition now?

RP: No, no, that's not what I mean. I mean, for a guitarist, the British blues tradition is something very important. But do I mean, "Oh, can I compare myself to people like Hendrix or Jeff Beck?" That's ridiculous, because they play like gods and I don't play like a god.

DT: Do you see yourself as playing a blues-derived style?

RP: Yeah, it's the same vocabulary for every guitarist. There are some legends like Hendrix and there are all the others, that's all.

DT: That's interesting, because you went down a different path than most others who would cite those people as influences.

RP: I can say that Hendrix was a major influence and yet it doesn't influence my way of playing. Who can play like Jimi Hendrix? Even watching what he's doing, it's impossible.

DT: Millions of people have tried.

RP: There are a million people who tried to do a copy of a copy of a copy. The more difficult thing is to do your original stuff, your original stuff that's only in your brain so that it can't be copied. So your brain is guiding everything. And when I say "your brain," it's of course including your soul.

I think the way I'm playing now, it's obliged to be the result of my whole life, you know? It's not because at fifteen I heard Jimi Hendrix, and at twenty I heard someone else, that I play like I do. I just play like the processes in my head. It can be good, or bad, or inside or outside. I'm just feeling it. Sometimes you feel you're going in a good direction because you're at a very high level. Sometimes you're not and you know it's time to stop, and you reflect.

⑧

LOVE THEME FROM
THE TWILIGHT ZONE

TOM VERLAINE

"Verlaine at his best . . . succeeds by clouding or shading the distinction between the dreamer and the dreamed, between the dream and the words that suggest it. 'All the rest is literature,' or so says our poet singing his 'grey song' in a minor key."
—Robin Orr Bodkin, on Paul Verlaine (1844–96)

From his days fronting New York City art dealers Television, Tom Verlaine has always been as elusive as his watercolor playing style. Raised on Ravel and the sci-fi theremin, he backed his way into rock via the same poetics as longtime intimate Patti Smith, mixing haiku and pulp fiction, jazz modality and twang. In a career spanning three studio albums with Television and nine solo outings, Verlaine cultivated powerful eccentricities such as the plunking anti-solo on "Little Johnny Jewel," the "switchblade" slide of "The Fire," and the film noir of "Call Mr. Lee." "I didn't ever have any interest in virtuosity," he says in his neurotic but laconic mumble. "You know?" Call it what you want, but when he plays one of his fluid skinsheddings, or explodes like a tiger into a roar of bells, it makes sense that Robert Palmer once proclaimed in the *New York Times*, "Tom Verlaine is the guitarist to mention these days if you're a young rocker with some pretense to intelligence and originality."

Along with his gifted foil in Television, Richard Lloyd, Verlaine authored one of the most intriguing two-guitar sounds in rock history, one that zippered like the streets of Times Square into too much contradiction. From the top of their jeweled debut, 1977's *Marquee Moon*, the stops and frills of "See No Evil" initiate a nervous cohesion that endures through 1978's *Adventure* and even survives a fourteen-year breakup until their sole reunion, 1992's *Television*. Often attributed to chemistry, this stitching was actually agonized over: "There was a hell of a lot of arrangement work in there," Verlaine told *Guitarist* just before the release of their final album. "It was by no means two guys jumping into a room and having this magical blend." But when you hear the interlocking neo-reggae upstrokes and neo–James Brown horn parts that open "Marquee Moon," all those dues the band paid—Television demoed with Brian Eno for Island Records as early as 1974—seem worthwhile.

Things would come easier for Verlaine with former Mick Jagger sideman Jimmy Ripp, his partner from 1982's *Words from the Front* on; their projects include guitar interpretations of "*cinépoèmes*" by Man Ray and Hans Richter collected in 2007's *Music for Experimental Film* DVD. Recording regularly as a solo artist, Verlaine also kept ties over the years with Patti Smith, did the occasional Television tour, composed the score for the 1994 film *Love and a .45*, and covered Dylan's "Cold Irons Bound" with the Million Dollar Bashers in 2007.

"Broadway looked so medieval," Verlaine sang in "Venus" (1977). "It seemed to flap, like little pages / I fell sideways laughing with a friend from many stages." This was just one example of the precision lyrics that matched the artistry of his playing. But his surname, taken half-presciently from a French symbolist, wasn't the only alias the former Tom Miller, born in 1949 and raised in Delaware, adopted. He was also half of Theresa Stern, an invented junkie prostitute created with "friend" and Television cofounder Richard Hell (né Meyers) who spoke in aphorisms such as "Like myself, my poetry is so alive it stinks." Verlaine would outgrow those proto-punk gags just as he outgrew the stage at CBGB—which, legend has it, he helped build. But he never lost a sense for how important the trash on the sidewalk was to his cityscapes. "These cold-blooded streets / They ain't no place to meet," he wrote in 1981, with hard-boiled Zen. "Oooooooo, darling / Mysteries come and go."

DAVID TODD: You always had your own sound, even relative to guitarists who cite you as an influence. One thing you might have in common with some of the others in this book is an interest in free-jazz people like John Coltrane.

TOM VERLAINE: Well, I wouldn't say Coltrane was an influence. He was a much better player of his instrument than I am on anything, first of all. Actually, the two I really liked out of that free-jazz revolution were Albert Ayler and [Eric] Dolphy, you know? But even before that . . . you know, if I do anything different, I really think it has to do with coming from having piano lessons when I was a kid, loving piano music and then loving jazz.

Rock music was really a regression [for me], coming from something that's schooled into something that maybe isn't schooled. And almost every guitar player I knew learned by playing along to records, you know, learning licks. And I never did this. When I decided to play guitar, I made a map of a neck and put it on the wall, and on each fret I put the notes, because I could remember from piano and sax what a scale was. So I put it together really quick, what a guitar was.

I never learned how to play guitar licks, ever. So that might be one difference in me, like I say.

DT: Instead of guitar licks, did you transpose things from piano and sax?

TV: I didn't really transpose anything; I just wanted to write songs. I mean, you can't sing and play sax very well together, so I thought, "I want to write and sing. OK, I'll play guitar."

I think I was too young to know what I was doing, you know? I remember I looked at a Bob Dylan songbook and I said, "Oh, there are only three chords there—what are they? Oh, what's *that*?"

You know, I still can't really play any Rolling Stones songs note for note. But those kinds of guitar sounds I also really liked.

DT: That was the other side of that coin for a lot of people. They liked Ayler types on one hand, and then on the other hand, they admired figures within rock like the Stones, the Kinks, the Yardbirds . . .

TV: The Yardbirds, yeah.

DT: The Who—maybe not as much for you.

TV: Well, the first Who record was a pretty cool record. That whole rhythm guitar style was amazing.

. . . I mean, that isn't to say I didn't like Coltrane. Just that, I think, the word "influence" is kind of dubious, you know? [*laughs*] If you say a guy like Michael Bloomfield was influenced by the blues, I'd be like, "Sure, he was. He was a blues player." But with so many other guys it's hard to say.

DT: Actually, I thought people like Coltrane and Ayler were more of an influence on your image of what a musician could be.

TV: Ah . . .

Hmm . . . I can't honestly say what I wanted to be. [*laughs*]

I mean, Coltrane did violin exercises. You know this? It's something I'd never have the discipline to do, but once I looked at them I said, "Oh, this is really interesting," because there's this strange link for a lot of jazz guys to the classical world at a certain time in their lives, like Charlie Parker tracking down Edgard Varèse and going to his house. In other words, the interlinkings of all these different things—when you start investigating them, it's pretty interesting.

There's also the whole Eastern interest that jumped up in the '60s with ragas, although they didn't go all that deep into it in American music, I think. I looked a little bit at Indian music, and there's this concept called *rasa*, which is based on somewhere between six and eight moods, and they're more interesting than you'd think. One's the family mood, which is something that doesn't occur to Western people, like, "What is the family mood, and how do you make music out of it?" [*laughs*] Then there's the erotic mood, and there are things that aren't in there that are controversial, because I think the angry mood, for instance, is not considered good to write from. I mean, I might be wrong, [but] I [don't think] the horror thing is in there, which is interesting because to many people there's something *horrible* about Schoenberg or about Varèse; to some, even, there's the hands-over-the-ears reaction to free jazz—"Let me out of here!" [*laughs*]

To me it just sounds good, you know. The tones of those players are so great. Ayler's tone is fucking fantastic.

DT: Was that tone something you could transpose in a way?

TV: I think the vocal quality of the playing, the kind of growling, was. Like sometimes when you're a kid you pretend to be an animal, like, "Now I'm going to be a bear!" This kind of frivolousness can be applied to guitar playing, you know. "I'm a shark!" [*laughs*]

DT: Can you think of a song where you did that?

TV: Well, the "Friction" solo. There's this line about "How does the snake get out of its skin," and I just thought, "This is how it *goes!*"

But, you know, I was so young when I was listening to that [jazz] music; the reaction was completely unconscious. I have no idea what this music was doing to me or why I liked it so much. My brother at the same time would be blaring Motown records—I thought those were pretty good, but they just didn't get across to me.

DT: What was the process like as you went from writing songs for yourself to writing for Television? How did you write "Prove It" or "Venus?"

TV: "Venus" . . . I was visiting my family in Delaware and there was a piano, and I looked at it and I thought, "You know, the left hand could be one guitar and the right hand could be another guitar." And I'm not a really good piano player, but I started messing around on the white ones in the key of C, and that's basically how that song got structured. I showed the right-hand parts to Richard [Lloyd] and I said, "Maybe you can do this," and we played around with it.

DT: That sounds like a jazz-derived concept.

TV: It's actually ragtime in many ways. It goes back to ragtime, although there's nothing ragtime about that song. It is pianistic.

"Prove It" was more about taking a very clichéd chord structure—because I'd actually written the lyrics to that first and I thought, "I want this really simple," you know? I just used that standard "Stand by Me," used-in-a-million-songs thing, and I put in these rhythm-and-blues parts for the verse. And then I wanted to change it dramatically for the other parts of the song.

The other thing in those days that was shaping some of the lyrics was just pulling shit from movies and TV. Like, "Prove it" comes out of the old *Dragnet* show with the cop saying . . . I don't know if he ever said that, but he said. . . . what was his big saying? You know, Jack Webb?

DT: That song has the line "Just the facts."

TV: Actually, that's it. [*laughs*] It's strange, because I didn't really like watching television when I was growing up; it was more fun playing in the woods or taking long walks to see what was by the railroad tracks or this kind of Americana, for lack of a better word, stuff.

The black-and-white element is also really strong, that weird silvery quality of all those old TV shows and movies—something in my mind really responds to that to this day. Also early '50s crime stuff, low-budget crime films, usually with really good dialogue. A certain amount of tough-guy stuff is really appealing.

DT: What do you like about that?

TV: Well, it's funny, is what it is. But it's also somehow skillful, and it indicates a certain attitude toward reality that you might have to take up just to brace yourself for all the crap that goes on in life. I think that's where that attitude comes from.

DT: It's a good survival mode.

TV: It's survival, yeah. Especially in New York City when you're young. When I first got to New York I didn't come off a farm, but I was in many ways a farm boy in the beginning. I didn't realize that women chased men, you know. I'd be invited to girls' houses and I'd think they wanted me to meet their pet cat or something. I was really naïve. [*laughs*]

DT: It seems like it did take some time for you to get going in New York. Did you have any concrete plans in your first few years?

TV: Uh-uh. I had tried to put a band together in Delaware, but nobody ever wanted to rehearse. So in September of '68 I just came to New York and thought I'd do it, and then it fell apart really quick, because everybody was doing drugs and stuff, and I wasn't finished taking drugs by then but I wasn't interested in getting stoned every day and jamming. Plus, growing up I didn't have any books, so my whole discovery of words happened in the first six months in New York, working at the Strand [Book Store]. Now it's all younger people there, but in those days it was half younger people and half people that had been there for twenty years, really well-read people. They'd be throwing shit at me, literally saying, "Read this, kid!"—you know, because they could tell I was just some kid from Delaware. [*laughs*] And it'd be a Baudelaire book or something, and I'd take it home and I'd be like, "Oh, God, this is amazing!" I mean, I never knew you could think in these ways. I didn't know you could write like this or have these kinds of thoughts; it was so inspiring. And this led to writing, that kind of freeing of your whole . . . like you develop systems without even knowing what your systems are, you know? Then when you come across these other things you go, "*Oh . . .*"

DT: Were there any breakthroughs like that for you musically?

TV: I think I just sort of went along. But in terms of standing alone on a stage and doing gigs, I think I only did two or three and they were twenty-minute sets, you know. And what was interesting about that was the whole performance thing of being there—I don't know what it does to you; it's so vastly different than doing it alone in a room! [*laughs*]

I remember the first time I thought, "I'll do this and see if anybody says anything." I was just wanting to have a reaction, but when I actually did it I thought, "Well, it doesn't matter what the reaction is. There's a certain clarity you get from just doing it and realizing what you don't want." And that being said, I probably wrote twenty [songs] that I thought I could do live at that point, and after doing three songs I probably threw out fifteen of them. I said, "Oh, I'll never want to sing that in front of people." There was something right away that led to developing some sort of . . . I don't know if it was an aesthetic, but it was a decision to present certain things and not present other things.

DT: What was the dividing line?

TV: I'm not really sure. What was the dividing line between the ones that got shut . . . ? [*laughs*] Let me think. . . .

The criteria, that's the word. What became the criteria to actually keep working on a song? Shit, I don't know. [*laughs*]

I think the things I threw away had to do with things that other people could do better or that had already been done.

DT: Was lyric-writing an area you thought you could do better in? You always seemed more serious about lyrics than most.

TV: I mean, I don't mind a good throwaway song if it has a certain enthusiasm, but I probably put in twenty times the amount of time on lyrics that I do the music, because I have to think, "Am I gonna want to stand up singing this for ten years?" But I don't know if there was any progress in the writing then. To me it was always about stripping things down, to see how simple they could get.

DT: The idea of stripping things down is something I wanted to ask about, because I tend to notice poets of the free-form type and then those of the sculptural type, and then a few who are equally both. I was wondering, as a songwriter who also writes poetry, how you see yourself.

TV: Well, I think it has to do with self-editing, you know. I mean, until Walt Whitman, people were writing in these schemes and rhythms, and then Whitman came along with this thing that kind of threw all that out the window and still was able to say something and have a feeling and not just be chaos, you know. Then that, of course, went worldwide, that influence. And I think a lot of lyric-writing has to do with distilling things and having a certain preference for editing too. "Marquee Moon" had about twelve verses at first, and then within two days I realized, "Well, these three are really good," and then I kept those three that I wanted to sing. Somebody else might've sung them all.

DT: Does that idea of editing or self-awareness also apply to your guitar playing?

TV: Yeah. For sure. I remember at some point, probably late '60s, I was playing an acoustic guitar: my thumb was hitting the open E, and I would just go through all the notes on the skinnier strings one at a time to see what they sounded like against the E, you know? And you hear the flavor of each note, like the high E♭ against the low E, the D, the C♯, the C. And when you do a couple in a row you realize, "Oh, that's what they do in Persian music, they use those two notes against the E"—all these things start to go through your mind. I mean, if I were teaching guitar, that would be the first thing I would do. I would say, "You have to learn what flavor each note has against the bass note," because it's going to have a certain flavor and you want to be able to choose that flavor, like you're cooking up something for somebody. "Do you want this flavor? Do you want that?" And then the next thing is, "What temperature do you want to serve this little soup at? Do you want it cool? Do you want it played hot? Do you want it played spicy ferocious? Do you want it very mild?" You know, those different touches on the guitar are what you hear in really good jazz solos, in the way that Pablo Casals will play a Bach piece. That's the kind of flavor a good chef has. He knows what flavors are available and he knows how to get them.

And also . . . how to combine those flavors. What I don't like about most rock music is it's just one thing in one scale—you know, one blues scale—and it's way too fast. I don't mind the tempo fast, but I guess the popular guitarists of the last twenty years are basically the fast guitar players. That's how it is.

DT: Were there any guitarists you thought had that awareness?

TV: A really good flavor guy was [Steve] Cropper. And in the '80s, someone gave me a compilation called *Beatles Love Songs*, this double-vinyl thing. I didn't listen to the Beatles; I always thought the Beatles were very twee. But I finally realized, yeah, "[George] Harrison was amazing!" He's another guy who had this flavor thing down—just the right touch and the right notes, you know. That's the kind of stuff I admire, and maybe try to do myself. Being able to, like, *know* . . .

Everybody fusses around on guitar when they're making records, but sometimes you get a song and you get the solo, and in three minutes it's done. Other times it takes forever to play a solo you like. But I realized that, yeah, by having this concept where you could think, "Well, look, do I want *this* kind of thing or do I want *that* kind of thing," you could narrow it down to what you want to put on there really quickly without endlessly experimenting.

DT: So it's good to have both approaches?

TV: I think it is. It's good to just wing it and think maybe you're gonna get lucky, and often you do—you just have the energy of something that you like. But it's good to have the other thing too, where you can really *make* the choice, like a guy chopping a stone, or [with] a painting where you *know,* "I'm not going to try purple and yellow because that has to be green." When you think, "Do I want contrast or do I want something that floats along with the basic mood of the vocal? Should it be like a trumpet or should it be like a violin?" Or again, "Should it be like a tiger growling?"—these other things where you can have to make that choice.

DT: As a listener, I think you convey things like the trumpet well.

TV: Yeah.

DT: In "No Glamour for Willi" maybe.

TV: The solo, or the guitar part?

DT: The solo, at the break. It has kind of a *wah* sound.

TV: Oh, shit, yeah. I know exactly what you're talking about.
   I mean, I don't know what thought I had when I did that solo, but I do know what you mean.

DT: It's like a trumpet with a . . .

TV: A mute, yeah. Or a muted trombone *wah*. [*laughs*] I wasn't thinking about that, but there is that kind of thing to that particular "announcement," you might say.

DT: Did you work a lot on those effects?

TV: Well, you get a vocabulary and then you know which little boxes do what, for sure. I actually don't use a lot of boxes.

DT: I mean effects in terms of the techniques you came up with too.

TV: Oh, the volume-control stuff . . .

DT: Yeah, and your left-hand technique overall, which is so . . . what would you say it is?

TV: I don't know. [*laughs*] Primitive.

DT: I think it's pretty evolved compared to most rock guitarists.

TV: Well, I don't really play hammer-offs. Actually, I was playing hammer-offs in the '60s; I was playing blues-rock when I was a kid for a certain amount of time. And then a Cream record came out and I said, "Oh the hammer-off thing, that's already been covered. I don't need to do that anymore." It was like a real conscious decision, so I was done playing that style by 1971, you know. I thought, "The world doesn't need that anymore."

DT: What about the vibrato you developed?

TV: Oh yeah. When I started playing, this guy I know who's a bass player said, "You play guitar with cello vibrato. Most people do not do that on guitar." Most people bend the string up; they don't go bridge to tuning pegs. It's much harder to do.

DT: You move your finger along the string, as opposed to pushing and pulling the string like little bends?

TV: Oh, no, I do that too. I do both.

DT: At the same time?

TV: No. Actually, I [sometimes] consciously try to do them both at the same time, but usually it's one or the other.

I remember in the '70s when I got the Jazzmaster, that's when I started to do it. I can see myself doing it in rehearsals in '75. You can hear it on "Johnny Jewel."

DT: What about the beginning of "Little Johnny Jewel?"

TV: That little weird, funky sound? It's muting the strings way up the neck with both the left hand and the right hand. So it's just little noises, little plunks. It's almost like a bongo drum sound.

DT: That's an interesting choice for your first recording, as a way of introducing yourself.

TV: [*laughs*] We got so put down for that record. Even our fifty fans at CBGB said, "Why didn't you do 'Prove It'?" I said, "Well, I think this is a good thing," you know. It was different.

DT: What about the Jazzmaster, then? How important was that for you?

TV: Well, the Jazzmaster thing's really gotten interesting over the years. When I came to New York I didn't have anything but an acoustic guitar for probably three years. Then in '71 I went to a pawn shop and bought this odd Japanese thing for $25, and then that got stolen. [*laughs*] So then the cheapest thing I could find was a Jazzmaster, because nobody wanted them in '74, it was ridiculous. And they were really problematic, because of the rocking bridge, and I was hitting it so hard that even with heavy strings I was constantly knocking it out of tune. But then that guitar became really popular among certain kinds of bands over the years, you know. And like three years ago, Fender called me up to do this celebration of the Jazzmaster, which was really funny. I said, "Well, who else is doing this show?" And they named J Mascis and Nels Cline, Thurston [Moore] and Lee [Ranaldo]. That was a kind of curious night, just with the amount of styles people were pulling off.

DT: Did Fender ever approach you for a signature model?

TV: Sort of. But I've gone off Jazzmasters for about twenty years. People don't realize it, but I really don't play them anymore.

DT: What have you been playing?

TV: I had a Jazzmaster neck and I gave it to a guy and said, "I need a three-pickup guitar with this neck." It's basically . . . I guess you would call it a

Stratocaster with Danelectro pickups, and I ended up really loving the sound. I've been playing that for fifteen years.

DT: It's funny, because players of the offset Fenders like the Jazzmaster used to be in their own world in a way.

TV: Yeah.

DT: Now those guitars are pretty popular.

TV: It's really strange, yeah.

DT: It does seem like a lot of that took off from you.

TV: Well, I don't know. I think a lot of it was because it was cheap, I swear. Because when we went to England, the punk thing was starting to happen there, you know. You still didn't see many Jazzmasters, but a couple of years after that you started to. Elvis Costello was on an album cover with one. I think that for the English bands that may have had something to do with it.

DT: Sure. But for the people in this scene, it's probably you.

TV: I don't know. That's what a woman at my record company used to say. She would say things like, "It should make you happy that all these younger players are listening to you and taking inspiration." And I said, "Well, I don't know about inspiration, but they are taking licks, aren't they?" And she goes, "Oh yeah, they really are." But uh. . . . but that's a thing I would never, ever, ever think about. I think it's even bad to think about whether you have an influence or not. I think it's bad for a person.

DT: Yeah, I'm sure it is. But as an outsider I also mean that, in a good way, it's as an influence that a lot of your impact was made, which is maybe why I asked about those free-jazz guys at the start. If you go back to Albert Ayler, the way he reached people was likely more as an overall influence than anything else, certainly more than as a popular musician selling records, but even in terms of having a style that people directly copied.

TV: Oh, sure.

DT: You mention him and your music doesn't sound like his.

TV: Uh-huh.

DT: I think you're right that people do take licks from you, but to me more people seem affected in an overall sense, so they might pick up the Jazz-master as a general profile as opposed to working on those left-hand techniques, which are pretty rigorous. I think it's fitting that if you started out with people like Ayler, you might've wound up being a similar type of figure.

TV: You know, I hear what you're saying, yeah . . .
      You want some of this cheesecake?

DT: No thanks. Nice change-up though.

TV: [*laughs*] It's something I eat maybe once a year.

DT: OK, well, how about this: The idea of two guitars. Did you always hear music that way?

TV: That's always the sound that I liked. Which is strange, because around '88 I thought, "There's no more two-guitar bands left," you know? You had R.E.M. and U2 and . . . what was that other band that was big for a while . . . oh, the Police, of course. They were the first one. But all these single-guitar bands came up, and I always wondered, "Did these guitar players not like playing with other guitar players?"

DT: But you were always inclined toward two yourself?

TV: Yeah, sure. 'Cause everything I liked as a teenager—"19th Nervous Breakdown" and the Yardbirds and the Kinks—everything was that sound. Two guitars. Even the R&B records had a couple guitars; even the James Brown things had two little funk chords going. Stax was different, Stax usu-ally only had one guitar, but the Motown records, when you go back and hear these things, you go, "Yow, this was really amazing guitar stuff going on!" The stuff was arranged super-well, mostly by jazz guys. [*laughs*]

DT: Did you ever have a clear sense of what the two guitars should be in your own music?

TV: Well, I thought they should be Fenders. Because in the '70s I was completely sick of Gibson sounds. Everything you heard was the same overdriven . . . Zeppelin, the Eagles, all that shit was the same fucking sound. I was like, "Nah, should be twangy Fender guitars," you know? That was the sound I liked.

I just wish some jazz guys would play with that tone. When I was a kid I hated jazz guitar. It sounded like fucking really bad corn syrup going by. Even though they were playing something good. I remember [John] McLaughlin on [Miles Davis's] *Jack Johnson* was the first jazz electric I liked, but for the most part jazz guitar was just such a shitty sound, you know, muffled, with the tone rolled off. I can't think of why these guys were playing like that.

DT: Yeah, but, Tom, for your music, though, did you have any particular arrangement in mind for what the two guitars were or how they worked together?

TV: I usually know exactly what I want to do with it right away.

DT: You mean it varies?

TV: It varies from piece to piece.

DT: It seems like in some bands there were certain roles the guitarists took on. Not necessarily lead and rhythm but something less rigid. Of course, maybe in the Stones Brian Jones was a freelancer . . .

TV: But you know what's weird? If you listen to *Got Live if You Want It!* he's playing the same fucking part on half the songs.

DT: Who is?

TV: Brian. I thought it was Keith [Richards] but it's all Brian. And his part is *"bum-bum-bum, chick-chick"*—he plays that on "Under My Thumb"; it comes up like four times. I heard that like two years ago and I was shocked, because I thought this guy was a big part of why I liked those early records, and listening back to it I thought, "It's probably not him at all." It's all Keith's little parts and riffs.

[*laughs*] But I like the sound of two guitars. I definitely do.

DT: All right. I guess I thought the two-guitar question would be the big one with you. If we went back to what you were saying about writing "Venus," what the left hand does on the piano usually serves a different purpose than what the right hand does, but there's no reason you had to do something like that.

TV: I mean, that's what my generation did. [*laughs*] All the '60s bands had two guitar players. I didn't even know how else to get those sounds. I remember hearing the first Hendrix record; I had no clue how he could play a chord and play a solo on top at the same time. I was like, "I give up. Nobody could play this but him." [*laughs*] And then like three years later this guy said, "Nah, man, he was overdubbing." I go, "What d'you mean?" He goes, "Well, he played one part and then he played the other on top of it on a different track." I was like, "Holy shit, so he's really not that good!" He said, "No, he's great, but he doesn't do it all at once!" [*laughs*]

DT: Did you ever see Hendrix play?

TV: No. I never did.

I saw him in the street once when I first got here. Actually his apartment was right around the corner from here.

DT: He just walked by?

TV: Yeah. Because I worked on West Fourth, one block away. I used to work at this bakery from midnight to eight in the morning, bagging bread, right?

They would bake it, it would cool from six to twelve, and then I'd come in and fill up bags and the truck would come pick it up in the morning. And they had a window to the street, and one morning he was walking by.

DT: What'd you do?

TV: Nothin'. I was like eighteen years old or something. [*laughs*] In '68.

He wasn't really tall, you know. You think of these guitar players as tall but all of 'em I've met are really short. Keith was tiny. Townshend's, like, medium. All of the English guys . . . Not that there's anything strange about that, just somehow when you're a kid and you see photographs you think of them as tall, but they're all surprisingly short.

DT: That's funny, because when you walked up I thought, this guy's actually as tall as he looks on the record covers.

TV: [*laughs*] Yeah. I'm tall.

⑨

THEY SAY THE NEON LIGHTS ARE BRIGHT ON THE BOWERY

CHEETAH CHROME

PHOTO BY ALAN RAND; COURTESY OF THE PHOTOGRAPHER

From June 1974 to August 1975, a band called Rocket from the Tombs played sporadic gigs in their native Cleveland, Ohio. Their repertoire included a few of their own antiescapist efforts, along with unholy covers of the Velvet Underground, Stooges, and MC5. The sheer audacity of their hope—that by reviving such fare they'd be any less ineffective than its

originators—doomed the scenesters to an obscure grave. But within their
art-punk aesthetic, soon to be broken up along the hyphen into two legendary groups, Pere Ubu and the Dead Boys, Rocket from the Tombs presaged
a great deal of the alternative future while dragging a lot of its past. Degen-
erate rock, Captain Beefheart and other postmodern sleazes, the line where
Alfred Jarry crosses over into Alfred E. Neuman, all would find a way into
their avant-garage.

RFTT was fronted by David Thomas (a.k.a. Crocus Behemoth), a will-
fully surly son of a college professor, who bleated tragicomically in a voice he
would later (jokingly?) describe as tone-deaf. The older of the band's two guitarists was Peter Laughner, another big fish in a small net whose amphetamine-
fueled networking skills led to encounters with his heroes, Lou Reed and
Lester Bangs (and soon after, a premature demise). The younger guitar player, hailing from the Twenty-Fifth Street projects, didn't share the
higher-brow leanings of his two relatively affluent bandmates, or their comfort articulating positions on rock in the pages of *Scene* and *Creem*. Rather,
Gene O'Connor (born 1955) had a more aggressive style on his instrument
of choice, evidenced by his spitting solo on "Transfusion" and his metallic
warping of "Raw Power." A tough, focused deviation of the Keith Richards/
Chuck Berry type, O'Connor had soul but preferred to rifle through arpeggios like Glen Buxton of Alice Cooper. He collaborated with Thomas and
Laughner on the classics "30 Seconds over Tokyo" and "Down in Flames"
but felt more akin to a scrawny, Iggy-devoted singer from Youngstown
named Steve Bator, who was skulking around the Rockets scene. As Rocket
from the Tombs rocketed down the tubes, Thomas and Laughner began to
peel off into Pere Ubu, while Bator and O'Connor started a group called
Frankenstein. Although the latter pair recorded some demos and put out
feelers to the emerging punk scene in New York City, their transformation
wasn't complete until Steve Bator became Stiv Bators, O'Connor became
Cheetah Chrome, and their new offshoot was rechristened the Dead Boys.

Pere Ubu was billed as Cleveland's "first concept band," but the Dead
Boys were a concept too: a punked-out Sensational Alex Harvey Band reign-
ing over unsuspecting *Schweinehunds* with black juju. By the time they got
to New York in the summer of 1976, they were rabid enough to be welcomed
into the prime punk role of CBGB's house band. A year later they released

Young Loud and Snotty, a debut as tight as the surging downstrokes Cheetah played on its famous opener, "Sonic Reducer." At the time the album was recorded, the group lived in a tenement with fewer mattresses than sleepers; they used to half-heartedly try to beat each other home in hopes of getting a bed. That's the kind of entropy that steams off "What Love Is" and "Ain't Nothin' to Do" and "I Need Lunch," one scuzzy speedball after another zooming by as Cheetah plays like a blood brother with Jimmy Zero ("one of the best rhythm guitarists ever," Cheetah told *SugarBuzz Toronto*). Like their heroes the New York Dolls, the Dead Boys were at their most elemental level a great rock band, and *Young Loud and Snotty* was their great rock record. Regrettably, their second outing, *We Have Come for Your Children* (1978), was also like that of the Dolls—too much too soon. Though "3rd Generation Nation" and "Son of Sam" were vintage tracks, the sheer accumulation of drug problems, near-fatal stabbings, and other classic Bowery foibles led to the group's crack-up in 1979.

Cheetah followed the Dead Boys by gigging with the Stilettos, putting out singles with his own band the Casualties, recording with Jeff Dahl, and eventually making a solo album, *Alive in Detroit* (2000). In 2002, Rocket from the Tombs' decaying tapes were finally released as *The Day the Earth Met...*, which led to a sustained reunion few could have expected. For these new Rockets, the band asked Richard Lloyd to fill in for Laughner—a twist on the old rumor that Laughner would replace Lloyd in Television. (In 2010 Cheetah joined the Dolls' Sylvain Sylvain in another of those overlaps as the Batusis.) If works like 2004's *Rocket Redux* proved anything, it may have been the unreliability of viewing the Dead Boys and Pere Ubu as two warring binaries that were never meant to coexist. "Cheetah and I have always shared common ground. We like raw midwestern groove rock. We like a good riff played hard and fast," David Thomas told *Philadelphia Weekly* in 2011. "Cheetah could have easily gone with me into Ubu and fit right in. Don't underestimate the artiness in Cheetah."

DAVID TODD: Of the punk guitarists, who stands out for you?

CHEETAH CHROME: It's hard to make a list; there's always somebody I shouldn't have left off. You know, Syl [Sylvain Sylvain], Johnny [Thunders]. Jeff Salen of the Tuff Darts. Both guys in the Dictators, Ross the Boss [Ross Friedman] and Top Ten [Scott Kempner]. Johnny Ramone. Ivan Julian. There were so many good guitarists, and all of them had something to offer. You know, punk rock was very much like the '60s, where you had so many good bands. It was like the Woodstock generation ten years later. Looking back on it, there was a big spirit to the community and the music.

DT: What about Brian James?

CG: Oh yeah. You know, he's got his own style. Some of it's sloppy; some of it's sloppy on purpose. The first Damned album he did with no guitar tone whatsoever. He pretty much plugged flat into the board, and it still sounded brilliant. [*laughs*] That's a sign of a great guitarist to me.

DT: Do you think of Brian James as being your kind of guitarist?

CG: I guess. I wouldn't necessarily bunch myself together with anybody.

DT: Maybe it's because you both played with Stiv, but I always thought you had something in common.

CG: Yeah. More so than Steve Jones [of the Sex Pistols]. [*laughs*] Steve Jones, he had a couple good riffs, but there was a lot of hack stuff in there too. I mean, his attitude and everything was great. He just wasn't setting the world on fire.

DT: The Sex Pistols were ripping off Johnny Thunders, who I guess was ripping off Chuck Berry.

CG: Johnny was ripping off Sylvain! [*laughs*]

DT: There's a real connection between Chuck Berry and punk rock though, isn't there?

CG: Oh yeah. There is for some of us. I mean, punk rock, it seems to me like there were two levels of it. There was one that was like Johnny Thunders, me, the guys from the Stooges, Sylvain. And then there are the guys who came right after us, the hardcore guys and all that. I don't see where they were influenced by Chuck Berry, whereas I see where me, Johnny Thunders, and Sylvain and a guy like James Williamson were. You know what I mean? Even if we weren't directly. A lot of times it was because we all learned from listening to the Rolling Stones, and Keith Richards was very Chuck Berry–influenced. So there was a direct line there.

For some reason, in the mid-'70s, probably after "My Ding-a-Ling," Chuck Berry became uncool. Bands weren't covering his songs, and if they did they were considered pretty naff, you know. So that got lost there. And so nowadays, you have to explain to kids who Chuck Berry was, which is a pity. He should be played all the time on classic rock radio, and he's not.

DT: Where there particular things you picked up from Chuck Berry, or was it more of an overall influence?

CC: Just overall. His songs were so easy with all the I-IV-V [chord] changes, and the classic riffs were all great. But the thing was more the attitude, the sense of humor, and the fact that you could do so much with so little. That was probably the biggest thing he ever taught anybody.

DT: What else did you listen to growing up?

CC: Oh, I come straight out of '50s radio and the British Invasion. I mean, Tamla/Motown, I heard all that stuff when I was a kid. Once I got into hard rock, I pretty much stuck with anything that came along that way. But, you know, I loved everybody for a while there. Steppenwolf was a big influence. Led Zeppelin. Big Brother and the Holding Company. Janis Joplin was a huge influence on me.

DT: In what way?

CC: Just attitude, musically. Listening to her taught me a lot about singing. I couldn't sing anything like her, but it influenced the way I thought about it.

DT: I liked your singing on the "Still Wanna Die" single [1979].

CC: Thanks. [*laughs*] Is that what that was?

DT: The Detroit bands were pretty big for you.

CC: Mmm-hmm.

DT: I know you saw the Stooges, but did you ever see the MC5?

CC: They played Cleveland, and I caught part of it. Just the very end of it, because it was a daytime thing, outside. But especially their *High Time* record, that was one I sat down and woodshedded with. I still listen to that one. My son Rogan loves it. [*laughs*] The Stooges were also great. I loved them from the first time I heard them. Between the time I got the first Stooges album and the time I moved to New York City, I probably listened to at least one Stooges record a day. One of the three.

DT: Did you differentiate between their guitarists or did you like them both?

CC: You know, it's comparing apples and oranges. They both were great. I tend to be more partial to James [Williamson], just because I like the songs better. You know, the whole songwriting style was different with Ron [Asheton]. But I probably learned as much or more from Ronnie style-wise, as far as taking something away from it.

DT: What about Zal Cleminson of the Sensational Alex Harvey Band?

CC: Oh, well, Zal Cleminson had the most insanely good guitar sound of anybody ever, to this day. [*laughs*] I don't know if it was his amp or what, but he had it live, he had it on record, he just had an insane sound. Plus, he could play really well. They were a very musical band, and there was a lot to learn from that. But mainly with him it was what not to play. Because he didn't play two notes when one would do.

Glen Buxton was another big influence like that, what kind of lick belongs where. You know, a lot of guitar players don't understand that when a song needs a lead someplace, you [have to] play something that fits. They just throw anything in there and think, "That's great." And if you're lucky, it is. But the thing is, you have to be able to tell if that doesn't work.

DT: Both Zal Cleminson and Glen Buxton played the Gibson SG.

CC: Yeah.

DT: Was that part of why you did?

CC: Back then in the '70s, that was the main guitar. You saw more of those—you know, Pete Townshend used it. Glen, both guys in Alice Cooper used it. Frank Zappa had one. Carlos Santana. They were all over the place. They just became out of style there in the late '70s, but they were great guitars. To this day, I still prefer one to a Les Paul. I love a Les Paul, but just for sheer crunch and tightness, an SG will do it every time. The Les Paul tends to be too much sometimes. It's overkill for what you want to do.

DT: You only play the SG now?

CC: You know, when I started endorsing the BFG Les Paul for Gibson, I was using that pretty much exclusively for about six months to a year. I really put it through its paces, used it on a lot of live shows. I loved it. But then I was recording something at home one night, trying to do a solo, and it just didn't have what I needed. And so I went and got my black SG out, and I plugged it in and immediately was like, "Oh my God. This is my baby here." [*laughs*] And I went back to using it pretty much exclusively.

DT: I liked Robby Krieger on the SG.

CC: Robby Krieger, there's another one. Did quite a bit with it. He used those Acoustic amps with a fuzz box, which was very strange.

DT: Another source for you was the New York Dolls. Was that also about attitude?

CC: Yeah, the attitude. You know, one of the things about punk was that back then the record companies weren't signing bands even if they were good. The bean counters were starting to take over and the egos were in place and cocaine was king, and a lot of good bands were starting to land by the wayside. So as a musician you kind of had to take the attitude that you were important whether you were or not. You had to approve of yourself before anybody else was going to. That had to come across. And so that was the attitude, and a lot of it came from the Dolls.

[*laughs*] Plus we were a bunch of drug-addict drunks, you know? A certain amount of attitude came from that.

DT: The Dolls had that too.

CC: Yeah. They didn't take anything too seriously. That was their thing. You had to have a sense of humor.

DT: Are there are other guitarists who impacted you?

CC: Oh, well, Jimmy Page, Keith Richards. Both of them were big influences on me. Mainly because they changed stylistically all the time. You know, I'm a sponge; I mean, I listened to all of them back then—the Beatles, for Christ's sake. I learned a lot from the Beatles about chord structures. It all comes in. A lot comes in, something comes out.

DT: A lot of those sources are sort of traditional in a way. So when you were finding your sound with the Dead Boys, as you were branching off Rocket from the Tombs, was it important to be "new," or did you just want to play how you wanted?

CC: We didn't want to bore people. We didn't want to rehash. In Cleveland you had to be on your toes, because there were a lot of good musicians there and they all played cover stuff. So when you stole a lick, they knew it. They were a very critical audience. So, yeah, with the Dead Boys we wanted to keep the originality there. Some of us had already been in Rockets and we had set a bar for ourselves with that, so we did not want to go backwards. We just wanted to take it in a harder direction, which was basically our natures anyway, so that came easy.

DT: Do you think the Dead Boys would have been different if you hadn't been in Rockets?

CC: I think we probably wouldn't have been as good. The one thing I learned in Rockets from David [Thomas] and Peter [Laughner] was how to rehearse, how to work on a song till it was done. And without having been in Rockets, I wouldn't have had that, so it probably would've been more amateurish.

DT: How did you work up those songs? For instance, "30 Seconds over Tokyo" you wrote with Peter and David, which seems like an interesting trio.

CC: I had the riff originally. I was watching *Kojak* one night and playing guitar and I just came up with that line. [*laughs*] I played it for David and he liked it too. After we got some lyrics, we played it for Peter and [bassist] Craig [Bell], and Peter came up with the bass line—which is just freakin' "Waiting for the Sun" by the Doors—and we threw that in. We kind of had an idea for the noise parts, but basically we all started building it up together. We'd just try things and if they worked, they worked. And we just threw them out if they didn't.

DT: Where did the noise concept come from?

CC: Some of it was the Stooges. Some of it was [Lou Reed's] *Metal Machine Music*, you know, car accidents on tape. A piano falling down stairs. [*laughs*]

DT: You and David Thomas also wrote "Sonic Reducer."

CC: That was one where David actually had the lyrics. He goes, "I wrote these lyrics, they're called 'Sonic Reducer,'" and he handed them to me. I looked at them, started playing, and five minutes later had it. I never know where anything like that comes from; just all of a sudden it's there.

DT: The Dead Boys and Pere Ubu are often depicted as these two irreconcilable counterparts. Is that how you think of it, or was RFTT not that easily divided?

CC: When Rockets broke up, all our stuff was there in a pile. It was there for the picking. I mean, the Dead Boys could've easily taken "30 Seconds over Tokyo" if Pere Ubu hadn't taken it first. I had actually planned to work on that song, and then when they did it, that was "OK, well, that one's gone." So we hurried up and grabbed "Reducer" while we still could. [*laughs*] A lot of the Dead Boys stuff like "Ain't Nothing to Do" had been presented to Rockets or was about to be presented to Rockets but never got worked on.

You see, [Dead Boys drummer Johnny] Blitz had been in Rockets too, a couple times. He actually wanted to rejoin and they wouldn't let him because he had already quit twice, you know? So when Rockets was breaking up, Stiv and I were hanging out, and we were like, "OK, let's get Blitz back in the fold. Let's start looking for another guitar player." So the Dead Boys was waiting in the wings, ready to go the day Rockets broke up. I just didn't want to quit, because I wanted to see Rockets through to the end, you know? But we saw the end coming, and when it came we were prepared. A week later we were in a rehearsal.

Pere Ubu, they took a while to get together. I think they didn't know what they were going to do. Peter was always pretty reliable, but he was starting to fall apart a little bit there and become more of a wild card. To tell you the truth, I wasn't all that aware of them, because I was busy with the Dead Boys. By the time Pere Ubu was starting to come up we were gone.

DT: When RFTT got back together you must've had to smooth over some of that, I'd imagine. How long did it take for everybody to loosen up?

CC: [*laughs*] Five years.

DT: When you first entered a rehearsal room . . . ?

CC: Yeah, it was very tense. Well, Richard [Lloyd] wasn't with us, and it was very tense at first. Right through the whole first tour. But after that, things got better. When we did the second tour in 2006, that was actually a pretty pleasant experience.

DT: What makes it worthwhile to go through all that?

CC: It's just a very creative bunch of people. Even without Peter, it's a challenge. It's fun. You know, something good always comes out of it. I remember this last songwriting session we did: We had been working for two days, and we had nothin'. There was nothin' in the tank. And we all just sat around in this room with our amps and our drums and guitars and said, "I got nothin." And then somebody started playing and we ended up coming up with one of the best songs we wrote out of just nothin', out of a scrap of a riff. We started messing around with it and the next thing you know, twenty minutes later we were going through our third take. So it's things like that, you know?

GUN, GUITAR, BULLHORN

LYDIA LUNCH

Prometheus brought fire, Lydia brought lunch. It was a nickname the runaway from Rochester (born Lydia Koch, 1959) picked up upon arriving in New York City at the not-so-tender age of sixteen. While her peers were gazing at rock posters, she was stealing food for the Dead Boys and Richard Hell and all the other Max's Kansas City/CBGB musos she admired. That is, before she dismembered them in the abrasive Teenage Jesus & the Jerks and the "horrorcore" Beirut Slump, just two of her musical projects that put the negation in the "no wave" movement.

Formed in 1976, Teenage Jesus didn't buy into the rosy retro power of the generic punks—"lousy Chuck Berry music amped up to play triple fast," Lydia called it in *Perfect Sound Forever*—nor the indulgent half-hour sets of the Ramones. They opted for seven-minute shankings with Lydia's untrained guitar flagellating Jim Sclavunos on bass and Bradly Field on "drum." On songs such as "I Woke Up Dreaming," the group clangs more ferociously than you'd think possible at dirge speed; in "Orphans," Lydia bipolarizes tough riffs with manic slide, complementing both with throat-pierced singing. Fortunately for Teenage Jesus, Brian Eno only had room for four of their songs on his 1978 anthology *No New York*; they would record only a dozen before their breakup a year later, but as untonal landmarks, those proved to be enough. With each of her works, as Lydia says in her interview, *"the point is the fucking point."* And the point was made as quickly as twenty-one seconds, in the title-indicative "Red Alert."

Teenage Jesus originally featured James Chance on sax, and his departure draws the line in their aesthetic: high-watt angularity, yes; James Brown party-vibe reverie, no, no, no. Lydia's other band of the time, Beirut Slump, was darker in a dripping blue-period way—there she acceded vocal duties to oddball Bobby Swope and blended her "baby slide" guitar work into the gloom of filmmaker Vivienne Dick's organ. Never one to linger—"My concept from the beginning was you find the collaborators, you do a few shows, you document it, you fucking go on," she told *3:AM Magazine*— Lydia moved away from the guitar with her 1980 chamber-dominatrix solo album *Queen of Siam*, sang with 8-Eyed Spy, acted in films by Richard Kern, published poetry and fiction, showed photography, and started a verbose spoken-word career with *The Uncensored* in 1984. Over the ensuing decades she also fronted 13.13 while living in L.A., on her way to San Francisco, New Orleans, London, and Barcelona. Her returns to the guitar have been infrequent, but they've included the Harry Crews project with Kim Gordon in 1988 and a Teenage Jesus reunion in 2008.

"The only thing worse than a guitar," Lydia once exclaimed, "is a guitar-ist!" (The sentiment so charmed her collaborator Nels Cline that he used it as the epigraph on his website.) Suffice it to say, her relationship with the instrument was always conflicted. Yet her balance of sensitivity and brutality led Teenage Jesus to moments of inspired shrill, and brought projects like *The Drowning of Lucy Hamilton* (1985) to poetic horror. Even after forsaking the instrument, her work with Cline, Robert Quine, and Omar Rodríguez-López—just a few of her alt-great collaborators—reflected her impeccable instincts. There is a difference between being a major guitar player and being a major artist who happened to play guitar. Neither is bad, but it may be too simple to place Lydia in the latter camp. Though she puts "the words" first, it's hard to deny the palette-cleansing effect of her playing—and easy to think of many careerists who failed to come up with comparable fire of their own.

DAVID TODD: How did you approach the guitar when you first started playing?

LYDIA LUNCH: Well, to me the guitar was strictly an instrument of torture to begin with. I went to New York when I was very young—spoken word didn't exist; I mean, this was between standup comedy and what spoken word was to become. But I went with writing in mind, and the band that really inspired me musically was Mars, and China Burg, who was an amazing guitar stylist. So I decided to start Teenage Jesus. But mainly it was just as a weapon to further the words. And the guitar just seemed the most heinous [*laughs*] and abusive thing to pick up. The words were abusive, my emotions were aggressive, and so the guitar made sense.

DT: Did you develop an affection for the guitar or was it always more of a tool for you?

LL: It was a tool. Definitely it was a weapon. But I loved the guitar; the guitar is so beautiful and so horrendous at the same time. I loved Bob Quine. I think I was one of the first people that ran up to him after the first Richard Hell and the Voidoids gig and said, "Fuck, you are God." And so then he took favor on me. [*laughs*] He was one of the few people who didn't run away from me at that point because I was too young and too aggressive and they didn't know what to fucking make of me. So, oh yeah, Richard Hell would run away, David Byrne would run away. Bob Quine just smiled and probably stroked the screwdriver in his pocket. [*laughs*]

DT: What was it about Quine's playing you liked?

LL: It was just *out*. I mean, that was it. He took the music somewhere else, because otherwise it would've been too-traditional rock. But he was able—

because he was so insane himself—to translate some of his own insanity into the guitar. I mean, he was really inspirational to me—and you know, Bob Quine ended up producing a lot of the early Teenage Jesus stuff, which was great. It was the best sound we ever got, for sure.

DT: And then he played on *Queen of Siam*.

LL: It was interesting; just the other day I had to write a little preview of a live performance of *Queen of Siam* I'll be staging for the first time—first and last time—ever, at a festival in Austria. I had to go and look for some reviews, whatever, to remind myself. And I came upon a lot of Lester Bangs stuff. And Lester Bangs just loved me; he called me one of the greatest guitar players. [*laughs*] I was one of his favorites, which to me was hysterical at the time, as it still remains.

DT: I don't think it's all that preposterous. But speaking of going back to earlier projects, I was wondering how you came to pick up the guitar again with Teenage Jesus in 2008.

LL: You know, we did this Teenage Jesus "retrovirus," as I call it, under the urging of Thurston Moore, who had put out basically this love letter to the no wave [*No Wave: Post-Punk. Underground. New York. 1976–1980.*]. Thurston said, "Why don't you do a Teenage Jesus show to support the book?" And I'm like, "Well, they're all dead except for Sclavunos," who is now drumming for Nick Cave. So then Thurston volunteered to play the bass. And I said, "Well, it'll be under the auspice of the wire coat hanger," which is how I got Teenage Jesus to be so tight; if they made a mistake, they would get whacked. But when I went to pick up the guitar again—I had picked up the guitar in the interim, but not for Teenage Jesus—when I went to figure out the songs, what was interesting was, I couldn't remember my own lyrics but I could remember all the slide parts exactly. And with the rhythm parts, I just couldn't figure out where I was coming from. I don't know chords, notes, any of that. I'm a total idiot savant with music, you know: just do what comes naturally. So I had to call Sclavunos, because he's got the iron trap of memory, and the answer he had was very interesting.

He's like, "Well, you didn't have a guitar; you would borrow one and some-one would have to tune it for you. And you didn't have a unique tuning; the guitar for Teenage Jesus was supposed to be tuned normally." [*laughs*] He said, "But a lot of the recordings"—you know, live recordings or what-ever—"by the time they accidentally happened the guitar could've been in its own tuning for weeks. So even though the slide was easy to reproduce, the basic chords could be impossible to decipher, because who knows what tuning the guitar had reached." So this was pretty interesting. This was quite the *contraire* of what you would imagine. And it reminded me of something with Nels Cline, another amazing guitar player. I had done this retrospective with him, [*Willing Victim*,] at the Sacher-Masoch Festival, and Nels Cline could not play "Orphans" correctly. I'm like, "Wait a sec-ond, this is one of the best guitar players in the world and he can't fucking play 'Orphans'?" [*laughs*] And the reason why was, I figured out years later, he was too in tune.

Teenage Jesus is not an easy thing for anyone to cover, because it's so skewered. I mean, I knew nothing about the guitar. I still know nothing. I don't want to know anything. [*laughs*] But it was perfect for that moment, for that sound, for that music, to express those emotions.

The only other time that I picked up the guitar—I'm just going to tell you the stories about the guitar, because I don't have that many—I recorded a record with China Burg called *The Drowning of Lucy Hamilton*, which was the soundtrack for [Richard Kern's film] *The Right Side of My Brain*. And that was great, because we just started playing together in her apartment. She was playing bass clarinet, guitar, piano, whatever. And this was very interesting to me, because as a contrarian it was the furthest away from the brutality of Teenage Jesus I could go.

But I like the guitar, because it's a mystical instrument when I'm just noodling around on it. I'm channeling something, because I'm not using chords, I don't play with rhythm for the most part. I have my style of gui-tar—actually I have two styles, the Teenage Jesus [style] and then this real slide sound. And, yeah, I pick up the guitar occasionally. [*laughs*] Don't tell anyone.

DT: I like *The Drowning* a lot, by the way.

LL: Thank you. I like it too. It's a small work but it really speaks to a certain side of me, you know? And it's instrumental, and I love instrumental music. I love space in music as well. Which, considering I've done a lot of quite noisy and propulsive stuff, might be surprising. [*laughs*] But yeah, space. That's what Rowland Howard had. Rowland S. Howard was a master of the pause or of the long note or of the suspense—of perfect playing, not under-playing but never overplaying. Just such beautiful, really space-ly, other-planetary sounds.

DT: I think you had some of that on *The Drowning* yourself. It made me wonder if you ever thought of going further with that type of guitar, or by that time were you already focused on spoken word?

LL: Well you know, one thing leads to the other. I'm a contrarian; everything I do contradicts what came before it. It's whatever suits the atmosphere of the place that I'm living in or my state of mind, what needs to be created. So, you know, New York at that period was just the right time to do more spoken word. And there might have been a call for me to do things like John Zorn and Glenn Branca, but that really wasn't my clique at all. I mean, the words were why I originally started doing anything. I kind of made the point with music, and then after that the words became the priority—because they were always the priority.

But also I started working with other guitar players, like for instance in 13.13, Dix Denney. Another genius. Another underrated, completely unam-bitious master of this vortex, this whirlpool, this hurricane of sound. Just a genius.

DT: Definitely in your case, not playing guitar freed you up to collaborate with so many of the best alternative-minded guitarists out there.

LL: Yeah, well, there's not really that many to choose from. I guess there's one guitar player I would still like to work with that I never have, and it was funny because at the Teenage Jesus retrovirus at All Tomorrow's Parties he ran backstage, threw the door open and said, "Beirut Slump changed my life!" And it was Paul Leary of the Butthole Surfers. Who I think is just fucking phenomenal. Absolutely amazing guitar player. And literally I just fell to my knees laughing—Beirut Slump changed his life? I'm like, "Wow. All right. Don't blame me." [*laughs*] And Beirut Slump, let's not overlook this. Because I have to say, this band makes me fucking laugh. It just makes me so happy, maybe because it's so . . . it's horrorcore, really. It's *horror*core.

DT: That's the perfect term for them.

LL: It is. There's no other.

DT: Those songs like "Try Me."

LL: Oh yes, "Try Me." It's just so weird—it's just so fucking weird. [*laughs*] What can I say? When Thurston and I were [preparing for the] Teenage Jesus [reunion], I said, "Well, why don't we try a Beirut Slump song just for fun?" We couldn't do it. We could not play Beirut Slump. I'm like, "This sounds like the worst piece of third-generation no wave bullshit I've ever heard in my life!" Because something just made Beirut Slump work when it worked. I mean, most of the lyrics—which I didn't write, I wrote the music and the guitar parts—most of the lyrics were quotes from bums. And we only played three times, and one of the three times a homeless person actually got up and started singing. And we were like, "*What!* It's his lyrics!" [*laughs*] It was amazing.

But yeah, Beirut Slump cannot be impersonated. Thank the goddess!

DT: Guitar-wise, you had some almost Black Sabbath–sounding chords on a couple of those songs, "Case #14" or "G.I. Blue."

LL: Why thank you! I don't know how that happened. [*laughs*] Really, it was so accidental. It's a mystery to me.

DT: Well, Beirut Slump also seemed to be where you started doing that *Drowning* style you mentioned.

LL: Absolutely. Exactly, exactly. That was when my guitar style, what's really indicative of my style of guitar playing, started to be birthed. Because it was still too razory or aggressive in Teenage Jesus, other than in "Baby Doll." You know, I had no desire to play rhythmical guitar, but I did have a desire to get out the razor blades and run them across the strings. [*laughs*] To sound pretty but horrible, and infantile.

DT: As you were developing this style, were you thinking of deconstructing the usual playing, or was it more instinctual?

LL: Absolutely instinctual. Just music to suit the words, to further the cause. And then when it came to the *Drowning* stuff, or even Beirut Slump, that was just, you know, the sound of that kind of monster. [*laughs*] I mean, that was it.

DT: One aspect of your playing I like is how you picked up the slide, which is supposed to be this connoisseur's device, played with taste . . .

LL: [*laughs*] Finesse. Sensitivity . . .

DT: Yeah. But you went the other way with it . . .

LL: Oh yeah, with a beer bottle, or a knife. Again, it's back to the sound of my torture being projected onto the audience. And it's interesting, because I've just done an album with Cypress Grove [Tony Chmelik], who was the last person to work with Jeffrey Lee Pierce before he died. And Cypress Grove is this amazing bedroom guitar player, just a genius. And it's kind of country, but I don't mean country-punk, I mean acoustic but still kind of swampy, just a different flavor than I've hit upon before. And I play a little guitar on this and it's more the sensitive slide, or as I call it the baby slide. [*laughs*] The sound of a baby crying. I guess that's what my guitar always goes back to. It's the sound of a baby crying, whether it's throwing a hideous temper tantrum like in Teenage Jesus, or like in *The Drowning of Lucy Hamilton*, the last gasps of a dying little girl. [*laughs*] The sound she would make is the sound of a guitar being strangled.

DT: Although your slide did develop as you were saying, it seems like you got where you wanted remarkably quickly.

LL: Oh yeah, I was there. [*laughs*] What's fascinating when you're thinking back on it is that it was just a hundred percent instinct. I mean, there was no one I took inspiration from. Everything I had liked in music was what I wanted to be against in creation. So, I mean, if I loved Bob Quine or if I loved the Stooges, I wanted my sound to be the exact diametric opposite of that. It wasn't deconstructing, it was demolishing all that came before it, and creating a sound you hadn't heard and maybe you never wanted to hear again. That was also important. "I never heard this before; I never want to hear it again!" Perfect! Goodbye.

That's why the Teenage Jesus shows were, at the longest, thirteen minutes. Seven to thirteen minutes. When we did the retrovirus we really had to stretch. I said, "OK, twenty-five minutes is the maximum. This is more than twice what a set was." You know, people weren't going to pay ridiculous amounts of money for thirteen minutes. Twenty-five I guess is OK. [*laughs*] That was every single song we had.

DT: It seems like there was a lot of instinct behind the song ideas in Teenage Jesus too, like "Red Alert." What made you say, "That's a song"?

LL: Well, it's like a siren. It's a perfect example of New York music, like a siren going by. And you hear it for thirty seconds, then it's gone. So, it was very much instinct, yeah. Not that there wasn't forethought, but, OK, this is the sound, like nothing you've ever heard. It's rhythm-based. Word-driven. *Word-driven*, yet there's a lot of instrumentals. So figure that out. [*laughs*]

DT: Just going back a bit, in essence moving away from the guitar was mainly about pursuing the writing for you, especially since spoken word was taking off as a form?

LL: Oh yeah, absolutely. I mean, I didn't know if I would do anything musically beyond Teenage Jesus. As I said, I went to New York thinking I was a writer, I was going to do spoken word. So I didn't think beyond Teenage Jesus, and then Beirut Slump, at the same time, I didn't think beyond that. And then Pat Irwin approached me for 8-Eyed Spy, and I had a lot of trouble with that band, because they were getting too jazzy, which I didn't really like, and surfy, which I hated. The band was just too popular, and I didn't like being popular, period, much less for jazzy/surf music—fuck off. I didn't like the look in people's eyes. That's quite frankly the bottom line.

DT: This need you have to keep moving seems to have played a big part in the way your career unfolded.

LL: Well, if you could call this a career. I call it crab-walking sideways through my life. But, yeah, I've managed to continue to create for thirty years by being stubbornly contrarian and doing the next thing, which is why I have to live in Europe now. I'd prefer to live in Europe anyway, philosophically, morally, politically, but even if it was just me and a bullhorn, I would still do what I do. And I see myself in that position, as the hermit on the hill, you know, at eighty years old, with a bullhorn and a shotgun screaming at the neighbors that aren't there. I mean, it's kind of what I always was, and I take great comfort in that image. [*laughs*] The hermit on the hill with the shotgun and the bullhorn. That's what I am.

DT: Do you think the writers you've mentioned over the years, people like Hubert Selby and Henry Miller, had much to do with developing that image of yourself?

LL: Well, to me what I read was far more important than what music I listened to. Because at a desperate period in my adolescent life—twelve years old, thirteen—when I'm reading these writers who took "reality," whatever that meant, and poetically, brutally slammed it on paper while traveling through life and the world . . . that just showed me that it could be done and that's what I had to do, that's what I needed to do. That's what I would do. It saved me the same way that music saved some people. I mean, music was very important, but for me it's always down to the words. Even in my photographs, even in my photographic exhibits, the titles are very important.

DT: Those words and titles give your work such clear intent. Not all artists want that; they might prefer more ambiguity or . . .

LL: No, no. Exactly what you're saying. That's what I do. You know, in a sense, I feel like I've always been making protest music. I'm repulsed, I'm revolting, always. I'm revolting against whatever power structure is obsessing me, whether it's personal, political, sexual, or a battle within my own psyche. This is always public psychotherapy; even when it sounds like good time fucking rock 'n' roll, you know, *the point is the fucking point*. And if I have to use the guitar to hit you over the head in order for it to penetrate you, whether you want it or not, whether you like it or loathe it, you're going to get it. Even if you don't "get it," I'm going to infect you. And the people who do get it, and who do need it—you know there's always one or two—that's who I'm playing for. I have a salon mentality. To me it's the one or two, at the most three or four, people who need these words, [for whom] something in one of the sentences you say is making life easier to deal with, the same way that Selby and Miller and [Jean] Genet and [Marquis] de Sade made my life easier to deal with. They made my life easier to deal with; they let me see a path, a trajectory, a way out, a way forward.

DT: Do you feel connected to those writers in the same way you do to your contemporaries such as Robert Quine and Rowland Howard?

LL: Well, of course. I'm very lucky that I've never been censored, that they haven't disappeared me yet. You know, this could've happened from *The Gun Is Loaded*, my performance piece under Ronald Reagan, until *Will Work for Drugs*. For the title alone. So I mean, I have a lot of empathy for de Sade's mania to continue writing under the worst of conditions—incarceration, imprisonment, etc. And Selby was to me a great balancer. Because when I first met him in the '80s, I think he was teaching school, living in this crappy West Hollywood apartment. Hadn't really done many readings. Never was paid to do a reading. And, yeah, one book took him sixteen years, one took him six months. But the work, that's what was important to him. And, Selby didn't have that great an output, but the impact of something like *Requiem for a Dream* is like a gut punch, a nervous breakdown on the page. That's the beauty of it.

DT: Did that set a standard for the impact you aspired to?

LL: Well, it set more of a standard for me to continue on and to not give up. That's where Selby was important to me, that he carried the fuck on, he carried on, he carried on. And it didn't matter who knew him and who didn't.

DT: Another way people like Selby and Miller might have been useful was how their works, whether they took months or years, at least appear to be spontaneous. That fits in well with spoken word and guitar.

LL: Well, so much of what I do is spontaneous outburst even though there is calculation involved. The guitar sounds spontaneous, the spoken word sounds conversational, and there is some improv, but it's pretty much written down. That duality is very much a key to my personality, is something that with guitar is brutally precise yet psychotic with slide, something that sounds spontaneous but has a manipulation somewhere underneath it, because there is an immense amount of control, yet it can also explode. So maybe just my personality is what infected the guitar, and that's what happens as a result. I mean, who you are is channeled through this instrument. My guitar playing is unique to the way I am because that's the way it is. [*laughs*] Because that's the way I am.

DT: I was thinking about that as it pertains to you, and I guess the central nervous system of whoever is touching the instrument has a lot to do with the total effect of his or her playing, and you can refine the technique but it's not going to change the feeling too much.

LL: Oh, that's perfect. And the thing is, nothing that I do is about refining any technique; it's all hitting upon the concept. The concept is the priority, [along with] finding the collaborators and documenting it. Those are the three priorities in what I do, and all three are important. And it is pretty spontaneous. I don't have volumes of unpublished stories or unrecorded songs. When it's time to do something, when the moment strikes that my version of hysterical/historical documentation about this moment, my emotional state, the light falling on the window across the street, needs to be documented, then it's birthed.

DT: When you use the word "concept," do you mean you see yourself as conceptual like a visual artist would?

LL: Absolutely, yeah. Confrontational/conceptual.

DT: Did you ever have a specific concept for the guitar?

LL: You know, the guitar is just another channel. I think that the reason I've had to create at the pace that I do, with the different collaborators, the different styles, is really just to splinter or compartmentalize myself. I describe myself as a hotel in which many monsters live. And if you understand that, then you understand why when a door opens, another kind of music comes out, OK? And that's the best way I can describe it: the guitar's just another room in this hotel that I inhabit called my body. There's the guitar, the guitar is in one room. Machine gun in the other. [*laughs*] Microphone in the other.

DT: A different part of your aesthetic comes out with each one.

LL: Absolutely. And look, I only play guitar when no other guitar player can achieve the sound that needs to be achieved for that specific project. I'm not going to start playing bad rock guitar; that's not what I do. It's not what's called for. So if my style of guitar is called for on very specific projects, then it's appropriate, but for the most part I'd rather have James Johnston, Rowland S. Howard, and any number of others—Nels Cline, the masters.

DT: Something that seems to come up with you is the way that artists with contrarian agendas are often perceived as only angry or unhappy when they express some frustration as part of their work. But as you're saying, these various media give you a lot of ways to vent, and these collaborators give you a community, and on the whole you seem to have a healthy integration of the difficult things you need to express with a contentment with who you are.

LL: Oh yeah. Look, I've done everything I've ever wanted to do with anyone I've wanted to do it with. I live where I want to live. I think I'm one of the most successful people I know—not financially, of course, but I live now at least in a country that not only encourages me to do everything that I do but allows me to travel quickly and cheaply to the places that have always supported me. And you know, it's not like I'm so different than I am onstage, but that's an extreme, that's going to the pinprick of the poison and exploding outwards. And I do have a lot of these vehicles, and basically on a day-to-day level, I'm pretty fucking funny. I can't say that I'm *happy*, because that's not the point, but I'm not as miserable as I could or should be because I see the absurdity, you know, and there's nothing I can fucking do about it.

I kind of like that. I like that it's "apocalypse forever"—part of my intellectual sadism is watching the empires collapse. Part of my sadism onstage, especially in spoken word, is when I know I've just riffed on a passage, on a sentence, on five sentences in a row, and one image is sticking out, and I don't know which one but there's one image that's sticking in your mind and you're stuck there, and I'm going forward, and that's where I get off. You know? *That's where I get off.* And maybe it's the same with the guitar: it's like, "How are you getting those fucking sounds? What the hell are you playing?" I don't know. So? Go figure it out, *Nels Cline*. I betcha can't. [*laughs*] So part of my joy comes in the mystery of that as well. You know, you don't have to know everything about me. I'll tell you everything, but I feel that the more I tell you the less you might have. Yeah, I'll tell you everything—you got it? I don't think so. [*laughs*] There's always gonna be the cubby hole in the attic door that hasn't been cracked yet.

(11)

META BOX

KEITH LEVENE

PHOTO BY MAUREEN BAKER, COURTESY OF KEITH LEVENE

orn in London in 1957, Keith Levene didn't fit into the high-punk era of recycled New York Dolls riffs and sweaty club shows, despite his childhood friendship with Sid Vicious and his front-row seat for the entire affair. After bailing out of an early version of the Clash, he got in early on the next wave, bringing his dub leanings to the ever-changing platform that was Public Image Ltd. Just as punk was presented as a reaction to rock, PiL was a reaction to punk: the group set out to break the formula wide open, letting go of tired forms (like the *song*) and working things out in the studio as opposed to onstage. For PiL, the whole rock project needed reprogramming, and vocalist John Lydon—a.k.a. Johnny Rotten—had the cred to get things going. And while bassist Jah Wobble (John Wardle) certainly played his part, it took Levene's guitar to bring it off musically. And when his guitar wasn't there, it took his synth, his studio skills, and his sense of knowing which off-tempo drum track would best work on one of their patchwork pieces. In a way, PiL was the ultimate put-on, three stoned gits taking their sweet time in Richard Branson's Manor Studio playing Space Invaders. But in the end, they were serious about the right things at the right times. The three and a half studio albums made with Levene—*First Issue* (1978), *Metal Box* (1979), and *Flowers of Romance* (1981), plus what became the 1983 bootleg *Commercial Zone*—are of a sharp piece, like the take-your-pick attachments of an army knife.

As their edict declared, PiL wasn't a band but a "communications company" with interests in film and other unspecified ventures. Yet gestures such as releasing *Metal Box* in 16mm film canisters may not be as interesting now as the music itself, which still has the shock of the new. What suited Levene to the group's futurism were the breadth of his musical interests (how many other punk-era guitarists were teenage roadies for Yes?), his regimen (. . . or practiced eight hours a day?), and his willingness to go down with the ship (he might have some competition there). Slim and pale, wielding an aluminum Travis Bean Wedge, Levene created parts that were weightless, like commentaries as opposed to primary tracks. In PiL, he proved to be the ideal foil for the snickering Lydon and the dread-gazing Wobble, carving hieroglyphs into their respective fogs. Despite the group's unconventionality, he was able to introduce a number of influential "Leveno" stylings into the guitar lexicon, as in "Theme," where he merged the dual outputs of his Electric Mistress into a single metallic coil, or in "Public Image," where he flashed chiming chords later copped by the Edge. Levene went thrashy in "Annalisa," dance reggae in "Death Disco" (a.k.a. "Swan Lake"), even picked Floydian arpeggios with crisp muscularity in "The Slab." There didn't seem to be anything he couldn't do with the guitar—that is, besides find it interesting enough to keep playing. (After barely touching it on *Flowers*, he often favored the bass or production in later work.) Still, over three decades after PiL's breakthrough, Jah Wobble exclaimed at TheQuietus.com, "No-one has ever come close to Levene in terms of playing the non-square, non-bourgeoisie, harmonically hip, 'guitar wash.'"

The original PiL dissolved acrimoniously, losing Wobble in 1980 and Levene three years later, leaving Lydon to carry on with a rotating cast that included former Magazine guitarist John McGeoch. Although Levene has worked somewhat steadily since—his solo releases include 1989's *Violent Opposition* and 2002's *Killer in the Crowd*, along with session gigs for Adrian Sherwood's dub label On-U Sound—his post-PiL reclusion has always made a certain sense, and not simply for the rumors that circulated to explain it. From those early days on, Stratetime Keith was always an apparition.

DAVID TODD: You've said that the PiL concept was close to your own vision. How was that the case?

KEITH LEVENE: OK, the original ethos of PiL was really complicated and serious. That was, "We're not a band; we're a company. We don't need producers; if we need to do a deal we'll get lawyers." OK? "And we can do other things." Now, we didn't know how to do anything except be stupid kids and possibly make some music. And it took off from there.

And we immediately were doing it. We made the first PiL album, and then we did other things like [side project] *Steel Leg v. the Electric Dread*. This kind of stuff happened really quickly. The idea would've been to put it all out through PiL, and at the time through Virgin [Records, the band's UK label].

Now, the reason we eventually went against our ethos was there was a lot more pressure than we realized; we didn't even realize the pressure was getting to us. And over time "us" became me and Wobble, and us became me, because Wobble left. But I'll give you this: the reason PiL failed is because of John Lydon—the PiL *ethos* failed. I feel like after me and Wobble left, they may have made two good tracks, but when it comes to a whole fucking album, I can't think of one.

DT: How do you rate the albums you made with PiL?

KL: I'm very happy with my time in PiL. The more I hear what's going on now, the more I think the whole thing was so worthwhile. Every other band at the time was saying, "What are we going to do now?" Well, we weren't like that. We were in the punk rock era and we didn't even have to perform and we passed the test. Not just because we had Johnny Rotten, but because we were who we were. And the fact was, we were really genuine

DT: "Genuine" is an interesting word for PiL.

KL: I was one hundred percent genuine about what I was doing. I mean all this [discussion among critics] about "Is it a trick with PiL?"—that was all bollocks. We'd get these reviews that were complete slag-offs. And all these things they'd slag us off for, if they were saying it was good because of them, it'd be a great review. So the same reviews would come out, and one was a slag, one was "This is wicked." And then there'd be the on-the-fence people: "Well, we'll have to see." In other words, "I don't know whether to say I like them or not."

What they didn't get was, we were totally fucking genuine. We obviously tried to do something different—we put a fucking record in a metal box. Really, it was a bleeding film can, but even for that we paid thirty-three grand back of our advance to get sixty thousand made, and Richard Branson went behind our back and made two million of them, literally. It was nuts.

You know about the music business, how maddening it is and how it contributes to situations falling apart. Look at Kurt Cobain—a lot of that is about the record industry, you know. You've got a royal fucking talent there and the kid's dead, and he was crazy, but you have to be crazy to do this stuff.

DT: In general, how were you able to deal with the industry?

KL: At the time not too bad, because we had all that "fuck off" stuff up front, you know. "You're doing a deal with a corporation." Having that, it was quite an interesting game. I felt like we were playing on our home court.

But when I learned about the business, I fucking knew I was learning an obsolete industry, just by the terminology they used. And of course I'd moan in interviews, "Oh, the future's going to be like this, and the technology will be like that." Well, now it is. And I still feel like the same kid, so I'm happy now, but when I look at the industry I think we were lucky to slip PiL through that system.

DT: It seems like a lot of your associations with PiL involve the business side as opposed to the music side. Are those the things you remember most?

KL: No, from my point of view, PiL, we did great. Even *Commercial Zone*. When we first did PiL, we were just kids—that's the best way to put it. And now I think it's hilarious, all our tycoon ideas, but we knocked a lot of walls down for a lot of musicians. A hell of a lot. Even though we weren't running our ethos like I said—of course we weren't, we were too busy taking the money, and who wouldn't, you know? That would've been insane. And we threw a lot of money away on the basis of "Let's see what it's like to make the wrong decision on purpose," you know? I gave apartments away. I wanted to say, "What would happen if I said 'No, keep it'?" And I found out.

We were pulled onto the Tom Snyder show and John went and opened his mouth about the one fucking business transaction we'd done, which was a soundtrack I had booked for [director Michael Wadleigh's film] *Wolfen*. I had it in the bag. And we went on Tom Snyder and when John finally answered the question, "Well, if you're a company, what other things do you do aside from gigs?" John went, "Well, we do tinker with soundtracks. Keith here will be doing a soundtrack at [Warner Bros., the band's US label] for the bloke that directed *Woodstock*." And I fucking knew the second he said it, "It's over for us with the record company." Because I knew Warners would freak out. They were freaked out already.

I might've looked like a stoned twat on that show, but I knew what was fucking going on. I was trying to talk about PiL, but my mouth was so dry because I'd never been on national TV before, and we'd just gotten off a plane and poured talcum powder over each other, so we looked insane. John got himself into a corner and he wouldn't let me do any damage control. And what John was saying was so funny—"Yeah, we're not fucking hippies, flap your flares"—he just went on such a roll. [*laughs*] But I was thinking, "We're going to be thrown off the record company."

DT: Why would you be thrown off the record company for doing a soundtrack?

KL: Well, Warners was deciding at the time whether to drop us, so John blurting it out like that on TV didn't help. They might've even called Wadleigh and said, "We can't let you use these punks on your movie," who knows? I never heard another word from Wadleigh and I can only connect it with that incident.

Warners didn't even limo us back to the hotel after the show. We had to get cabs. Then the next day, we got a rise-and-shine from them 'cause the interview got special TV ratings, thanks to our candor.

DT: What's the difference between you now and in those days?

KL: It's so much easier [now], because I don't care about the things we had to talk about like incorporation; it's not an issue anymore. And it was all an issue then. It's like, if we did that Tom Snyder interview now, he'd sit there and have a really great conversation with me going, "Wow, I like that," and I'd say, "Well instead of using money as a currency, in fact, I don't work for money anymore, because I've had so much trouble getting paid. I do the work because I love it." We're in the data age now, and the data age really suits me as the Public Image guy.

DT: So you do still feel connected to that PiL ethos.

KL: I always said with PiL, you don't work *for* PiL, you work *with* PiL, and I've always kept that. I kept a lot of what you might call these days the PiL ethos. We never actually laid down a manifesto, not like Devo: "You either are Devo or you're not, and these are the reasons." They were great. But I think we were a bit more serious and purposeful.

DT: It seems like there was so much theorizing about the business model with PiL, but what about the music?

KL: No plan of action. Knew what we didn't want.

DT: What didn't you want?

KL: Well, I can't tell you [now] what I didn't want. I knew what I didn't want [at the time] because it was there. Like, I knew I wanted Roland synthesizers; I knew I wanted old Moog modular systems. I knew I wanted the new [EDP] Wasp—that was a plastic synth I bought every member of the band, and that got us through the *Metal Box*—but I knew I didn't want a fucking Fender Strat. I didn't want to look like Jimi Hendrix; I didn't want to put it across like I was some fucking guitar god. When I was sixteen, sure, but for me it wasn't about refining what somebody did in 1965. I didn't want that kind of plan of action. I didn't want to stick to the plan, and therefore I didn't have one. And because I didn't have a plan, I would look at a situation and think, "Well, what's not working?" If everything was fine, I'd carry on, and if it wasn't, I'd make changes. That's pretty much the way we made music.

DT: It seems that one thing PiL didn't want to be was punk.

KL: Yeah, definitely. PiL is post-punk, without a doubt. The whole point to the first album is like, "All right, we can do the Sex Pistols, but we're not going to do anything like that. *This* is what you're going to get." And then *Metal Box* is like, as one of the guys I work with calls it, our stake in the ground, and even *Commercial Zone* was wicked, though it didn't get the right airing. And *Flowers of Romance* was too esoteric, really, but it's a lot of people's favorite.

DT: I've heard there was a lot of pressure on the band for not being consistent enough stylistically.

KL: How about that? "You're changing. You're too new." How can you deal with that?

DT: Was change essential to the group?

KL: Yeah, that was the whole idea. That's why I stayed in PiL, because it changed all the time. And as far as I'm concerned, the constant was me and

John, and that's why when I left, PiL was done, and I think a lot of people feel that way.

DT: Was it unavoidable that the changing would lead to the band splitting up?

KL: It's funny, I think I could've continued with John—[PiL's 1986] *Album* could've been wicked. Come to think of it, that potentially could've happened, although I don't know how John would've reacted to it. And that was the whole problem, wasn't it? "What's up with John?" It wasn't "What's up with Keith?" which is what some people think. Or "Is Keith on smack?" Our problems were never about smack. I might've had some problems, but with PiL it was never about smack.

DT: I understand.

KL: I'm just saying, because that comes up. And, yeah, it's fine if Keith Richards does it or Lou Reed, but talk about me and it's like, "Oh, that naughty Keith Levene was doing smack all the time."
  The drugs weren't helping the situation, but I could still prorate my life and figure out what was happening in reality. There was nothing that far-out going on.
  So anyway . . .

DT: People might've thought the problem was worse for you because although you were in New York and L.A. for much of the '80s, they didn't see you with other bands.

KL: No, [they didn't].

DT: Were there bands you could've seen yourself playing with?

KL: Not really.

DT: Nobody?

KL: I didn't want to join Guns N' Roses. [*laughs*] I don't know, it's not so much joining a band, but I could've seen myself working with people. I was surprised I didn't end up working with Eno or Bowie or a number of people—Peter Gabriel. They were all around and I never got offers from any of these guys. No one.

DT: Did you make yourself available?

KL: I'm not the easiest person to find. It's not like I go out of my way, I just make myself difficult to pinpoint for numbers of reasons. But there's no way I wouldn't work with Eno, of course. And there's no way I wouldn't work with Bowie, even if he was ninety. We're talking about a guy I'm very fond of and . . . I couldn't imagine living without, to be quite honest. I can't imagine being me without Bowie. I mean personally, I've got a lot to thank David Bowie for.

But I'm just saying, I would have expected more interest from a lot of people so . . . who fucking knows?

I'll tell you what I think, right? I do think I had a reputation and I do have more than a sneaking suspicion that I was locked out of certain situations too. Virgin had this habit of stopping me doing deals with people, and that lasted seven years that, let's face it, career-wise was my hottest time possible.

DT: Another factor is that you were working a lot of those years, doing sessions in London for On-U Sound.

KL: It's really annoying, because people would assume I was doing that. I definitely had a lot of people who didn't ask me because they figured I was busy.

DT: It made sense to me that you wound up on a dub label, given your playing style with PiL.

KL: I had that one. And I've had people say, "Well, I didn't think you'd do it." And I'd say, "Well, the way to find out is you ask." You know what I mean?

DT: This is getting away from PiL, but it's interesting to me how often names like Peter Gabriel and Brian Eno come up with you.

KL: There are a few [names that come up], in very diversified areas. Paul Simon comes from the generation before me but he sang the fucking same shit I'm thinking still, which is wonderful. I can listen to Paul Simon, I can listen to Eno, time and time again. I can listen to their new stuff and be quite comfortable with it and wear it like a velvet coat.

DT: What do you like about Paul Simon?

KL: Simon, I consider like my big brother, you know. I like his consistency. I like the fact that I can listen to *Graceland*, which was the '80s, and then listen to 2006's *Surprise*.

DT: Didn't Eno produce that?

KL: No, he didn't produce it, he did electronic landscapes—in other words, he played on it. Paul Simon produced it, and it's a great fucking record, just like *Graceland*, just like "Bridge over Troubled Water," and that's why I cite Paul Simon, that's why I cite Eno and I cite David Byrne, Peter Gabriel. There's more out there but I don't want to bore you to death; we've got to get on, you know.

DT: I think it's interesting, your take on Rhymin' Simon.

KL: Oh, he's so fucking important. Shit, man—same as John Lennon—I wanted to put a Paul Simon record on my Myspace.
    Leonard Cohen. When I was eleven and I used to listen to "Suzanne," I was thinking, "That's that weird Jewish guy with the deep voice," you know. When we were punks we were like, "Fuck you and fuck the record you came in on," but I knew he was important. I mean, I wasn't particularly that punk anyway. I'm more with the general public, but not within what I'm doing. Anyway, there's definitely a spectrum of people like Paul Simon and Leonard Cohen that affected me.

DT: What do you think of the state of the music industry today? Well, maybe I already know the answer to that . . .

KL: Yeah, it's fucking terrible. The industry right now is so manufactured, because they're scared of talent, they don't want talent to get out there. There could be a government fucking ruling for all I know but there isn't; it's just the way people operate. They want everything on the table, and that gives us a definite "Don't fucking go there," you know. That's the billboard it sends to me.

Go to any hits channel, you see these wankers standing there, not even doing it well. You know, if you're going to do it, do it, and turn me on.

DT: Every year it seems like Jerry Lee Lewis is that much cooler.

KL: Fucking-a. Exactly! Give me a debauched fucking reverend's brother any day of the week.

DT: OK, I do want to ask about your guitar playing. We were talking about PiL as post-punk, and I was wondering if the type of guitar played in punk bands was one of the reasons you wanted to go "post-" that.

KL: Look, when I learned to play guitar, I learned to play like Johnny Thunders. I mean, he was older than me, and that made a difference, like, "He's never going to see it the way I see it." But I dug what he did, and so I played that way. Because, really, the New Yorkers invented punk; it wasn't the fucking English people. The English people have a way of picking up on a look, and actually I found that look with Sid [Vicious] before anyone was doing that shit. But, yeah, with post-punk and the punk guitar thing, there's Johnny Thunders, possibly a couple others. Tom Verlaine would be the more intellectual—it's more Tom Verlaine that crafted the shit we're talking about. All Johnny did was play really great rock guitar and have his own style within the parameters that are dictated to you by the records that you learn to play with. But Tom Verlaine, I mean, he's the one. He's punk era. He's pre-punk era. He's Patti Smith era. And Patti Smith influenced so many punks. I was right on the punk scene, and she influenced the Slits, she influenced fucking Mick Jones. She influenced me.

DT: She influenced you as a guitarist?

KL: I play guitar like she does vocals. Just the whole open thing—the way Lenny [Kaye] plays with Patti is the way I had to play with John to make PiL work. I conducted the band by knowing what the number was and not having any parameters for it, and I had to assess how long Wobble was going to play, and be prepared for John to come in, be prepared to turn around or not depending on what he came in with, and all that kind of thing. Well, I could do that because I'd watched Lenny and Patti. That's how Patti Smith influenced me, you know.

DT: One guitarist I know you get asked about a lot is Steve Howe of Yes.

KL: That's all right.

DT: How did he affect you?

KL: Steve Howe? Most creative, hardest-working guitar player I've ever heard. He was totally aware of all the guitaring that was around. And he was always original—he only ever sounded like him. And I loved the way he looked. He was never my hero, but I liked him as a kind of role model, and then by the time I was sixteen, I was working for him. So I hadn't particularly wanted to meet him, but I ended up meeting him, and luckily he was a straightforward guy and he was a fucking amazing artist and . . . I don't know. I think his enthusiasm influenced me, just the way he approached the guitar. I think that's what made me practice for eight hours a day, because I figured, fuck, I bet you have to practice for eight hours a day to be as good as that. And I was right. You do.

Another thing that was great about Steve was that he stopped me from closing up. He kept me open to things, because he played nylon, he played sitar, he played mandolin. He didn't play in 4/4 time. He didn't play in any time. And then he played in very specific times: 13/11, 7/9—just, like, mad shit. And that obviously influenced me, but not directly, just as a general overruling influence.

I've obviously gone out of my way not to copy anyone, and that's been one of the biggest struggles between myself and what I was doing on guitar. And because it was me, myself, I just thought my own playing had to be shit. And it took me twenty years to realize the *Metal Box* wasn't shit. I fucking pulled it off. In fact, I aced it. But honestly, it took me twenty years to see that.

DT: When you said you pulled it off, what does that mean?

KL: I used to say, "Don't call me an artist," and "Don't call me a musician." And I still don't consider myself a musician. I know I can play all these instruments but I fucking hate musicians. That's the punk in me.

DT: Does that go for guitarists too?

KL: Well, look, I was a guitarist, and by the time I got good I was thinking, "Fuck, man, this is over. Guitarists are a dime a dozen." And at the same time I was thinking, "There's no fucking way this is over. This has only been around since the Beatles." So I was like, "What can possibly make this exciting now?" And it wasn't Jimi Hendrix that was making it exciting, or Jimmy Page, or the up-and-coming punk bands. So, yeah, I was into music as a nonmusician that could play guitar.

DT: It also seems like you were better versed in rock guitar than a lot of the other people from that time, having practiced so much.

KL: Well, that's why I knew what I didn't want, you see. I covered what I thought I wanted and then realized, "Well, I've done that now, and come to think of it, so has every cunt that made the records I got it off," you know?

What I had going for me is, I was there for the first generation, when this stuff was really new. When I was three, the Beatles were new, yeah? When I was thirteen, Led Zeppelin were new. And in between that, Pink Floyd, the whole fucking gamut of it, I was listening to since I was seven. I went through all that bollocks, *Ummagumma* to *Dark Side of the Moon*. So I had all that and I was thinking, "Well, I can't do any of that." And then I got [Eno's] *Here Come the Warm Jets* and that was amazing, and then [Bowie's]

Diamond Dogs, which was fucking incredible. I went into the Clash armed with that, and I was listening to [Robert] Fripp, and I was thinking, "Wow, I can't do what he's doing." And when I started getting records out I was thinking, "Oh, I'm fucking glad I didn't do any of that. I could have done that but I didn't, and I'm glad."

DT: I hear you on that, but we're back to that same question of what you did do.

KL: Well, now when I look at the *Metal Box*, I realize we were so free, post-punk punks getting away with fucking murder. I had that grounding and I was in a very chaotic situation and I was getting all that kind of awareness as it was going on. I was listening to "Theme" recently—and I don't listen to PiL every day, it just happened—and I was thinking, "My God," because I remember when I did that, feeling like, "Wow, I don't know if they're going to think I'm taking the piss; I don't even know if I am taking the piss." I just knew what I didn't want. That was the bottom line. And I'd always say it in interviews, "I certainly know what I don't want," but when it comes to what I do want, I don't want to pin it down, because there might be something out there and we don't even know what it is.

Really, I was just treading out into this world of mine, which was very difficult to access. Because I was tired of all that old shit—it was like obsolete data, you know. And you could take the same data and reconfigure it or you could add a few bits to it that were never there, and so that's what I did. And when I found the thing that had never been there before, it didn't matter what it sounded like, because it was going to be repeated, you know?

DT: I always wondered whether you were setting out to be innovative or provocative or piss-taking, and I liked how it was all of those at the same time.

KL: That was a big thing with me, too. I've never spoken about this on the record, but what was going on with *Metal Box* was, we'd already got the first album out and we were kind of getting into what we were going to do next. And I was going through that thing with my guitar playing too, OK? A lot of the stuff I was finding it remarkably easy to do, but I was finding it remarkably hard on a mental level, because I was thinking, "Well, what are you doing?" And I was thinking, "Well, the fact that I don't know what I'm doing could be exactly what I want. And I'm not hearing any complaints, and I'm not disliking it." Between me and myself, I knew about guitar playing, but I wasn't sure if I was . . . I just wasn't sure what I was doing, and therefore I wasn't sure if it was good or bollocks. I didn't even fucking know. I was thinking, "Should I go back into Eddie Van Halen mode or should I go back into Joe Walsh mode?" If I was thinking too much in a rehearsal I might start playing that stuff, but it just sounded so alien, and then I realized, "Wow, if that sounds alien then basically what's alien is the boat everyone's just got off. *That* sounds out of place." So I just went with my instincts and I dubbed myself. I subtracted and subtracted anything that was like Jimi Hendrix.

Now, as time went on I got more confident and more blasé and I was thinking, "Well, I don't care if Jeff Beck drops in on me for a split second—so be it." And if I missed a note I wouldn't stop the fucking music, because it wasn't all about me; it was about the whole thing that's going on, you know.

DT: For you, was there an evolution, then, to *Metal Box* from an early song like "Public Image," which could be seen as more traditional . . .

KL: It's totally traditional. The bit that wasn't traditional for me, though, was that I thought, "I will just repeat this." I didn't do anything else. And it wasn't a minimalist thing. I was just thinking about Eno, who doesn't play guitar; I wasn't thinking Phil Manzanera, who does. I was thinking, "I'm staying here. Why go anywhere else? I just want to hear this." And it worked. It worked, and that's it.

By the time we did "Theme," it was maybe the third or fourth first-album track. We'd done a gig and I saw how it worked, and I saw how the recording worked, and I was really pleased. "Theme" was great for me, and I got a retrospective off it, pretty much 20/20 hindsight within three months, and it really helped me become who I was on the *Metal Box*.

When I got to the stage where people were saying, "Keith, this isn't like Hendrix, this is like you. You're going to be like him," I was like, "Well, I'm probably not going to be like that, but I get what you mean and thank you,"

you know. And then I was thinking to myself, "God, Keith, this is like you." And like I said it took me twenty years to really be able to view me as me and not as another guy. I've only just gotten used to that in the last five years.

DT: What was holding you back?

KL: It was really weird. I mean, it's not about having money but about viewing yourself differently. OK, so I did the first album and I'm getting all this feedback: "How'd you do this? How did you do that?" It's like you know something's going on, so that makes it more difficult to believe it's you. I didn't believe I was me, and it really took me from leaving PiL to about twenty years after that to be able to assimilate them both, how I saw myself and how other people saw me.

DT: Didn't you like what you were doing?

KL: I don't think I liked myself too much. I don't think I was comfortable with myself. It's probably part of growing up—it's probably part of leaving school the day I was fifteen as a birthday present to myself, you know, taking the path less traveled or whatever you want to call it, and the kind of things I sought out. I wasn't doing those things because I didn't like myself, I was doing them because that was the shit that interested me. But I realized they were taking a toll on me, and the question I had to ask was "How much of this was me experimenting and how much was being forced on me?" And then I had to deal with getting out of these situations, and obviously as I got out of certain situations I realized I made those choices to be in them and that's what makes me me. And then I had to come out and say, "Well, I like me. Fuckin' hell, I'm fucking Keith Levene," you know? And even though I am me, it's like . . . well, you get it. I can't really say it any clearer than that.

⑫

PURLOINER

ROWLAND S. HOWARD

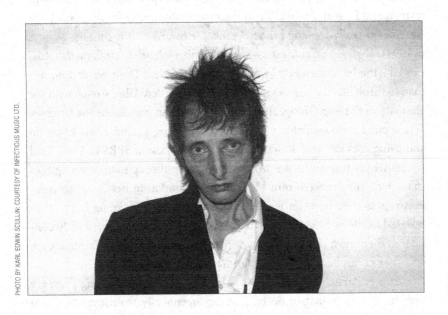

PHOTO BY KARL EDWIN SCULLIN: COURTESY OF INFECTIOUS MUSIC LTD.

n July 1982, Australian post-punkers the Birthday Party car-smashed German TV to promote their second album, *Junkyard*. They launched into the title track with unnerving mise-en-scène: singer Nick Cave perched on the drum riser like a love/hate preacher, bassist Tracy Pew gyrating with rough-trade panache, multi-instrumentalist Mick Harvey looking sideways at the whole spectacle with who-knows-what regret . . . and guitar atmospherist Rowland S. Howard, a cigarette dangling from his lip as if sculpted by Giacometti, seizing with every abuse of his whammy bar. "I am the king!" Cave cawed. "*Eeeyuh!*" Although it sounded like the black crow was damning the audience's souls, Howard punctuated each shriek with chilly reverb. His ancient white Fender Jaguar—fused to his hip at birth—

slithered above a dirge that was bloody, arty, massive, primal, uncompromising, utterly life-and-death, as if belted out for a coliseum full of Romans. This was the Birthday Party in full effect: a swampy, avant-Testament brand of hellfire.

Debuting in 1980, the Birthday Party raged against being relegated to the second wave of punk abrasion, especially since they could've outdone anybody in the first. Hailing from Down Under, they railed at their countrymen and English snobs alike, at their own *disgustingly fawning* fans ("We were never really looking for acceptance," Howard told *Prehistoric Sounds* in 1994). Thriving on contrasts—smart/dumb, violent/spectral, raw/sophisticated—the band formerly known as the Boys Next Door wanted no less than to throb like the Stooges, play the angles like Pere Ubu, stretch with the elasticity of the Pop Group, and leap out of cartoon panels like the Cramps. "We wanted to do something with rock music using a standard rock line-up and using rock clichés," Rowland said to Lee Bajzek of 3PBS in 1996, "and yet somehow transform it into something new through sheer strength of character." They moved from Melbourne to London to Berlin . . . so compulsive was their need for fertile alienation that they broke up just as they released a pair of 1983 EPs, *The Bad Seed* and *Mutiny*, that are widely considered their most realized works. Still, they'd moved so far so fast that even now they continue to cast a long skinny donkey shadow.

As a guitarist, Rowland S. Howard was an equally looming presence over his less imaginative peers, shifting ingeniously from overchords to verti-peggios to war-whoops all in the Birthday Party's "Sonny's Burning" alone. He had his signature—springing reverb skimmed off the tops of chords, trapped in the vacuums of his Fender Twin—but he also summoned the howling fog that opens "The Friend Catcher" and the pyschobilly gunfire of "Dead Joe." A video of the *Mutiny* sessions captures Howard overdubbing on the murder ballad "Jennifer's Veil," showing how masterfully he could *use* the guitar on top of how well he could play it. In the beginning, it's hardly a "part" he crafts, just some electric weeds he taps out as if half asleep. Then he calmly throws down a series of crushingly dramatic chords like a straight flush one card after another. Then it's back to more harmonics and fragmented tremolo, all of which seems random as he creates it but settles over the finished track like a frame. In a field dominated by overplayers,

Rowland realized that the easiest way to make a song bigger was simply to pump more air into it, to inflate with more space, more silence, more of his flickering self-consciousness.

Sure, it was Cave who ascended after the Birthday Party split, enjoying success as Howard battled his opiates in less posh quarters. But both of them, as well as their many imitators, drew from the same well of antipodean suffering, whether it was Nick with his kill-crooning Bad Seeds (with guitarist Blixa Bargeld, on loan from Einstürzende Neubauten), or Crime & the City Solution, a group formed by Mick Harvey and singer Simon Bonney that welcomed Rowland for a pair of releases in the mid-1980s. For Rowland, there was also These Immortal Souls, the band he led circa 1987–92 with his brother Harry on bass, and a solo career initiated with 1999's *Teenage Snuff Film*. Rowland's second solo album, 2009's *Pop Crimes*, was recorded during his battle with liver cancer and released just before his death on December 30 of the same year, a passing that occurred only shortly after this interview took place, and was an indie tragedy that reached far beyond the St. Kilda neighborhood of Melbourne where he lived like a demigod.

DAVID TODD: You said before the interview that "virtually every part of the guitar is playable, thus making it a very easy instrument to subvert." What did you mean by that?

ROWLAND S. HOWARD: Well, the electric guitar is a really primitive electronic device, and by virtue of that the whole thing is basically miked up, you know. You can get sound off it anywhere. And I think this is one of its great strengths, because a lot of the new digital instrumentation sounds exactly the same no matter who plays it. It's very hard to subvert because you can't actually get to the mechanics of the device and make it do something that it wasn't supposed to do. Whereas with an electric guitar you can just hit it on the ground, there's all sorts of very physical things that you can use to get these strange sounds out of it. And, you know, you still hear sounds coming out of an electric guitar that you've never heard before, and when you think of how many millions of people are playing it, that's pretty amazing.

DT: Was that your goal from the beginning, to get new sounds?

RSH: The way I play was born of necessity, in the sense that I had ideas about what I wanted to do but I didn't have the technique to pull them off, so I had to find ways to approximate them. I think the big lesson punk rock taught me was that you didn't have to be a virtuoso, that it's all about trying to do something that differs from most people. You know, if you're any good you should be able to be picked out in the first few notes. There aren't a whole lot of guitarists like that, but when you hear them, it's a wonderful thing.

DT: Were there any of those guitarists around when you were starting out?

RSH: When I first started playing professionally, the really interesting records were the Public Image stuff and the first Pop Group album, which has an amazing use of space. I think that's something that a lot of people never learn, how to utilize space, and guitarists are probably the worst of them. The Pop Group would go from making some tiny noise to this maelstrom, and there were a lot of groups around then that utilized space in that way. I think it often happens that people come to the same conclusion in a field of art at the same time because they're reacting against what had been going on before, and that involved a lot of progressive rock where everything was virtuoso. But, yeah, those two bands in particular illustrated to me how important something like space is.

DT: A couple of other guitarists you've mentioned are Syd Barrett and Fred Frith. What was important about them?

RSH: I was interested in that English-eccentric music. All those people like Kevin Ayers were doing things in their own little worlds and made these incredibly English records. When I first started buying records, there was this shop near my school that used to sell deleted records very cheap. I could buy three a week or something with my pocket money. And consequently I got exposed to all these records like Eno's *Music for Films*, a lot of Krautrock, Neu! I used to buy anything that the cover looked good on. Because there was no way to hear them. The stores wouldn't play them for you, and there was very little in the press about these people. You just had to search. You know, I feel like it's unfortunate that kids these days just have to look things up on the Internet and it's all there. I remember looking for over a year for a copy of *Raw Power* and eventually finding it, and nobody else I knew had one.

DT: Did you have to search like that for the sound you're known for, the Fender Jaguar played through a Twin Reverb amp? How did you arrive at that combination?

RSH: Pretty much like a lot of things in my life, just by chance. I remember going to buy a guitar and the Jaguar was the one with the most chrome on it—that was attractive to me. [*laughs*] There were all these hideous wood-grain guitars around in the early '80s; they looked like pieces of Scandinavian furniture or something. And the Jaguar was about as far away as you could get from that. I just knew I wanted to make a sound that was the complete opposite of a Les Paul, and that's pretty much a Jaguar.

DT: When you started playing that setup, was there a moment of recognition for you?

RSH: Yeah, definitely. I mean, I got the Jaguar and I already had a Fender Twin and it just seemed to naturally go in a particular direction. I'd always had a fondness for spaghetti-Western, twangy guitar, and I knew I wanted to do things that were new without using a whole lot of effects to achieve them. It's like, I saw Jane's Addiction reformed on TV the other night, and . . . what's that guy's name in Jane's Addiction?

DT: Dave Navarro?

RSH: Dave Navarro, yeah. There was so much digital delay on what he was doing that it didn't really sound like a person was playing it; it just sounded slick and professional, like another digital sound. And I don't understand that desire to create a sound that has so little of yourself in it. Because anybody with the equipment can do it.

DT: What techniques did you use to come up with new sounds?

RSH: Just the tremolo bar and reverb on the amp, you know. I mean, they were all very simple things like playing the harmonics really softly so the reverb comes off bigger than the notes. It's just a matter of using them judiciously.

I'll tell you a funny story about that, actually. Well, it wasn't very funny to me at the time, but it's funny in retrospect. I did an interview with an Australian newspaper once and they said, "So you've obviously been heavily influenced by Blixa Bargeld." And I said, "*What?*" And they said, "Well, you only have to listen to his harmonics on the Bad Seeds records and then listen to the last Birthday Party record to see where you got it from." I'm like, "Hmm . . ."

DT: That makes me think of something that surprised me while I was reading up on you, which is that the Birthday Party received some criticism for not being proficient.

RSH: Well, to say that we weren't proficient is ridiculous, because we were really tight, you know. We wanted to be tight enough to have as much impact as we could. But on the other hand it depended on the song—some songs were deliberately sloppy. And we barely ever rehearsed, because we always wanted to leave a large amount to chance. You know, you can rehearse and rehearse, but something only really takes off when you put it in front of an audience, and that's worth a thousand rehearsals. The adrenaline boost makes you do things you wouldn't have thought of with your cognitive mind.

DT: You wanted to have to be engaged in your performances?

RSH: Yeah. Very much so. I actually wrote a piece for a magazine called *Word Art* where I was trying to point out that the only difference between performance art and rock 'n' roll—or good rock 'n' roll, rock 'n' roll as it should be—is the way people look at it. You can go and see some band play and it'll be one of the most affecting things you'll ever see in your life, and far more profound than a so-called performance art piece.

It's like the difference between method acting and classical acting: you draw upon your own experiences and your own frustrations and angers to make something that is really ferocious. But that doesn't mean that at the same time it can't be intelligent. With the Birthday Party, we wanted to prove that you could be an intelligent and yet incredibly aggressive band. That was the connection that Nick and I had.

DT: Is that why you weren't necessarily punk?

RSH: Yeah. As much as there are some records that I might describe as punk rock that I think are great, they're much more sort of one [of those things] than [the other]. The Stooges are a very intuitive thing, and I certainly don't get the feeling that there was any intent to show their literacy. I don't feel that was on their agenda.

DT: It's rare for even the best bands to have too many substantial sides to them. Compared to the Stooges, the Velvet Underground were more literary, but . . .

RSH: They weren't physical.

DT: Stylistically, too, you tend to get bands that are either traditionalists or want to rip it up and start again. Patti Smith might be one of the few people I can think of who embraced rock at the same time as she tried to make it new.

RSH: Yeah. I think you're right about Patti Smith in that regard. And, you know, having worked with Lydia [Lunch] over the years, nobody would ever know that in her heart she's this enthusiastic, cheerleaderish American girl. And I love her for being that. I wish that she would express more of that side of her personality in her music, because I see nothing cool about relentless negativity, you know. I was pleased to hear that she'd revived Teenage Jesus, because she tends to have this attitude to her records like, "Well, I don't even care if this is going to be available in six months." Well, *I* fucking care. You know, I think a large part of it is a defense mechanism, but it harks back to what you said about Patti Smith. Lydia does have that remarkable ability to celebrate all that is American while at the same time criticizing it.

DT: It's interesting you shifted that from rock 'n' roll to America, but I can see why you would.

RSH: It's impossible to overestimate America's importance culturally on the rest of the world, because it's just so iconic. It seeps its way into everything, almost as the default setting for life. I do it all the time; I find myself not reading books because they're Australian, you know. I'm far more likely to read something if it's from America, which is appalling, the worst kind of snobbery.

DT: I can see where some American writers like Cormac McCarthy have an aesthetic that's relatable to yours.

RSH: Well, most of the art that I am exposed to is literature. I wrote a novel about, I don't know, ten years ago, and I'm halfway through one now. Mind you, I haven't written anything for about a year. But, yeah, I read a huge amount.

DT: Who are you into these days?

RSH: I really liked the last two Nick Tosches, *In the Hand of Dante* and *King of the Jews*. They're remarkable books, quite unlike anything I ever read before. *In the Hand of Dante* has a crime-oriented plot, but then in the middle of it he'll go into a rant about his publishers and how they say his books sell "thirty thousand copies," not thirty thousand and two or thirty thousand and three hundred. [*laughs*] It's just this incredible mixture of a novel and diary, and it's got a lot about Dante as well, a lot about the Bible. It's extraordinary.

The other guy I discovered recently is Thomas Ligotti. He's American, and he only writes short stories. And they're genuinely the strangest things I've ever read. They're like horror stories but there's no morality, no good versus bad. There's just these really bizarre scenarios.

I'm a big fan of Jerome Charyn, who has an incredibly literate series of crime novels written in such a particular way. They don't rely on the normal conventions like tension and suspense. The characters are so fascinating that it's sort of about being with them. And the principal character, who's the chief of police in New York, he's called Isaac Sidel, and he has a tapeworm that steers him in the right direction for solving cases. [*laughs*]

DT: It's funny, because I can see a lot of what you're saying about those guys in your music. Like with Nick Tosches, do you think that's how you approach songwriting, there's a certain element of genre and then a subjective side where you come in?

R$H: Yeah. I think when you've been writing songs for as long as I have, you have to find something in it that continues to intrigue you. You know, most songwriters have very few themes that they work on, and it's about finding ways to keep those things alive. If you look at Leonard Cohen, lyrically he's got about three nails that he hits over the head repeatedly. And they're probably all three pieces of the one nail. I principally write the same song over and over, and I guess it's a song of the sadness of the world. But convention and conceit allow you to write it as a song to a single person, and that makes it much more moving.

DT: Do you have a sense of why you're so pulled toward sadness?

R$H: I guess I just see so much in the world that makes me feel sad, and I don't understand why other people don't, and why it should be such a crime to point it out. But, you know, that's just me.

DT: To me that's more than just a theme, it's a way of looking at things.

R$H: Yeah. I think that when you work on anything artistically you have to be expressing something that is real to you. If you want it to be rich and substantial, it's got to be something you know is strong, and I think this applies to my guitar playing as well. If there's a similarity between my songs and my playing it's because that's the voice my guitar has, just as a singer has a voice.

DT: That's one of the points of this book, that a guitar is a voice like any other. I don't know if people always get that.

R$H: No, I don't think they do at all. And I don't think they understand that ultimately it doesn't matter what guitar I play, it's still going to sound like me.

DT: If you think of Leonard Cohen, he's known for his lyrics but so much of his effect is in that low, bleating tone.

R$H: Yeah. He's somebody who I look at and think, "You can get it right. You can write lyrics that express all these shades of different things." And, like I said, "You can just keep hitting the nail over the head." He has this fantastic ability to write songs that are really scathing but don't come across as being mean-minded or critical. They just express basic human emotions like jealousy, you know. And that's very rare, to be able to retain your humanity and be as—it's not a phrase you usually use with Leonard Cohen—popular.

DT: He's popular in certain circles.

R$H: Well, I was surprised to hear how much money he'd had stolen from him.

DT: Now that he's touring again?

R$H: Yeah. I just saw him live the other week. I have to say, I wasn't hugely impressed.

DT: Why not?

R$H: Well, his whole performance was really slick, and the band was just unspeakable. He had this old guy playing a bouzouki, and he was great, but it was like he had "Mark Knopfler Jr." on guitar and some guy playing a five-string bass with his thumb. And I think the way he uses backing vocals on his records is beautiful, but [in this performance] he did this curious thing where there were three backing vocalists and each one of them got to sing a song [solo], which . . . you're not there to see the backing vocalists sing. And the other thing was that he introduced the band in this really lengthy manner where he gave each member a sort of spiel. And then there was an encore, and then he came back and he did the introduction of the band thing again. And I thought he must be losing his grip, but I was later told that he does it every night, that the stage show was exactly the same down to the last detail. It's sad. When you listen to an old concert that's just him and an acoustic guitar and he's quite drunk, he sounds so fantastic and raw.

I mean, the audience loved it, but it was like Leonard Cohen doing show business, which isn't how I want to remember him. But, you know, I would've much preferred to have seen that than to see the Velvet Underground reunion, which every time I hear a song from it makes me never want to listen to Lou Reed again.

DT: You have a love/hate thing with Lou Reed, don't you?

RSH: It's just that he was so great and to become so incredibly . . . oh, I don't know. I find him really grating these days. But it's only because I admire what he's done.

DT: He's in a tricky place, being that big.

RSH: Yeah, but you don't have to go out and act like you're God's gift to the world, that's what you don't have to do. I mean, he just seems to feel like we should all be thrilled to get the small portion of his life that we're given entry to.

DT: Did you ever see [Lou Reed's appearance in the film] *Blue in the Face*?

RSH: Yeah.

DT: He's talking about Delmore Schwartz in the cigar store . . .

RSH: Yeah, in his fucking denim waistcoat. [*laughs*] Anyway . . .

DT: Yeah, anyway . . . But as you're saying, both Lou Reed and Leonard Cohen are so good at just having what they do and doing it. Lou Reed even had those musical obsessions like the D chord that were so pure.

RSH: Yeah.

DT: Do you think your guitar playing has evolved a lot, or are there certain things you keep returning to there, too?

RSH: I guess, because what I do now no longer revolves so much around aggression, that I'm not as concerned about that anymore. I think in a way I've learnt to just relax. Like, I never really do any of that harmonic work we were talking about anymore, because from the first Bad Seeds album Blixa had picked it up. So I just felt like I shouldn't be doing that. And I guess I'm relaxed enough and confident enough now to do whatever I think is best for the song. And that's ultimately what I want the guitar to do, is just serve the song rather than anything else. There is a song on the new record where I do some of that harmonic stuff, and maybe it was just the first song where I really needed it.

DT: Did you feel like you had to get away from your sound with the Birthday Party after they broke up?

RSH: Sort of. I didn't want to be in a band that was a sub-version of the Birthday Party, even though I was aware that what I did was a large part of the way we sounded. You know, the time from when the Birthday Party broke up to the time when I moved back to Australia was very hit-and-miss for me. I did a lot of things but they were all sort of all over the place.

DT: What did you want to do?

RSH: I don't think I really knew. I guess I would've liked to have had more faith in myself and to have been able to make *Teenage Snuff Film* ten years earlier. But things happen when you're ready for them, I guess. You can't make your life hurry up.

DT: At least with These Immortal Souls you were getting closer to that.

RSH: Oh yeah. I think These Immortal Souls did some really great stuff.

DT: By the time you made *Teenage Snuff Film* you were around forty. Did you find that by that time your idea of what you'd do as a solo artist had changed?

RSH: I think everything that you take in affects what you do. On my new record, the songs are all personal, as they always have been and probably always will be, but some of them are written from a more global viewpoint, which I certainly never had before. I think it's just the impact of the world, like this sort of preapocalyptic atmosphere that is being developed now, the idea that we should live in some kind of fear. I think stuff like that's changed, because I didn't start out to write like that, I just recognized it after I'd written these songs. And I think that all those things affect you without you necessarily being aware of them. You know, often the record you make is not always the record that you want to make, because you have the limitations of budget and stuff like that. And because I've been very ill while I was making this record, I was only in the studio for about four hours a day. So unfortunately that meant a huge part of the budget got eaten up by time when I couldn't be there. But, yeah, that's got nothing to do with what you're talking about. [*laughs*]

DT: No, it does, though. It must factor into the music a great deal.

RSH: Oh, it factors in. I mean, I've got two songs left to write, two sets of music, and I've just found myself procrastinating and procrastinating, because I guess some part of me thinks that it might be the last record I ever make, and that I don't particularly want to finish it or something like that. You know, if you understand.

DT: I understand. I hope that's not true, though.

RSH: Well, you know. These are just things that run through your mind when you spend too much time alone and you're not well. But they are all things that sort of . . . Basically, what I'm saying is that there are so many things that influence the way that you do things and what the end product is.

I feel like I did that [Birthday Party sound] and now the way that I write songs these days is not in any way as confronting, just because, you know, you use the tools that you have at the time. I'm not Nick Cave; I can't go out there and pretend to be him and I can't present things in the way that he does so incredibly well. But, you know, with every group the personality it assumes is the equation of the people's personalities. A sort of group personality arises. And what I do now, because I'm sort of solo, is a lot more like I am, I guess. It's a lot more fragile with sporadic moments of violence and it sort of has a self-deprecating sense of humor. It's just a representation of what I am.

DT: Humor is the other thing I wanted to ask you about, because it seems essential to your music, especially to how you can pull off the subject matter you've been talking about. It's also been one of your obstacles, getting people to see that side and not dismiss the music as "depressing."

RSH: Yeah, I suspect that I need to offer something free with every copy of my records so that people can find out what the punch lines are. But I think for a lot of people, anything that calls up any kind of real emotion is too much for them, and it's not what they want from music; they want something that they can listen to while they're doing the housework or whatever, that they can tap their feet to. They don't want something that's going to revive some feeling that they would rather have never felt in the first place, or to have to think about "Where is this coming from?" and "What's it saying?"

I'm happy that my music is at times sad, but I don't find sadness to be essentially depressing. I think there's a huge gap between the two things. You know, sadness is just part of life; it's something that I think is a necessary thing for people to feel. I think you need to feel all these things to be a good person.

But, you know, I do the best that I can. I can't sort of write down to people or whatever. I write the songs essentially for myself, so they have to be entertaining to me before they're entertaining to anybody else. And I probably have more interest in what I'm doing now than I've had for a long, long time. I get a lot more young people at my gigs than I have for years; I get people coming to see me who probably weren't even born when the Birthday Party broke up. I get all this mail and e-mail from people. Things are quite strangely good.

THE $HI(F)T

FRED FRITH

PHOTO BY HEIKE LISS; COURTESY OF INTAKT RECORDS

"Losing control is a discipline like any other." —Fred Frith

When British guitarist and improviser Fred Frith arrived in America in 1978, he already had half a life's worth of experimentation behind him. He'd survived a decade with prog collective Henry Cow and their defectors, Art Bears. He'd released *Guitar Solos* in 1974, a record of free-form sketches done with extended techniques—using alligator clips and brushes, and finger-tapping on a neck split into separate "keyboards"—that reconsidered the very practice it was named for. He'd exercised his formidable intellect writing columns for *New Musical Express* and helped organize the Rock In Opposition alliance of European agitators. Once in New York City, Frith eased into projects like Material's

193

Memory Serves (1981), in which he alternated guitar duties with Sonny Shar-
rock, and John Zorn's *Naked City* (1990), which found him on bludgeoning
bass. He continued this rootless cosmopolitanism over the next few decades
by playing with bands Skeleton Crew and Keep the Dog, recording with fellow guitar doubter Henry Kaiser, composing for the Rova Saxophone Quar-
tet, and improvising with Bob Ostertag and Phil Minton. When asked how
he manages this pace, Frith—who currently teaches in the esteemed music
department at Mills College in Oakland—shrugs it off. "I get up early in the
morning and I don't like to waste time," he said to *Bagatellen* in 2003. "It all
just kind of happens."

Born in Sussex, England, in 1949, Frith was isolated geographically during his childhood but stimulated at home (one brother, Simon, is a music
writer and sociologist, and the other, Chris, a psychologist at University College London). Though earthy in appearance, his music is lucid and deft, filled
with cleverness and always leaning toward a gypsy-folk sensibility he picked
up among inspirations including John Mayer's Indo-Jazz Fusions, Berio's
Visage, and Ornette Coleman's *Chappaqua Suite*. But rather than try to take
in all four hundred (reputedly) of Frith's recordings at once, it's better to let
Henry Cow's serious playfulness guide you to the Art Bears' Ono Band cabaret, to let Frith's "guitars on the table" techniques take you into stately strings
or atonal jigs. "You could say that everything the musicians have learned and
known over the years, all of their technical resources, are in a dialogue with
the things they are discovering every time, as if it was the first time," he told
the *Long Beach Union Newspaper* regarding his gregarious improvisation.
"So there's a tension between this kind of knowledge and this kind of discovery that's going on in the performance." The same tension heightens the
listener's process of uncovering Frith's work—one piece leads to another, but
each gives you something new, which expands what you bring to the next,
with a kind of guided unpredictability that is among his signatures.

One of Frith's ensembles that might suit rock-leaning souls is the power
trio Massacre. On their 1981 album *Killing Time*, the title track buzzes like a
Jesus Lizard outtake of a decade later, with Frith's solo springing against Bill
Laswell's rollerball bass. That polite number drifts into the metal-howling
"Corridor," which bottoms out in the desolate "Lost Causes" before beget-
ting the tribal introspection of "Not the Person We Knew" and fading into

the death ambient "Know." Against these shifts, the agile guitarist is both battering and graceful, throwing feedback, Frithertronics, and scratchiti all over the canvas. "The cubism reference is about seeing the same object through many different perspectives at once," says Frith, whose ability to catch words within words even as he types them into an e-mail response provides the title to this chapter. "There are no rules, and no givens." With Massacre or his current ensemble Cosa Brava, he approaches the guitar from the points of view of a noise sculptor and free improviser and rock-trained soloist and astute observer all at once.

DAVID TODD: Were you always interested in guitarists who were looking for ways around the usual rock styles?

FRED FRITH: At the beginning, "rock" style for me pretty much meant "blues" style. Starting, in my case, with Alexis Korner; then the John Mayall school that produced Clapton, Peter Green, Mick Taylor; and then going to see Muddy Waters and B. B. King, which was revelatory. A bit farther away from my own purist tastes of the time were the Yardbirds and Jeff Beck, and players like Roy Buchanan or Link Wray who seemed to have something else going on. Anyway, after I saw Hendrix it became clear that he was the yardstick against which everything else was going to be measured. That was the context for rock guitar in my world.

DT: How did you relate to all that?

FF: I can't say I aspired to any of it, really. I didn't feel I belonged there. I didn't try to copy the electric players the way I had spent hours learning Bert Jansch or Davy Graham songs from LPs. I guess I was more of an acoustic player, and I played mostly in folk clubs.

As an electric player I began with the Shadows and then the Beatles. I related more to the pop end of things, much as I loved blues. I liked George Harrison and Pete Townshend, the way they used the instrument. And I was a big fan of Syd Barrett, and through him Dave Gilmour, who I think has always been underrated. I must have seen Pink Floyd a dozen times between 1968 and 1970.

I think Gilmour and Daevid Allen and Pete Townshend were probably the three biggest influences on my electric guitar playing if I'm being honest about it, and they were all "looking for ways around it," whatever the "it" was. But as I said, it took me a long time to get going on the electric guitar. I didn't really have a clue about amps and how to get a sound, and all that. Slowly I became more comfortable, mostly from seeing Dave Gilmour up close and understanding how little you need to do to be effective. He was a good teacher. It was all about sound with him, simple gestures combined with pure passion. I remember him sitting cross-legged in front of me during a Henry Cow gig in 1969, how nervous I was. I hope I gave him something back!

DT: What was it about acoustic players like Bert Jansch or John Renbourn you liked?

FF: The Renbourn-Jansch axis goes back a few years earlier. I learned Renbourn's first LP note for note; Jansch was harder for me to grasp off records but I managed a couple of things. I've never actually seen either of them play ever, to this day—nor Davy Graham, oddly enough. I was a teenager, and living far away from the center of things. But I knew their records backwards.

To give you an idea of how isolated I was, I learned stuff that was in open tuning without knowing that such a thing was possible, so I can play [Mississippi John] Hurt's stuff in regular tuning only, which is pretty funny. I was also drawn to [Snooks] Eaglin, I think, because he learned everything from the radio, didn't get out much. I related. But I did understand very early on that the electric and acoustic guitars are completely different instruments and require completely different approaches and techniques.

DT: But you could combine those approaches in Henry Cow, couldn't you?

FF: When Henry Cow started, I reckon, my guitar playing combined those two sets of influences. One set coming from folk and folk blues—including the Incredible String Band, who I loved. And the other set British pop, namely the Beatles, the Who, and American groups like the Mothers of Invention, the Band, Captain Beefheart. Actually, I guess you can throw the influence of new jazz, especially John Coltrane, into that mix, but I didn't really have the skill to do anything other than bathe in its intensity, or in the case of Charles Mingus, to wonder at its constant flirting with chaos. But I was definitely listening to them a lot.

DT: Do people like Keith Rowe of AMM and Derek Bailey fit into this?

FF: I'd heard AMM when their first LP was released, but I had only a hazy idea of the players on that record as instrumentalists—I don't think I had improvisation sorted out as a "thing" yet. Having said that, I absolutely loved that AMM record and I think it had a big influence on my improvising.

Derek Bailey was another story. Lol Coxhill told me to check him out, and I did, in 1971, as the only audience member at a solo performance of his in London. Inevitably, we became friends. Derek was fantastic; he was a rather unique combination of ruthlessly single-minded on the one hand and generous and open on the other. When I first met him I'd just moved to London from Yorkshire, where I grew up and where he also came from, and it meant a lot to me to have someone with whom I could drink tea and eat pork pies and discuss cricket. It felt like home. But it's worth pointing out that my engagement with the "improvisation scene" at that time was non-existent—his concert was the only one I ever attended at the Little Theatre Club, and I didn't really know who the other players in that scene were until much later. So I didn't rush to embrace that music, rather the contrary. I was busy being in a rock band.

Actually, if you want to know who inspired me at the time of *Guitar Solos*, it was Barre Phillips. I'd heard his first solo LP called *Unaccompanied Barre* and it blew me away. I wanted to do for the electric guitar what I thought Barre had done for the bass—in other words, turn it into a completely different instrument.

DT: With Henry Cow, there seems to have been a subversive element from the start, musically as well as politically. Where was that coming from?

FF: We developed a lot over our time together; I don't think there was anything particularly subversive about us at the beginning. When we began we were trying to learn how to play our instruments and imitate some of our role models, like Zappa or the Soft Machine. Then again, I suppose those were pretty subversive role models! It was also a time when everything was being approached with a kind of wide-eyed, open-minded curiosity. We just wanted to try stuff out, and we did. And we kept on doing so.

Our subversiveness grew as we became thoroughly alienated from the music business, and it manifested itself in our version of the leftist rhetoric of the day. But the music wasn't like that at all, which is interesting. We hung onto our core experimentalism and saw that as the true revolutionary path.

When contemporary writers now characterize us as "dour Marxists," as they tend to do, it's clear that they've been reading our bombastic PR, and perhaps listening to our lyrics, but definitely not actually listening to the music, especially not the instrumental music. If you're talking about musical form, it's clear that we were all over the map, trying out every conceivable approach, constantly challenging ourselves and questioning what we'd already done. I still find that an admirable model for how to proceed.

DT: That sounds like the kind of insight that might come up in your classes at Mills College. I know you've taught a course on rock music there.

FF: Rock is a more or less meaningless term when you're using it to describe "music." None of my students can tell me what it is, and most of them would characterize it as something from the past, anyway. What I try to get at in my rock course is first of all an analysis of where we're at now with the whole "high" and "low" culture divide, which I think has long ceased to have any relevance to most people. And to talk about the divide at an institutional level, because that's where it still means something—who's giving money to whom, and why? And then rather than do what most rock courses do—which is to point out interesting musical qualities in popular music that your students are likely to know, in order to get them interested in, you know, "real" music, serious music—instead of that, actually look at how vernacular music has impacted serious composers at the high culture level, and whether the ways they have been influenced have been at all interesting when compared to the models they're drawing upon. Obviously you can go back and look at the impact of folk music on Bartók, or jazz on composers like Milhaud and Poulenc, but I mean more the moment when La Monte Young's *Inside the Dream Syndicate* spawns the Velvet Underground, the moment when Steve Reich says that "composers who ignore rock music have their heads in the sand"—these are very interesting moments. When Zappa situates himself as a disciple of Varèse and yet plays in the context of rock, a new chapter is definitely beginning. And the fact that in the pop and rock world exists a far more provocative understanding of the possibilities offered by the invention of recording, and that this is still ignored by a classical world that sees recording largely as a dishonest way of creating the illusion of a "perfect" realization of "the score," which is the classical world's primary unit of value. Anyway, you get the idea.

DT: That's the course?

FF: That's just the beginning of the course.

DT: I assume you can plug a lot of your ideas into that high/low divide, like this concept of "dirt" you favor, or never liking to think of something as finished.

FF: Another one is attitude to sound. I tend to be drawn to sounds that are quite difficult to control and that typify a struggle that goes on between me and the instrument. I use beautiful and well-controlled sounds as well, but there are these other things that happen where you just scratch your head and think, "Hell, now what?" I don't think this has anything to do with "rock" or "classical," which are pretty much useless as categories anyway. It's more about attitude, whatever world you think you inhabit. Accepting what's happening, being in the moment, treating a musical performance as a unique and ever-mutating conversation between yourself and your instrument, as well as with the other players and their instruments, and yourselves and the listeners. That's when it's interesting for me.

At Mills we're geared toward what it is that students are trying to do and then working to help them figure out what tools they might need. What I can provide is a lot of questions—"Why are you doing this? Why are you doing it in this way? Why are you using experimental notation when you could get the same results more easily with conventional notation?" And so on. In all cases they are questions that I have asked myself.

DT: It seems like the best lessons often aren't technique-oriented, in that way. You've spoken about a childhood violin teacher who encouraged you to simply breathe.

FF: Breathing is technique, the most important one of all. I was profoundly lucky to have as my first teacher someone who not only knew this, but was also prepared to invest a lot of frustrating time trying to communicate it to a five-year old. But think about it—starting to learn an instrument for the first time with a deep appreciation for how it involves your whole body, your whole being, that's an amazing gift for a kid.

It was never about "technique" for me—I guess that's why I never became or wanted to become a "virtuoso"—but about the pleasure of making sound, and constantly learning and relearning how to refine the sounds that you make, to be in control of them, to be able to deploy them however you want to. I encourage my students to take dance classes for the same reason, because the body is the center of both dance and music.

DT: You mentioned an "ever-mutating conversation between yourself and your instrument." Was that the idea behind *Guitar Solos*?

FF: Recording *Guitar Solos* was a process, sure, but it was mostly a challenge I offered myself. Virgin wanted a solo album, and I thought they were assuming I would do what rock guitarists tended to do when they got to make solo albums, some kind of guitar-heavy rock 'n' roll stuff. Which didn't interest me, really. On the other hand, I thought it would be an opportunity to redefine for myself what the instrument might be, to find a path to set out on. I gave myself a two-week deadline, and during those two weeks I sat around at home thinking and looking at "the electric guitar." And then I went into the studio for a couple of days, which was all I had the budget for, and I recorded as much material as I could.

What was really the focus was the separation of the electric instrument into a number of discrete sound sources, but with it still played in the "regular" position, except for on one piece. I had a stereo guitar, but I also had (and still have) a pickup mounted over the nut, which enables the player to amplify the notes generated to the left of the left hand. It provides not only a different channel, as it were, but whole different scales and tone colors. With a capo I could treat the two halves of the neck as separate sound sources, making them appear and disappear with the volume pedals.

I think there were about eight or nine tracks being recorded in real time. It allowed the guitar to become a kind of orchestra, and that was what I was really interested in. My preparation for the sessions was all about learning how to control the separate sources and make them blend into each other. It was also inevitably about what's now called tapping, since I had to be independent with each hand. Looking back, I think it was really a set of suggestions, avenues of exploration for future reference. I've been working with them ever since.

DT: Have you modified that design much?

FF: I didn't add to the design. I actually stopped using the standard stereo altogether.

DT: What exactly is the standard stereo guitar?

FF: Stereo guitar is simply having each of two standard pickups going to separate channels of a stereo system, or two amplifiers. I believe the idea was introduced by Gibson in their [ES-]345 model in the 1950s. I bought my 345 in 1969 and used it as designed for a while, up to and including *Guitar Solos*. Afterwards I had it modified to put the pickups back in mono again, since the stereo idea wasn't of any particular use to me. It made sense to me to make the additional pickup, what I've already described, one half of a stereo picture and the two regular pick-ups the other half. That's the system I've been using since 1975.

[In my system,] each "half" is routed through a different set of pedals. What [that] offers is all kinds of things: a different set of notes. A different range of timbres. And with delays, the ability to cross-fade from one half of the instrument to the other, which makes for greater continuity. But, of course, you have to relearn and reinvent the basic playing techniques of the electric guitar from scratch, which is a lot of work. I assume that's why nobody else has ever really developed it.

DT: I was wondering about the relationship between composing and improvising for you. Do you find that you use a lot of the same techniques as you go from one to the other?

FF: Technique is simply what you need to be able to do to realize your ideas. If that means being able to control the velocity with which a grain of rice hits the A string, then so be it. When you improvise, things tend to happen that you may or may not be able to control. If you want to be able to repeat them or use them again in another way, you have to learn what happened, and how you can make it happen again. Thus, an accident is always a potential technique.

The relationship between "technique" and "lack of technique" lies at the center of every improvisation, in my opinion. But this is not necessarily the same as experimentation, and whether or not an idea is "new" is entirely secondary to whether or not it is useful, and alive.

DT: So you don't necessarily separate these things, or have different modes you go into depending on the form you're working in?

FF: I don't see the creative process in a particularly finite way. Anything I could say about it today could easily be contradicted tomorrow. That's why I like it so much. The trick for me is never to get stuck in one way of thinking about or doing things.

I think it's often true that if you end the process with what you thought you would have when you started, you've probably failed, but even that's not a hard-and-fast rule. Obviously, setting goals is also important. You just have to be in the moment, whatever you're trying to do, and understand that what worked before may not work again, or not in the same way. It's a fluidity, a flexibility, which is always exciting and mysterious to experience.

DT: Well, one reason I asked is because I thought it might be a way of addressing your career as a whole, which is not easy to do given all the projects you've taken on. And not to belabor the discussion, but it did get me thinking about differences in the types of texts or scores that are produced by improvising as opposed to composing. What's entailed in that shift as you see it? Does that involve any change in sensibility?

FF: It's all composing; the only difference is the time frame. And a lot of the shi(f)t between them has to do with politics and money, because improvisation is not privileged with copyright. When Coltrane played *My Favorite Things* the money went (and rightly) to Rodgers and Hammerstein, but what happened to what Coltrane "composed?" Because of this problem we have the weird phenomenon of electronic music composers creating "scores" of their pieces after they have been realized, in order to be able to get paid when they're broadcast. But the score isn't actually the music. It's a peculiar contradiction!

I write music down, and I also make it up spontaneously. Each of these activities has inevitably influenced the other. Sometimes they overlap in the same pieces. And sometimes they are completely separate from each other. I've always done both, and I don't have any sense that one is more important, politically correct, or insert-cliché-here than the other. I like what I can do in each medium. That's really all there is to it. I don't see how I could avoid the same sensibility coming through in both of them even if I wanted to.

I am the sum of my experiences. Every time I compose or improvise, everything I know is available to me if I need it, and in both cases what I don't know has a habit of imposing itself and making its own demands. Obviously, the key difference is that when I'm improvising I'm doing it myself, and when composed pieces are being performed that isn't usually the case, so then we're dealing with other people's experience and knowledge, which are different from mine. But I enjoy the fact that this inevitably changes the picture, otherwise I wouldn't do it. On the other hand it's nice to be in a band, because I can be part of the process of realizing my compositional ideas. That's why I got so much out of Henry Cow and Skeleton Crew, and why Cosa Brava is so important to me.

DT: Before we end, there's a scene in *Step Across the Border*, Nicolas Humbert and Werner Penzel's 1990 documentary on you, that I wanted to ask about. In this segment you come home and begin unloading some food into bowls.

It looks like you're preparing for guests, but then you start pouring these items over your guitar strings. My question is, once you start deconstructing things in this way, does that tend to be a self-reinforcing mentality? Does it start a process that's hard to stop?

FF: That whole scene was a reconstruction that was done at the request of the filmmakers. They heard about my solo concert at the Kitchen ten years earlier. For that concert, I thought, "Well if I'm going to play at the Kitchen, it makes sense to take some ingredients with me." So I played with rice and pasta and salt and pepper and all that. It was kind of a gag.

But, yeah, deconstructing the purpose of things is a part of the way I've gone about making music. It's also why I stopped playing the guitar for a while, not long after the Kitchen concert, because the guitar seemed to me to have become irrelevant to what I was trying to do. I built my own crude string instruments instead, instruments I felt more comfortable "abusing," if that's the right word. I believe in allowing the process to suggest its own possible conclusions. It's a logical mind-set for an improviser. As for whether it changes the way you look at things, well, sure, of course. I think it encourages you to be open to possibilities, to find potential in unexpected circumstances, to invent, to let go of habits and preconceptions. At least, I hope so.

THE SHAKESPEARE SQUADRON

GLENN BRANCA

PHOTO BY JAMES WELLING; COURTESY OF ATAVISTIC WORLDWIDE

O n June 13, 2001, no less than a hundred guitarists assembled in the shadows of the still-existing World Trade Center, fronted by a visionary who didn't conduct so much as compel by sheer force of his pompadour. The guitars weren't tuned to E-A-D-G-B-E or D-A-D-G-A-D—no, they were in menace settings like A-A-A-A-A-A and F-F-F-F-F-F, whole sections of them creating a magnificent swarm of overtones. The piece was Symphony no. 13 (*Hallucination City: Symphony for 100 Guitars*), devised and led by Glenn Branca, a New York–based guitarist-cum-composer, and even though it would eventually be rewritten entirely, the gist of it was in place, that being the operatic clash of Branca's "small" six-to-ten-guitar compositions magnified to epic scale.

The revised Symphony no. 13 begins with a March, in which waves of guitars stomp on a lone drummer (props to whoever dares). Soon more guitars layer chorused hums over organ-like sci-fi swirls. That is to say, within a few minutes enough warring elements have been established that the piece is already in a state of crisis, the guitar factions—alto, tenor, baritone, like sections of any orchestra—veering into suspended conflict. Dismissed early on by John Cage as a "fascist," Branca is in reality less Mussolini than de Sade, a trained dramatist with a feel for S&M ("I liked to mess around with the idea of feeding plot elements to the audience and then not paying off on them," he says of his early days writing plays in Boston. "It was all very mean-spirited.") But unlike most tormentors, Branca (born in Harrisburg, Pennsylvania, in 1948) doesn't withhold so much as overprovide, in pieces that soar into catharsis and stay there.

Starting circa 1977 with his first bands Theoretical Girls and the Static, Branca pursued inventions such as his three-octave tunings and mallet guitars, infused with the energy of a Soho art scene that was about to see its stock split. His starkness is reflected in the Robert Longo cover for *The Ascension* (1981), one of Branca's first multiple-guitar recordings, which served as a bridge to what he described in the *New York Times* in 2007 as his "full-blown orchestration." For Branca, this shift was natural, because he was never a traditional guitarist to begin with, but one who saw the abstract potential of the instrument first as a scoring element in his plays, then as the foundation of his extended pieces for small ensembles, then as the deep structure of orchestral works like *The World Upside Down* (1990). "It's easy," Branca says when asked how he composed no. 13 for so many performers. "It's written in exactly the same way I would write for an orchestra. And I think that's why it's unique. Usually when somebody writes for guitars, you assume you're going to have something rock. There is no rock in this piece. It's a symphony."

Although his onetime rival Rhys Chatham explored similar tunings, and former protégés Lee Ranaldo and Thurston Moore went their own way with such techniques as Sonic Youth, there is something unique to Branca among these strategists ("What I most respect about Glenn Branca is that he's an absolute original," no less an authority than Steve Reich told the *New York Times* in 1995.) Known for being difficult, one wonders whether he could've made it without thick skin, dismissed with bad reviews and existing on the fringes of multiple audiences, not fully inside the haughty world of symphony commissions and yet not one with the snotty rockers. As an interviewee, Branca is prone to bold pronouncements, but damned if he doesn't go out there and invent the techniques and work them into compositions, find the day players, spill his minimalist-by-way-of-no-wave blood, and back them up.

DAVID TODD: You came to New York City from Boston, ostensibly to do theater. How active were you in that when you arrived?

GLENN BRANCA: I went to at least two or three plays a week. I saw everything that was going on in New York in 1976. And there was great stuff going on. Of course, Richard Foreman, the Wooster Group . . . but what happened was, I met another guy who was into theater. We kept running into each other all the time; we finally had to become friends because we didn't have any choice in the matter. And so Jeff—Jeff Lohan—he had a ground-floor loft in Soho, two thousand square feet. So we decided to turn it into a theater. In those days you could do that. So we started painting the place black. And we both had plays that we were going to produce there. But one day I couldn't help the idea of starting a rock band, which was something that had been in the back of my mind for a long time. I had always imagined doing an avant-garde rock band. And part of the reason I wanted to come to New York was because I was so into the punk scene, especially Patti Smith.

So this friend of mine, Jeff, had studied music, and he had started composing. We were both basically becoming experimental composers. But I wanted to start this band, and I didn't imagine that Jeff would be interested, but when I mentioned it he immediately said, "Let's do it." And he had a friend who was a very well-known performance artist named Dan Brown, who loved punk music. Dan said, "I'm doing a performance-art piece at Franklin Furnace in about three weeks. If you get your band together you can play after my show." So in three weeks we wrote all the songs, we threw the band together. It was me on guitar, Jeff on keyboards, and a drummer that we borrowed. It was a gigantic success. I mean, within a matter of two months, we were one of the hottest bands in New York.

DT: And that was Theoretical Girls?

GB: Theoretical Girls. So what happened was, we had this kind of skewed punk band. But both of us still wanted to do theater. The whole thing was like, "OK we'll do this band for a while, and we'll get back to painting this loft black and doing our theater." The problem was, the audiences got bigger and bigger and what we realized was, "OK, we're on a stage, we're in front of an audience, this is our theater." And so we went from being a skewed punk band to doing experimental music in the context of rock instrumentation. And we didn't care whether people fucking liked it or not.

The problem is, the more outrageous the shit we did, the bigger the audience got. So we found ourselves stuck. I mean, what could you do?

DT: Did you think the rock audience was better for you than the theater audience?

GB: Yeah, it was a combination of that and . . . I'll tell you what it was. First of all, you have to realize that we were very much an art-world band. I mean, when we played audition night at CBGB the place was completely packed out the door. They couldn't believe it—"Where did these people come from?" It's because we had been playing in lofts and galleries, and we had built up this tremendous audience. But it was the first generation of artists who had grown up listening to rock music. You know, the list goes on and on, Robert Longo, Julian Schnabel, Cindy Sherman, you name it, we were their favorite band, because we were thought of as the conceptual art band.

DT: Could you have done a rock band if it hadn't been in that atmosphere?

GB: I never would've done a straight rock band. Never. If I was going to do a rock band, it was going to have to be a serious fucking band. And that's what we turned Theoretical Girls into. I mean, part of our reputation was, every time you go to see Theoretical Girls there's going to be at least a couple of new songs. We wrote like crazy.

The band only lasted in a meaningful sense for six months. We just went nuts for six months. And then Jeff started getting ideas about doing a Philip Glass thing on his own, because he was a trained pianist. And then when he started pulling away, I started another band, the Static. So there was a point at which both were going at the same time. And then I started getting ideas about doing things that were too big for a band, like *Instrumental for Six Guitars*.

Again, things would happen coincidentally. Theoretical Girls was invited to play at Max's Kansas City Easter Festival in the spring of 1979. I was out of town touring with the Static. And Jeff got the call and said, "Well, listen, how about if I just do a solo gig? And I've got my friend here Rhys Chatham, how about if you let him do one too?" So when I got back to New York, I found out that these guys had basically taken this gig, so I called up and said, "Well I want to do a solo gig too." So in two weeks I wrote *Instrumental for Six Guitars*, and that was where it started. Because I used that as an opportunity to do a piece that I'd been thinking about for a long time for lots of guitars, using different tunings. And the piece—again, it was like Theoretical Girls—was just an immediate hit. But the fact that it was a hit was not what was important to me, it was the fact that it sounded so fucking incredible. I mean, I was an experimentalist, and it was one of those moments where your experiments jell perfectly. Sometimes these things happen. And it happened. And, I mean, no one had ever heard anything like that. It just sounded unbelievable. And so I just threw everything else out the window and said, "I'm doing these multiple guitar pieces. That's it."

DT: When you say you were experimenting, do you mean working off some kind of theory or literally experimenting?

GB: No, I was literally experimenting. I was hearing things that appealed tremendously to me, like I'd somehow stumbled on [Krzysztof] Penderecki. Because at the time I didn't read music, I'd never studied music, so it's not like I was looking at Penderecki's scores. But I had stumbled on it. And I knew how he was getting what he was getting because I heard it in my music.

DT: On the *Songs '77–'79* collection, early Static pieces like "Don't Let Me Stop You" have so much of your later style.

GB: Well, for one thing, that was the first band that used that octave tuning. That had a whole hell of a lot to do with it. Even before I wrote *Instrumental for Six Guitars* I was already using that. Everything the Static did was in this three-octave tuning.

DT: Where'd you get that?

GB: It was just one of myriad ideas that I had. I liked the sound of open guitar strings, so I wanted more of them. And I wanted to have a guitar that had a lot of strings playing the same note. The problem is, when I wrote, I didn't want to have to go through the trouble of changing the strings, because that would've been too much of a hassle for other musicians. So I figured out a tuning in which you could get three unison octaves without having to take the strings off and put on new ones.

DT: Do you mean different strings for baritone or tenor or whatever the specific guitar is tuned to?

GB: You've got the baritone and the tenor and the alto, and they're all different sets of unison strings. And actually, that's a two-octave tuning, not a three-octave tuning. Because then I get more unison strings. It's like a string section of an orchestra: you get that sort of slightly out-of-tune unison sound. Not to mention that I can get clusters very easily, and it's difficult to get a real three-note cluster in a guitar that's tuned E-A-D-G-B-E. You'd have to be, like, a Berklee-trained musician. Whereas this way you just go "*boom,*" and it sounds evil as hell. I love that fucking evil sound. I love the devil's tri-tone, you know. It just sounds cool.

DT: So you just came up with these things and tried them out?

GB: I tried all kinds of things. That one sounded amazing. And I will never forget the first time I was at a sound check and the soundman just stopped:

"Wait a minute, dude, how are you getting that sound?" And, I mean, it was about a year of that.

DT: What were the specifics of the original unison tuning?

GB: Well, the two low strings are tuned to the low E, and the two middle strings are tuned to an E an octave higher than that: you tune the A down to the low E, then you tune the D up to the E an octave higher than the low E, then you tune the G down to [that same] E. And then the [final] high E string is right, but you've got to take the [preceding] B string and [*squeak*] tune it up. But it works. It works and it doesn't break.

DT: It's all Es?

GB: Well, that was the original tuning. The tunings I use now are different, but they're still unison tunings.

DT: Before the interview we were talking about *Indeterminate Activity of Resultant Masses*, which was a piece for ten guitars you premiered in 1981. How had your tunings evolved by then?

GB: Well, in that case, every guitar is tuned to a different pitch of the twelve-tone scale, except all six strings [on each guitar] are the same note. So this was the ultimate unison tuning, except every guitar is tuned to a different note. So that was a little challenge unto itself.

DT: Were those alto/baritone/tenor tunings?

GB: In that case, no. In that case, they're broken down simply E, F, F♯, G, G♯, and each one of those guitars has six G♯ strings, six A strings . . . If you listen to the middle section, which I could call the bell section, it's very easy to recognize: everyone is just playing "*rang.*" They're all just playing open chords. Except since each guitar is tuned to a different pitch, the open chords are all blending in a different way.

The tenor and the alto was a different thing. I was using that for my so-called Ascension Band, you know, the band that Lee Ranaldo was in. Why did I do that? I don't fucking know. I wanted to try out what it would sound like to have a bass and a baritone and a tenor and an alto. I think at that time I called [the alto part] a soprano. Lee played the soprano; he was the ass-kicker, a truly great, gifted guitarist.

DT: On top of the tunings, you had the idea for these ensemble works first, then symphonies as you went along.

GB: When I wrote Symphony no. 1, I thought I was putting my head on a chopping block. You know, "I'm writing a piece for loud, punk-style guitars and I'm calling it a symphony. They're gonna crucify me."

DT: Were the tunings as important as the ideas for those compositions? The instruments too, for that matter?

GB: Yes. Yes, yes, yes. The instruments that I created, created the pieces that I wrote. I mean, I created the harmonic series of instruments, and that's a whole other story that we haven't gotten into. My harmonics guitar is on a whole other level.

DT: As you started with these new musical ideas, did you just leave theater behind, or did people like writer/director Richard Foreman stick with you?

GB: Richard Foreman is one of the most important people in my entire life. Period. End of story. Right to this very moment. I loved Richard Foreman before I had even seen Richard Foreman. And then when I saw him, I was like, "This is everything I've dreamed of—he's already fucking done it."

You know, I mentioned [before the interview] that I had written a play when I was in London [in the mid-1970s]. It did get produced. Lunchtime theater. [*laughs*] But I remember when I came back to Boston, a guy that I met read the play and said, "This is like Richard Foreman." And of course I had never even heard of Richard Foreman at the time. And then I started reading stuff in the [*Village*] *Voice* about him. That's how I discovered Patti

Smith. I read that she was doing a benefit for [avant-garde Marxist group] the Situationists and I figured anyone who's doing a benefit for the Situationists has got to be super-cool, man. [*laughs*]

But there are times when I'm still tempted to do theater. I still have this deep-seated love for theater.

DT: Do you think of what you do now as theater?

GB: Yes, I do. I do see what I do as theater. Maybe more than ever now. But I saw it as theater from the beginning. My Symphony no. 5, I can tell you, it was theater. I can show you some reviews.

DT: Do you think people like Richard Foreman had an effect on your music?

GB: The music is very much of itself. It organically grew from itself. When it comes to Richard, I responded to his work the same way that I responded, for instance, to Burroughs's. And I couldn't find a way to say how Burroughs had specifically influenced a piece, you know.

DT: You're a big Burroughs fan, right?

GB: Gigantic Burroughs fan.

DT: We were talking about this before, too, the idea of life without Burroughs. It seems like the whole culture would be different.

GB: No, I think you're making a good point. The one set of books that sits right in front of my desk where I can see it at all times is my Burroughs collection, and I'm always ready to reach out and read one at any time.

I mean, *Naked Lunch*, which is only one of many great books he's written, it's still ahead of its time. What blows my mind is, how the hell did he know all that shit in 1957 and 1958 when he was writing that book? A lot of people would like to think of him as a conspiracy theorist or something, except there's only one problem: he wasn't fucking wrong. And on top of that he was a poet. And when you put together his brilliant mind with his incredible poetry—I mean, he used repetition a lot, for instance; this is something that novelists didn't do. I mean, you know Burroughs.

DT: Do you know his concept of the Shakespeare Squadron?

GB: No.

DT: It's an expression he used for the hard-core writers like Beckett and Genet, "lifers" you might say, like, "You can't walk out on the Shakespeare Squadron, Bill."

GB: This isn't a term that he used in any of his novels, right?

DT: He used it in his essays and journals. But actually that was one of the main concepts behind this book, the Shakespeare Squadron of guitar.

GB: Well, yeah, I'm in the Shakespeare Squadron all right, if that's what he meant. I'm going down with him. [*laughs*]

DT: Even if there's no direct impact on your music, it seems people like Richard Foreman and Burroughs set a high standard for you.

GB: Well, I need those standards. I mean, musically my standard when I first came to New York was Philip Glass. Because he, for me, was the first person to go all the way out on a limb, do something incredibly extreme, and succeed. And you have no idea what that meant to the New Music scene at the time. I mean, you could *do this*, you know. And make it work. You needed that guy who got there first.

You know, forget John Cage—I don't want to criticize John Cage, but it was really Philip Glass who went out there. And you have to realize, I'm a gigantic Steve Reich fan. In fact, I think Steve Reich may be the best composer working in the world today. But Phil Glass just pushed and pushed and *opened the doors*, is the way they say it. This whole world, this whole [New Music collective] Bang on a Can thing . . . even Sonic Youth wouldn't fucking exist without Philip Glass.

DT: Do you think your work is like Philip Glass's, from the performer's angle, perhaps? There's a lot of rigor involved.

GB: Yes, there's a lot of rigor.

DT: Is that what John Cage was responding to in his famous "fascist" critique of you, putting the performers through these motions? Or was he worried more about the sustained climax?

GB: Both. He was talking about both of those things.

DT: Where did your concept of the climax come from? It seems like most experimental artists avoid that.

GB: Well, the thing was developing from itself. I would hear something and I would go with it. It was as simple as that. And if I heard something good I kept doing it and kept doing it until it stopped sounding good. It wasn't that I wanted to keep people at a climactic level; I was making something that I was getting off on, man, big time, and I know the audience was.

And it was of the time. You have to realize, there was a time that came [later] when I could do exactly the same thing and it had no effect whatsoever. Zero. On me or the audience. It's very bizarre, but there are things that are of their moment, that have their time and place. And there was this time and this place when people needed that, when I needed it. It was like this mental excitement that just didn't exist anywhere else, and it felt like something more than just entertainment.

DT: What was it specifically about that time?

GB: Well, it was the beginning of the Moral Majority, of the Reagan era, and you have to realize, we thought we had left all that. I was coming from the '60s—we thought that was all over, and all of a sudden what we got was fucking Hitler!

But you know, minimalism is all about losing a sense of climax; that's what John Cage was so wrong about. It's accepting, it's immersing yourself in it, and then entering a new world that has all of the same climaxes except at an entirely different level of perception. There's a piece by La Monte Young that is just a single extremely high-pitched tone—this is on a record!—and I would take that baby and crank it to the top of my fucking stereo and there was the most unbelievable amount of music inside of this single tone that you could possibly imagine. And it had nothing to do with anything Bach or Beethoven or Mahler or any other composer has ever thought about, including even Harry Partch. It was a new way of listening to and experiencing music.

DT: Do you feel like your work is minimalism?

GB: I mean, yeah, it's minimalism. I've tried to tell people, "I'm a minimalist." Period. End of story. I'm not a postminimalist, I'm not a postmodernist, I am a minimalist, and I feel as though my work should be seen in that context.

I'm not doing what Philip Glass is doing. I'm not doing what Steve Reich is doing, or La Monte Young, or Phill Niblock, or Charlemagne Palestine—there's a long list of good minimalists whose work is different from mine. But what I'm doing is definitely minimalist, the way I see it and the way I think about it.

DT: I get that, but how are you defining minimalism then?

GB: [*laughs*] Well, OK.

It's hard to . . .

See, this is not easy to explain. I mean, I felt that there was a potential with the idea of repetition, which is something that interested me tremendously when I was younger, and was a connection that I saw between rock music and minimalism when I finally discovered Steve Reich and Philip Glass. You know, in the early '70s, I had a feel for repetition. I could hear the effect that it had. Led Zeppelin used it to great effect, and many other rock bands. And then to find these other people using it in a new way, especially Steve Reich, and then manipulating it and drawing you to another place, it became like a spiritual experience. And I saw the potential, especially in those days.

And . . .

There's music within music. That's what the message of minimalism is. There's music that you haven't written down that goes on while the music that's been written down is playing. And it's both psychoacoustic and . . . well, it's both acoustic and psychic. It's something that happens not only inside your ear but inside your brain. Music is a subjective take. Now of course you could make an argument that *everything* is, but music is truly an abstract expression and is more subjective than anything else. And minimalism opens up the potential of that subjectivity. And that's what I was going for. I was interested in how far you could take manipulating—not in a fascist way [*laughs*]—I mean, manipulation is the wrong word; I mean how far you can construct a piece of music that creates an ambiguous landscape but also feels as though it's going somewhere. And, see, this is what minimalism could do; it was always going somewhere. It was taking you somewhere. But you could kind of decide where that was.

Now the fact is, I didn't feel as though minimalism stopped in 1967. Or 1968. Minimalism still had potential to keep moving. You don't just shift from minimalism to modern classical music. You don't just adapt this sound and this style to a conventional orchestra, you reinvent the orchestra and evolve.

In the early '80s, when I was writing my early symphonies, I was hearing shit that was unfuckingbelievable. And since then I've dreamed of somehow writing this stuff down. I know it can be done, and I know that someday somebody's gonna do it. But there is a music that sounds like it hasn't been written, that sounds like it's happening inside of your ear, that you're dreaming it. It sounds like five orchestras and six choruses all playing at the same time but perfectly and utterly integrated into one piece of music that has so many levels and so much depth. And I've heard this music, and it's difficult to not go for it, you know. It's difficult not to try to figure out how to put it in a bottle and put it on a piece of paper in such a way that it can be reproduced. And the whole world can hear this magical thing that has never been heard before by human ear. And this is what my music is about, and it's why I've so often failed. Because I reached too high for too much. And, you know, sometimes the temptation is to not reach so high. And the fact is, you never know how you're going to get there.

DT: I appreciate you defining that. It certainly accounts for so much of your approach.

GB: Well, I won't go on about it. But that's where I'm headed. And I've come closer to describing it, actually, in the last minute and a half than I've done in any interview that I can think of.

DT: Since you were coming after the prime years of minimalism, were you able to feel like part of the no wave scene, even if it wasn't exactly what you were doing?

GB: Absolutely, I loved the no wave bands. I thought they were fucking fabulous. I was a fan of DNA, the Contortions, Teenage Jesus & the Jerks. And the idea of being part of a scene—I mean, forget a scene, part of a *movement*—I thought this was the coolest thing I could ever imagine. You have to realize, I'm coming out of theater and it was like, "You mean to tell me I'm in a scene that's like absurdist theater? You've got to be kidding me." It was incredibly exciting, yeah.

DT: So you felt like an authentic part of that?

GB: Yes! One thousand percent authentic.

DT: So why did you decide to leave that no wave scene creatively? Was it the musical challenge of working with your guitar ensembles, or were you more compelled by the risk-taking side?

GB: Well, I have to admit, risk was the most fun part of the whole damn thing. It was nothing but risk all the way down the line. I had nothing to lose. Nothing! So my life happened on that stage, and that's the way I played it, one hundred percent. It was like I gave everything I could possibly give every time. And I remember, I'd be sitting around thinking, "OK, I have to write a piece now." And I'd get out my notebooks: "OK, I've got ideas for this piece, and I've got ideas for that piece—no, no, no, I'm doing them all right now. I'm not saving up anything, I'm going to put every idea I've ever had into this one piece, right now." And it fucking worked, man. And then when I would get on stage, same deal. If it wasn't sounding right, if it wasn't working, I made it work. That's where the conducting thing started—I mean Symphony no. 1, I was the guitar player in that piece. I wasn't conducting, I was giving cues with my guitar, the same way I used to do with the band, and about halfway through the first movement I'm giving my cues, I'm trying to get people going, and it's not happening. I took off my guitar, I put it down on the floor, and I started to conduct. I said, "I'm gonna make this get where it's supposed to go."

I mean, that was it. That's what kicked the piece off. And I never picked up the guitar again.

STARTING WITH THUNDERS

BOB MOULD

"I'm sure there are guys who can play circles around either one of us, but do they know what the instrument means?" So asked Bob Mould in a 1992 interview for which he was paired by *Musician* with another indie anomaly, Black Francis. "Technique sort of sucks." As the two traded opinions on Nirvana's success, a thread emerged among Mould's responses, namely a healthy resistance to guitar mythology: "I was listening to the new Pixies record. I thought that some of the guitar things were so unorthodox and I could never do that because, unfortunately, I learned to play the instrument. . . . It's hard to unlearn." As he pursued it, this unlearning became the key to Mould's many guises, driving him from one city, one lifestyle, one instrument, to another. As his first band, Hüsker Dü, fades (just a little bit) into history, Mould remains intriguing not only for his sustained songcraft—especially his signature balance of pop accessibility, singer-songwriter introspection, and punk power—but also for his willingness to challenge it. "I just do what I do," he told *Harp* flatly in 2005. "I play music, I change directions."

Born in 1960, Mould survived post-punk, hardcore, and Reagan death kitsch (*"I'm not easily amused,"* one might say) as well as a public outing at the hands of *Spin* (". . . *and I'm not easily amazed"*). Though hailing from upstate New York, his aesthetic is better located by the Twin Cities axes from which Hüsker Dü emerged, honing their metallic-grey sound on albums such as *Zen Arcade* (1984). Over *Zen's* four sides, Mould and drummer Grant Hart thrashed and harmonized their way to the vanishing point between pop psychedelia and nihilism, alternating haunting Harters such as "Never Talking to You Again" with howling Moulders such as "Something I Learned Today." Hüsker Dü were received within the framework of punk, but their fourteen-minute "Reoccurring Dreams" redefines the genre by reducing it to wordless feedback. Completed in one eighty-five-hour blur, *Zen* was an exercise in immediacy, defied only by the band's ability to maintain that pace with four more LPs over the next two years.

Mould followed Hüsker Dü with the solo *Workbook* and *Black Sheets of Rain*, taking his songwriting and guitar playing into new, moody directions circa 1989–90. Still, it seems he'd been taking notes on how to work within a band format, which he put into practice with a new group, the aptly named Sugar. If Hüsker were ahead of their time, Sugar were deeply of it, their 1992 debut *Copper Blue* a poppier companion to the *Nevermind* tracks it joined on the radio. "That's the one where I hit my stride as a songwriter," Mould told Fuzz.com in 2008. "The stars lined up." *Beaster*, a doppelganger EP released the following year, took the tunefulness of "Hoover Dam" and "If I Can't Change Your Mind" and tested it against the mystifyingly bleak lyrics of "JC Auto" ("I'm your Jesus Christ, I know / Bleeding to death again"), and proved the formula still worked.

By the 1998 solo album *The Last Dog and Pony Show*, Mould was tipping his hand with titles like "I Hate Alternative Rock." "Sometimes I get so sick of what I do," he moaned in *Mojo*. "Two weeks into this record I was like, I hate this. . . . Why don't I have the nerve to do something else?" Mould retreated into club culture, reemerging in 2002 with *Modulate*, the album that finally polarized the audience he'd been trying to provoke since the good old days of Hüsker's thirty-five-minute, one-note encores. In 2003, under the pseudonym LoudBomb (an anagram of "Bob Mould"), he released *Long Playing Grooves*, which further mystified the faithful, even those who'd seen the writing on the wall with *Last Dog*'s techno-rap "Megamanic." The "shock" of his homosexuality, what little there was upon *Spin*'s announcement, dissipated quickly, yet it seemed a bigger queering to watch Mould veer into electronica—and not arty, bleeps-for-snobs IDM but high-energy dance. Relocating from New York to Washington, DC (and later San Francisco), he began to collaborate with producer Richard Morel on the bearish Blowoff project, a series of raucous DJ parties that's still running—alongside Mould's songwriting, of course, last captured on 2009's *Life and Times*.

DAVID TODD: One of the points to this book is to reevaluate some lasting perceptions about rock guitar. It seems you have a few things ready to go.

BOB MOULD: Well, right off the bat, my motto with guitar players is, good rhythm guitar players are always more valuable than great lead players. I think historically the instrument has been glamorized by people like Hendrix and Page, and I think people have always looked at it as "Oh, lead guitar, it's this fluid expression of melody." I understood that notion growing up in the '70s and listening to heavy metal. My friends were into it, I was into it, like KISS or Foghat or that kind of stuff. But to me rhythm guitar is way more important, because it's the underpinning of what makes a song move. I didn't pick up the guitar thinking, "I'm going to be like Hendrix"; the thing that got me going was the Ramones, which is rhythm playing. When did the Ramones introduce leads, the third or fourth record? Maybe you heard a couple flubbed notes. So to me, the value of guitar is in the rhythm.

The other records that left an impression on me would be Johnny Thunders's. Not so much with the New York Dolls, although that's great stuff, but in the Heartbreakers, the way he and Walter Lure played off each other. They were both playing this seemingly simplistic rhythm with sophisticated, almost Chuck Berry leads. I thought Thunders was great, and he influenced so many people, like Steve Jones.

Again, those are the two people that really got my ear perked up. The two different approaches to the New York sound.

DT: Both those guys were very New York, but not in the cerebral sense one might think of.

BM: Yeah. And within that I think they're very different, because Thunders was loose, and you know Johnny Ramone was the biggest tight-ass in the history of guitar playing. [*laughs*] All the way around he was very strict, and Thunders was more cerebral. But, yeah, it wasn't like what you think of as cerebral playing.

DT: Did you think of yourself as borrowing from those guys?

BM: I was emulating, I think, out of necessity. You know, with Hüsker Dü starting up in '79 as a three-piece, I had to cover a lot of sound. So the way Johnny Ramone approached rhythm guitar was attractive to me because there wasn't a lot of intricacy; it was more of a propulsion.

I mean, I picked up guitar and then two-and-a-half years later Hüsker Dü started, so there wasn't a lot of time for me to get great. When I could step off-mike—with Grant's songs, where I could open up my guitar play-ing—then it got into more of an involved situation. But early on with Hüsker there was a lot of feedback involved; it was just this sheet of noise to keep something active.

DT: Being in trio and doing a lot of the singing, that would be a challenge to also being inventive guitarwise.

BM: It was, you know. [But] there's precedent for it. Chuck Berry did it; [Pete] Townshend had to do it with the Who. [Roger] McGuinn covered a lot of sound for one person.

DT: Were you interested in Roger McGuinn's playing?

BM: Yeah, I think later on as my playing evolved and the production got a little more sophisticated—I think especially starting with [1983's] *Metal Circus*—there was opportunity to add a little more to the sound, and that's when the more chorused sound that I was working with for a number of years came in. There was a piece of equipment that was kicking around, the Eventide H910, and that was what I was using to get that. It was one of the state-of-the-art harmonizers that people used on voices, to make things fatter. So I used that on guitar. And it was weird, because the time clock in that piece was inaccurate, so you couldn't get like a pitched voice. It tended to float, so when you listen to "Real World" or "Diane," those things where you hear that sound, it's because the clock is irregular. And I think concurrent to that was my revisiting a lot of the '60s folk/psychedelic stuff, especially Roger McGuinn's playing with the Byrds, you know, the twelve-string. I picked up a twelve-string guitar and started to incorporate that as well. He had a lot of that over-ring, a lot of harmonics, sort of making it more than it was.

DT: When you say "over-ring," is that basically overtones?

BM: Yeah.

DT: How did you get that effect yourself?

BM: You can get it from a twelve-string or using a harmonizer or just overdriving a sound [to] where everything just starts shaking and tones start generating. Again, to me it was always trying to make the sound bigger than it really was.

DT: Is that need to fill the space why you came up with your drone technique?

BM: Yeah. Just out of necessity. As Hüsker Dü went on it was like, "OK, make the sound bigger; make it more melodic." As things slowed down and my playing got better, I was able to articulate things inside of that drone pattern.

DT: Could you describe that, how it evolved?

BM: In '82, '83 was when I developed what people look at as my technique, which is droning in first position with what I call cowboy chords, first-position chords like the ones we learn from Mel Bay books. The technique is setting up a primary drone at the top three strings, then using the lower three or four strings to move the melody along. For a lot of things it's first-position G: usually the two highest strings are parked on the third fret, and then I'm creating all of the voicings with the lower three or four strings, using the thumb to wrap around and walk a bass line while I'm playing the stuff on the inside. So it's really sort of a high drone, a low bass part, and then the voicing in the middle. It's arguably three parts at once.

I was doing a lot of stuff in first-position B as well. If you go back and you listen to those records, a lot of songs are in those two keys, B and G. They're the keys I still work with a lot.

DT: B is an interesting guitar key.

BM: It's a great guitar key. It's one of the ones that nobody really knows how to use very well, but it's one that I used over and over.

DT: Can you think of an example of that?

BM: [*Zen Arcade*'s] "Chartered Trips," where the song is in first-position B. I walk the chord progression of the signature in the lower strings, and keep alternating on the open B and high E strings as well.

DT: How did you work that style out?

BM: It's by feel. There was no real methodology behind it other than "This sounds good."

DT: It's so economical.

BM: Yeah. I mean, out of a B position I could probably, without moving my hand whatsoever, do about twenty different chords. You know, why would you not use it, especially when singing? It's a position where I don't have to look down. I make a lot of moves; I can do a lot of stuff inside of that position.

And also, because I'm not moving around, it's a rhythm-based style. It's a rhythm-based style that overlaps melody on top.

DT: For you, is a rhythm-based style also a songwriter's style?

BM: Yes, it's a singer-songwriter style. I'm not a big rock guy doing bar chords; I'm writing in a folk motif that delivers a story. I'm sure when Roger McGuinn was writing songs he was pretty much in first position or first position with a capo. In your writing, you do that in order to let a story be told.

But, again, I always say I'm a better rhythm guitar player. I don't consider myself a good lead guitarist. As Hüskers went on, I started playing more conventional leads, something I like but I'm not big on. *Flip Your Wig* [1985] was the record where I started looking at solos as more than just a flurry of noise.

DT: Did Johnny Thunders influence you lead-wise, or were you starting with other people?

BM: Starting with Thunders and then moving on. The Hendrix style, using controlled feedback, low feedback, that stuff came later. That came in '83, probably.

DT: Is that when you reached a mature point?

BM: That was when I got to the next point. Where my playing really made a jump was 1988.

DT: What happened then?

BM: I had downtime. I got out of Hüskers and I wasn't recording, I wasn't touring. For the first time as a musician I had a moment to reevaluate what the instrument is. Because one thing is—and you can ask most players who are really active—it's hard to find time to come up with new things. You might have a moment where you grab a new sound and tuck it in there, but when you're in a band, you're out touring and playing your catalog. But when I'm sitting at home in 1988 with nothing to do but play guitar all day and night, that's when I had that opportunity to turn my style around. I spent eight months relearning the instrument, sitting there going, "OK, get rid of almost everything I know. Get rid of the distortion, stop hiding behind that. Learn how to articulate. Learn how to voice." That period was pivotal for me personally on a couple different levels. It would have been really easy to continue doing the same exact guitar sound and the songwriting style that I'd established and made a name for myself with. But I had no interest in continuing writing songs in that style, because I'd done it for many years. Had I just continued doing what I was doing, we wouldn't be talking, more likely than not. We wouldn't be having this conversation. You know, by spending the time to really craft my playing and come up with a new voice that was separate from the band, that was what told people, "OK, this guy wasn't just in a punk band. This guy's a real guitar player."

DT: Didn't you think you were a real guitar player by then?

BM: At that point I was twelve years into playing. I went from hearing the Ramones and the Heartbreakers and folding those two styles into one—a combination of rhythms with a simplistic lead approach—and I added these other pieces, whether it was effects like harmonizers or a cowboy-chord, folk-song approach to conventional lead playing. And now I'm up to '88. I'm sitting at home trying to relearn how to play. And the big thing was, I was living up in northern Minnesota at the time on a farm that I had bought right before the band broke up, and I had gone down to the Twin Cities to do something. I don't know what I was doing that day, but I stopped at a music store halfway to the farm on the drive back. There was one of these generic music stores—I can't even remember the name of the place—and I don't know why I stopped, but I walked in and saw the guitar that I still use twenty years later. It was my main guitar, that Lake Placid Blue Strat, the American Standard Strat Plus. On the rack. Nothing fancy about it. I just went over, played it unplugged for about thirty seconds—and it was completely different. I had been playing those Ibanez Flying V Rocket Roll Seniors, you know, with the rosewood neck; it's sort of a soggy guitar. And I picked up this Strat and it's brittle, it's a heavy piece of wood, it's a completely different feel. And I'm going, "Whoa." It forced me instantly to articulate. There was no softness to it. And I was like, "Wow." And I plugged it in, and put it in Strat position. It was the first time I'd ever played in that position with no distortion pedals, no nothing. And I'm like, "OK."

The other guitar I bought that year that was a really big informer of what was to come was that Yamaha APX series twelve-string acoustic. I had had twelve-strings before, but that one had a certain tone and a resonance to it; it just had this crazy shimmer, this thing that I always called the bag of dimes. So I bought the Yamaha twelve-string in March of '88 out at a music store in Boston and then the Strat in the early summer of '88. And those two guitars, I sat with those and capos and open tunings and completely turned my playing into a different thing.

DT: What style did you think you were heading into as you did all this?

BM: What was I going for? I mean, if you go back and listen to a song like "Up in the Air" off of *Warehouse* [1987], the last Hüskers record, that's a mandolin song. Mandolins are tuned in fifths instead of fourths, upward in five. I had beater guitars around the house that I was tuning in fives, and I started doing a lot of stuff with dulcimer tunings wherever there was D and A, because I had picked up a dulcimer somewhere along the way. And I liked that, because that was that droning, you know, almost like what Joni Mitchell does. So I started tuning guitars like that.

DT: What did the tunings themselves offer you?

BM: By changing the tuning, all of a sudden everything you know is wrong. And then you're forced to deal with your brain again instead of doing muscle memory movement. You know, muscle memory in songwriting will get you to *this* point and then you're there, and you've done almost everything you know how to do. Once I started changing the tunings, I had to learn everything over. And then all of a sudden it's like, "Oh my God," and then there's inspiration and then it opens up the songwriting. And that's the beauty of the guitar as compared to other instruments: it allows you to open up all these different voices.

So in the summer of '88 I was sitting there with these guitars that had completely different sounds than what I was used to. And with the dulcimer and the mandolin tunings I had all these new drones—bluegrass, Celtic music, even deeper into folk music than campfire songs. It was a whole different thing for me.

DT: How you do think these developments played out on the album that followed from that period, *Workbook?*

BM: My writing style changed quite a bit at that point. I went away from writing for a punk band—which was signature "verse, chorus, verse, chorus, and you're done"—to what I call my narrative style. It's a style that I don't use a lot, but when I do it's really effective. "Brasilia Crossed with Trenton" was three chords, but how long is that song, seven minutes? How those songs come about, it was words first and then the music was improvised, so it's a really different way of writing and it gets different results. *Workbook* stands out from the rest of the stuff I've written because it's more of a narrative style.

DT: How about the opening song on *Workbook*, how was that new for you?

BM: "Sunspots"? That was standard tuning, a fourth fret capo, so you know it moves everything up to G♯. But that was all just finger-picking, which is something I'd never really done.

DT: OK, because even though that's in standard tuning, it seems to clear the palette of your earlier music, where you left off with Hüsker Dü.

BM: Yeah, I was trying to reset everything. You know, you look at [that song], the first note is the root. The second note that you hear is minor. So you're down, it's darker, it's a little more introspective. Then the second song, "Wishing Well," comes at you and it's like, "OK, where am I now?"

DT: It's interesting that you were working on this new style in isolation, because that period was when the Richard Thompson comparisons started for you.

BM: I didn't even know about Richard until I played those songs for a friend of mine and he said, "Have you ever heard of Richard Thompson?" I said, "No." And he goes, "You need to listen to these records." And I went home and I listened to them and I was like, "Oh, shit."

DT: This is a good time for the obligatory "How amazed are you by Richard Thompson?" question.

BM: I mean, he's the guy. Of everybody you've got on that list [of interviewees], he's the guy. He's the guy. He's the guy. The rest of us are just, "OK, you win." And anybody who says different is lying.

DT: Nobody has said different.

BM: He's the guy.

DT: Can you say anything more specific?

BM: I've seen Richard play solo, [and] in a band, and I've met him since then. When I saw him solo, I was just like . . . it's ridiculous how much sound he's covering. Some players have a wide grasp of different styles, but no one uses the knowledge as effortlessly as Richard. He has a complete mastery of the instrument. And it doesn't sound studied or stuffy—it's completely natural. He is so in touch with the instrument in ways most of us never achieve.

And the thing is, someone might get to his level technically but try to add on the catalog of songs. He still has that body of work.

DT: Do you think you and he have a similar aesthetic?

BM: There are slight similarities in our songwriting styles. Our singing voices are not dissimilar. I mean, once I was aware of his work it was like,

"OK, this is what the good players do." But Richard's style . . . you know he didn't come off of punk rock. His path and mine are similar, but I don't know what got his playing to the level it reached. I'm guessing that a lot of it was, again, having to facilitate multiple parts at once.

DT: Is that notion of facilitating multiple parts, or of emphasizing rhythm parts, why we don't hear as much of an influence of post-punk guitarists on your playing?

BM: Like who? Andy Gill, Keith Levene? Angular stuff?

DT: Yeah.

BM: I liked what Joy Division did. That informed my playing a little bit at that time. It just wasn't a route that I followed, because all those guys were standing players. They weren't singing and jumping and carrying on, so it was easy to do more of a funky style. I respected it for what it was, but it wasn't the way I wrote; it wasn't the way I sang; it wasn't part of the deal.

DT: Do you think you could've kept playing the kind of music you were doing with Hüsker Dü after 1988? I'm not asking in terms of a reunion, I mean physically would it have been possible to carry on?

BM: I always say side two of *Zen Arcade* is the reason I would never look back. I barely remember writing that stuff. I barely remember recording it. It's awfully visceral, you know. It's awfully angry. It's awfully of a certain point in time. I don't know too many people who would want to go back twenty-five years to revisit their emotional states. I think the shortcoming of most reunions is that your body just doesn't operate that way anymore, and people can see it. I feel my age as a player. My knees don't bend as much as they used to. There's a limit to how much I can do. And it changes the way I look at the instrument. And anybody who tries to recreate something in an unbecoming way leaves a bad memory. And I'm aware of that as well.

But the physicality of it—I mean, in your twenties you have absolutely no brains at all. You can wreck your body, you can go as hard as you want all the time. And I think I was operating at that high level—that high level of anger, that high level of frustration, that high level of denial, that high level of everything. You just go, go, go. You destroy, destroy, destroy, create something out of what you destroyed.

DT: That's what strikes me when I compare Hüsker Dü to your music since then. It's almost hard for me to see it all as the work of the same person. Do you think some of that aggression was a function of the type of outlet you had—basically, hardcore in the Reagan era—as well as your age?

BM: Yeah. It was all about the time and place and age and energy level. You're creating an environment; you're destroying the notions of what modern music is, the formalities of modern music. You know, you're in a VFW hall and the PA sucks and you can barely hear anything; how do you get your point across?

DT: We've been talking about some of the larger shifts in your career, and obviously one of those is your decision to set the guitar aside around 1998. What was behind that?

BM: When I put the guitar down and started working with samplers and software, that was, in a completely different way, as valuable a period as 1988. Because when I looked at constructing a sound and stories without one of my main tools, it forced me to completely reevaluate everything again. You know, *Modulate* is great, because it was such a polarizing record. It meant a lot to me, whether people like it or not. I think sometimes people don't understand evolution from the creator's side; they only see it from the audience side. And I'm guilty of it with other musicians. Neil Young was great on this subject. When people challenged him about *Trans* and *Re-act-or*, he said, "My son was autistic and I was trying to find a way to get through to him." You know, it's not always about feeding the fan base. Sometimes we do things for our own peace of mind.

DT: In 1998, electronic music was probably more interesting than what was going on in rock.

BM: It was a lot more interesting than what was going on, and having been there from the get-go, it was frustrating to see what was happening in rock. I mean, did we really need another band that sounded like Bush?

DT: Is there a reason you mention Bush specifically?

BM: I'm not knocking those guys; I'm sure they're nice. But they were just the major-label embodiment of all of the good things that had happened in the ten years before, wrapped in cellophane. They were the embodiment of a plastic type of music. And then they spawned a generation of bands that were imitating them and created this catastrophe. So then I was like, "You know what, Paul van Dyk and Sasha & Digweed are a hell of a lot more interesting than another band that sounds like this."

DT: In some ways, a songwriter is the last person I would expect to become an electronic musician or DJ, because the notion of the song is so different. There's much less sanctity toward it, so to speak.

BM: Yeah, well, with the electronic stuff, when I started hearing the idea of remixing and chopping stuff up, that was what I liked. That's the first time I'd let go of that idea of sanctity. And, you know, that's part of our culture, too. That's part of a short attention span, that sort of recycled, purpose-built music, as opposed to the true narrative, the church music of rock. I mean, look at a concert versus a club night. In a concert, here's the stage, the storyteller looks out, and the listeners look back at him. You look at a club night and sometimes you have a DJ away from the audience. Everything else is 360. It's social interaction. As a DJ you're creating a soundtrack for people to socialize. You're not telling a direct story, you're creating an environment where all these small stories that you're not privy to rotate. So it's a completely different way of creating an environment. It's not a narrative; it's more like you're painting. More like Jackson Pollack.

DT: And that filtered back into your sense of a song?

BM: Yeah, totally, because with dance music you get to the essence of a song. It's really heavy repetition. And that's what I liked about it when I first heard it. You know, like *Xpander* by Sasha. I was like, "This is just a riff over and over and over."

It's just the mechanics of getting in and out of songs. As a DJ, one of the frustrations is when you can't match two songs up together, because they're in completely different keys; there's just not a way to get them together. So DJing taught me how to string songs together, how to tell a story to an audience, in a different way.

DT: DJs are much more responsive, wouldn't you say?

BM: Yeah. Definitely. That's it. Being aware of what kind of sound is moving people. When I'm DJing, if I'm on a kick that I want to go on and I'm looking out and people aren't really feeling it, it's my job to adapt. Again, it's different from storyteller and audience, where they know the message already and they want that message again. With the idea of a DJ presenting other people's music in a series to get an audience to a place, you've got to make it up as you go. When I'm performing I'm delivering one person's message. When I'm DJing, I'm curating. That's the difference.

It's been a challenge. I've gotten much better at it. I've still got a long way to go but I've gotten better, and it's a whole different thing.

But you know, that period from '99 on, it wasn't a complete abandonment. I was still writing on the guitar—a lot of things that showed up on [2005's] *Body of Song* were written in that period—but I was really trying to force myself off of it. I was really focusing on the electronic stuff, and that led to *Modulate* and the LoudBomb record and people were just completely baffled. And then I sort of looked at that and said, "OK now, how can I incorporate this new language I've learned into the old language that I know so well?" And then in revising *Body of Song* and finishing it, I got that hybrid that I really enjoy. You know, *District Line* [2008] is a continuation of that, tipped more toward guitars, because I was out touring again, playing again with guitars in my hands. So *District Line* leans even more toward the guitar.

DT: Do you think there are more possibilities for mixing the guitar and electronic music?

BM: I like some of the people in the electronic world—like Christian Fennesz's stuff is definitely interesting. It's different; it's not for everybody. Guitar-wise, I still like a good song. I think at this point in my life, I'm really more of a song guy, and it doesn't matter how it comes at me as long as it's a sound I like that tells me something, that adds value. I mean, I still like power pop when it's done right, you know.

DT: Song crafting.

BM: Song crafting. Sound crafting, too. As a DJ, I hear what people are doing sonically and it informs what I do. I've gotten to be a much better producer, I think, because of it.

DT: Was there anything else that brought you back to the guitar over the last few years?

BM: Just came back to it. It wasn't any kind of master plan. Just started playing it, writing on it, and enjoying it. I wanted to get *Body of Song* finished, and that led to touring, which I didn't see myself doing again, but did, and it was fun. And then it became the main instrument again.

DT: Well, it is your instrument.

BM: Yeah. I'm a singer-songwriter-guitarist.

(16)

INFINITY SUITCASE

LEE RANALDO

"Do you want to see the reflection of how it used to be?" asks Sonic Youth bassist/guitarist Kim Gordon in a song from the group's 1987 album *Sister*. "Beauty lies in the eye of another's dreams." Though buried under the usual six feet of indeterminacy, her focus could've been on the group's process, how they mined concepts like the missing twin whose death pushed novelist Philip K. Dick down a Benzedrine typewriter ribbon. "What kind of themes are on the *Sister* record?" a KTRU interviewer inquired at the time. "Um . . . kind of . . . cyberpunkish," Gordon coughed up as her husband, guitarist Thurston Moore, wondered, "Themes?" In other words, what exactly was so interesting about Dick's loss wasn't clear, necessarily, just like it hadn't been two years earlier when the

237

band murkily resuscitated Charles Manson with *Bad Moon Rising*. What was important was that out of Manson had come a black orgasm called "Death Valley '69," and now from their dark scannering came "Schizophrenia" and other tracks that laid the groundwork for their most mature work, on 1988's *Daydream Nation* and thereafter. "We jack into the matrix," *chimed* in Lee Ranaldo, another guitarist in a band that reshaped the instrument like metallurgists melting an old ring.

"Imagery zapping in from the philosophical minds of P.K. Dick, Sun Ra and Black Flag," boasted riff/quote machine Moore in *Sister*'s liner copy, "culminates with all that is sonic pop and holy." That is to say, this is a band that was at its best in the middle of everything it could take on: sound, art, video, poetry, fliers taped to Bowery telephone poles, disaster tours with prehistoric Swans, even New Music and classical compositions. "The conceptualist avant-garde from the 1960s was the outer space of music," Kyle Gann wrote in his *Village Voice* review of *Goodbye 20th Century*, Sonic Youth's 1999 album covering Cornelius Cardew and Pauline Oliveros. "It's hard to imagine that music as anybody's 'roots,' as though John Cage and his cohorts were involved in some quaint ethnic tradition." Still, the Youth eased into *Goodbye*'s graphic scores as comfortably as they shadowed the Beats in *NYC Ghosts & Flowers* in 2000. Perhaps most important, the band cracked open the guitar's DNA by gutting old Jazzmasters, shoving screwdrivers between strings, double-strumming in F♯-F♯-F♯-F♯-E-B and E-G♯-E-G♯-E-G♯ through songs built like Godard films—in short, combining punk energy with the art heroics of no wave, aspiring to the over-shrill of a thousand power drills. When Robert Palmer identified Ranaldo and Moore as heirs to the Velvet Underground/Television tradition in his 1991 essay "The Church of the Sonic Guitar"—"to attend a show by one of these groups," Palmer rhapsodized, "is to immerse oneself in a clanging, droning, sensurround of guitar harmonics"—he was as right as he could be at that point. Lee, Thurston, and company are a living link to those wayback times, but also a portal to so many subsequent connections that it would later take a six-pronged touring exhibition called Sensational Fix to document them.

Which brings us to the subject at hand. Born in 1956 on Long Island, Lee Ranaldo was raised on 1960s rock, began warping on art and film at SUNY Binghamton, then went abstract upon his arrival in New York City in 1979, first via a Rhys Chatham show at Max's Kansas City and second through a stint in Glenn Branca's Ascension Band. These shocks prepared him not only for his love/*EVOL* ride with Sonic Youth but also for free-form solo albums such as *From Here to Infinity* (1987), prose works such as *JRNLS80s* (1998), and projects with wife Leah Singer, including their book of poems and photos, *Road Movies* (1994). A dyed-in-the-wool experimenter, Ranaldo can be caught improvising with Text of Light, his sound collective that reacts to films by Stan Brakhage and Harry Smith, or found in recent installations suspending a guitar like a pendulum, playing it with a bow as it swings. "It's like a gong—if you're holding it in your hands, it's dampened," Lee says. "But as soon as you hang it, it's resonant."

DAVID TODD: As a way of starting, I wondered how important you think the alternate tunings you've come up with over the years are to Sonic Youth's sound and songwriting, to everything with the band.

LEE RANALDO: I think they're super-important to what we do, for a lot of reasons. You know, the perspective on them has changed over time. For the first decade, the tunings were very unique. Nobody was doing anything like that. And even still, to this day, you can always tell a Sonic Youth song right away, because it has a different tonal center.

When we all got to New York, we started to do some things with Glenn [Branca] and Rhys [Chatham], and they were working with differently tuned guitars, and some people think that that's where we got that stuff from. For myself, I had been working with open tunings for a long time before that, but more coming out of the folk guitar tradition, whether it was Joni Mitchell or Keith Richards or Reverend Gary Davis. When you first hear those records, they sound like these very complicated pieces, but when you learn how to create that stuff with the open tunings, they're really simple. So it's a way for inexperienced players to sound much better than they are. And in a way, that's still part of what goes on with the way we play. A lot of what we do is simple; we're not Yngwie Malmsteen players—far from it. We're kind of ham-fisted, but we know how to do the stuff that works for us. A lot of times I'm hitting bar chords, just one finger or something like that. We get all these beautiful complex tones just by the tunings.

But to go back to the question, I think as a rock band through the '80s, the tunings really set our music apart. We didn't realize it at first, because in New York everybody was doing something weird. That was the norm. But we started to go to Europe early on, and over there the reaction was like, "Wow, I never heard anything like this." And it made us see how strange what we were doing was. Through the '90s and [the following] decade, more and more people have done weird digital creations; sound has gotten more complex in general, so it's not as particular. Still, if you listen to Wilco or whatever rock bands there are now, they're playing G and C and D, and in some songs we're playing those same chords too, but we're playing them with, like, three strings tuned to the same low D, so it's very different in terms of what comes out. So I think for us it's been one of the most important things that set our music apart.

As players, the cool thing about starting with the tunings was it immediately removed us from that entire map of people who were playing in those traditional forms. Once you're playing Gs and Cs, you inevitably fall into I-IV-V [chord progressions], [but] as soon as you start with open tunings you're in this whole other galaxy. Not being trained players, we're playing by ear mostly, and whenever you have a new tuning you have to create from scratch a sense of where your fingers go on the fretboard. So it's all this sense of discovery. We don't know what chords we're playing and if they're an augmented seventh or whatever, although sometimes they are those complex chords. It's just seat of the pants, so it keeps us on our toes too. Of course we've got tunings that we've had for a long time where we've got plenty of ways we can riff with them, but the fun of it is when you start with a new tuning—you're really starting from scratch.

DT: Because the members of Sonic Youth have such diverse interests and so much creative ambition, it seems like those tunings were an ideal device to group yourselves around.

LR: Do you mean in terms of the tunings themselves?

DT: Just having something unconventional at the center of the group.

LR: Yeah, I think so. But like I said, when we started what we were doing, New York was this hermetic little box. There were no record labels, there were no magazines covering the scene, and there was no way to get out and play your music across the country. So you were really dealing with this audience of your peers. And everybody had come to New York as a film- maker or a writer or a visual artist, but everybody was drawn to music from the fact that you kind of grew up with it. Everybody had it in their blood. It was very immediate, and it was easier in the end to get a gig in Max's or CBGB than it was to get your novel published or whatever. So the rea- sons people were drawn to it were obvious. But, you know, everybody was experimenting, Teenage Jesus and DNA and the Contortions and those no wave bands—that was such radical music, and although people in New York loved that, it was still the music down the street from you, and it seemed so normal. And we were kind of right behind those people. All of the groups that came up at the same time that we did, many of which never became household names or anything like that, were trying something weird, from Swans with the double bass to this group called V-Effect, all these other groups. And nobody thought twice. You didn't come up to each other and say, "Wow, that's some really radical shit you're doing," because it was just like that.

The other thing that made our sound possible was the fact that in New York you had this melding of the art community and the music community and all these different aspects of culture. Because Glenn's and Rhys's first successes, and ours as well, were in gallery spaces. So you went in know- ing, it wasn't like you had to please a paying audience that were planning to come to a rock concert. It was about making artworks in a way, in this case with electric guitars.

DT: When you were first starting out, was the process of working out your tunings arduous?

LR: It's never been arduous. It's always been fun or interesting at the very least. You know, when Sonic Youth first started, we didn't have a lot of good guitars. This is the classic story: we had some cheap guitars that wouldn't

have held a standard tuning if you tried. So we were doing stuff like sticking sticks under the strings and contact miking them, seeing what kind of
sounds we could get. So it just evolved out of that. I mean, our first record is
all normal tuning, and immediately after that we abandoned that, because
we found that with all this other stuff the textural and tonal possibilities
were way more open. And texture is so much of what our music is about.

DT: When you've been asked about guitarists you find interesting, a lot
of them were in bands with two guitars: Television, Sleater-Kinney, the
Voidoids . . .

LR: The Dead.

DT: Is that kind of interplay another thing you're into?

LR: I definitely am. I'm not usually very interested in power-trio-type music.
I really love that kind of interplay of instruments. It was the most beautiful
thing about Television, that's for sure, and in a way about the Dead. Some of
those bands are also models for the way Thurston and I play, and now we're
at three guitars again. We've been on and off a three-guitar band, and we are
right now, and that's really cool. In the early days people would ask, "Who's
the lead guitar player and who's the rhythm guitar player?" and those terms
don't mean anything to us. Within one song there'll be points where I'm
playing the lead and Thurston's playing the rhythm, or we're both playing
the lead or we're both playing the rhythm. It's all over the place, and it's all
about this snaky, intertwining thing, and that's the most beautiful thing to
me. We consciously try to mix the music like that. We like it better when the
things are meshed.

DT: Is that similar to how you write too?

LR: Usually. Either someone brings in a sketch of an idea—Thurston brings
in a lot of them, more so these days because we're all separated geographically and we don't have the same amount of time—but up until six or eight
years ago, we would get together in our practice space four or five days a

week and just *play*. And every once in a while there'd be something that you were like, "That sounded really cool. Could we repeat that?" So we built up structures just by having the music start and seeing where it took us. And still people say, "What was your concept for this record?" I mean, we don't have concepts for records as much as we start with music and let it take us somewhere, and the accumulation of ten or twelve pieces becomes an album. We'd just be hanging out, playing, and things would start to happen.

I would say since the very beginning that's the way our songs have been created. It's very rare that anybody brings something in, like, "Here it is," start to finish. Even when Thurston brings stuff in, he'll bring in a part of a song and then we'll work it over for a couple of weeks, expand it and contract it, restructure it until it works properly for the band. Again, it's this process of adding, subtracting, taking away, and then molding all the coolest parts into a song.

The other aspect is, we almost always create our songs as instrumental pieces. Usually the words aren't worked on until the song is tracked, so that means we've been playing it for weeks, and then we are in a studio maybe overdubbing on it, and maybe at that point you figure out who's going to sing it and they start thinking about lyrics. There's no sense of the music needing to be beholden to anything, like, "This is where the verse is. This is where the chorus is." So I think that's one thing that keeps our pieces strong, is they have to be dynamic instrumentally to begin with. Sometimes later it's a pain in the ass for whoever's singing it, because you've got a section that's only three counts instead of four or you have to squeeze vocals into strange sections. And sometimes we've made things more normalized after we've recorded something, like, "There needs to be space for one more line here"—we've taken a snippet and looped it in the studio. But I think it keeps the music really strong, and it's way different than when the music is just a backup for a vocalist.

DT: It's interesting what you were saying about not making concept albums, because I think the band has a good way of meditating on ideas together. I wanted to ask you about one record where that might apply, which is *NYC Ghosts & Flowers* [2000]. That seems to stand out in your body of work.

LR: That record was interesting in that . . . you know, usually in the year period or whatever that you're creating a record, there are certain topics that you're talking about a lot. Things you've been fascinated by, whether it's some artist's work, or around *Bad Moon Rising* we were reading all those books like *Helter Skelter* and *Heroes and Villains*, just getting deep into that point when '60s idealism crushed up against the opposite of it with Altamont, and it really informed a lot of that writing. The same thing happened around *Ghosts and Flowers*; somehow early on we found the concept of looking at New York City as this creative place where we all lived, and this cultural movement from the '40s and '50s when the Beats started, and moving forward from there. It just kind of happened. Usually it's a more subtle thing where somehow topics and books you're talking about get embedded in different lyrics. With our last record [2009's *The Eternal*], we put out a press release that had blurbs for each song, and there are a lot of names dropped that you wouldn't necessarily pick up on just from hearing it. So then every critic is like, "What's this about Uschi Obermeyer in 'Anti-Orgasm'?" [*laughs*] But *Ghosts and Flowers*, I mean, that's a weird record in our canon. Some people do not like that record very much. It famously got a zero rating from *Pitchfork*, but who cares, you know? I think it has a particular feel, and some of the stuff on there, "Nevermind" and "Small Flowers Crack Concrete" and the title song, I think they're great pieces.

We go through these periods when how rocking a record is [becomes] more or less important, and I think for a record like that it wasn't very important at all.

DT: I like the introspection myself. It's not just shoegazing to me, and if you're going to explore something, that seems like a rich subject to tap into.

LR: Yeah. Well, that's our take on it, for sure. That's what we feel about that.

DT: I like the ghost element, too, because it seems like that's all that's left of that world.

LR: Yeah. And that's why we used [William] Burroughs on the one side of the cover and Joe Brainard on the other: they're different eras but they're both significant in their contributions to New York City culture. And right around then I was getting friendly with [Allen] Ginsberg and a little bit later we all met Burroughs, so we were tapping into these cultural heroes. And we were looking deep into the St. Mark's poetry scene and Ted Barrigan and all these people from that period too. So I think that record has a certain poetic bent to it.

DT: I know you're a fan of the Beats and get asked about them a lot. But one of the connections I see between Sonic Youth and them is the notion of being open.

LR: Oh, Ginsberg especially, he was open to everything. He was everywhere before anybody else. [*laughs*] The more I read about his life—I mean, he was discovering all these things, from eastern mysticism to drug use, way before they became part of the counterculture. They were searching for weird hallucinogens in South America and all that stuff. It was pretty amazing.

DT: I think it helped the Beats that they were doing those things before there was a counterculture, so to speak. Like Stan Brakhage, too; he could be adventurous without having to be nihilist in the way that most things after punk were.

LR: Certainly Brakhage was very much a Colorado hippie. He lived almost his whole adult life there; he taught at Boulder forever. But, you know, he was part of that generation that was formulating new ways of living and values different from their parents'. It's also the beauty of early rock 'n' roll: it was all being formulated on the spot. It was before it all was kind of codified and had these ritual . . . I mean, these days most rock 'n' roll is an anachronism.

DT: Well, the Beats seem to get typecast as these personae that people don't always bother looking past.

LR: Sure.

DT: Do you think that happens with Sonic Youth?

LR: I think it happens all the time. We're a band who are famously heard of but not heard. Tons of people know there's a band out there called Sonic Youth. We're referenced all over the place, but the portion of people who have actually heard the music is like a tenth of the people who know the name. So it's a little bit like that; we're classified by people who think they know what it is just because they've heard about it for so long. And maybe it's to be expected when you're as gregarious as we are, as multifaceted or whatever—we've got our tentacles into all these different things. You know, we've got this huge museum show that's traveling around Europe, Sensational Fix, and it's a whole other aspect of the group. And it's something we're really tied into, like a cultural look over the last thirty years through our prism, in a way. I think it's a really interesting show. And yet some people find it surprising. People don't have any idea that we're involved in all that stuff or that we do that kind of work ourselves.

DT: How did you assemble that show? Did you choose the artists together?

LR: Well, we each had certain people who we felt were important, and we had some people who we all felt were important. A lot of people we collaborated with, obviously—Tony Oursler, Mike Kelley, Raymond Pettibon, people who have had this cultural significance far beyond us but crossed paths with us at one point or another. There are people like Robert Smithson who I've done a lot of stuff with personally. There's a current artist named Tacita Dean whose work I like. Just different people both young and old. There are a lot of young people that nobody's ever heard of, noisicians who do artwork and we were like, "Let's put some of this stuff in the show." So there's one section of the show that's more tacked-on-the-wall stuff rather than fancy framing. And it was important to us to exhibit the poetry side of what we do. Thurston's a big super-collector of all that mimeo-fanzine stuff from the '60s, so there's a whole section of broadsides—[Gregory] Corso, Patti Smith, some of mine. Again, some unknowns, some very-well-knowns. But it was important for us to structure it like spokes on a wheel, like a lot of different tangents. So there's the real fine-art stuff and then there's art made by musicians and then there's this poetry spoke, there's a lot of video, people like Richard Kern, just all different kinds of things. It adds up to a really fun show.

DT: That idea of the spokes, is that what holds it all together?

LR: The thing I've come to see about it is that for us as a group, the most important thing from the very beginning has been the fact that we exist within a community. It's never been important for us to feel like we're the top of the pyramid. It's always much more been about, "Here's a constellation that we work within," and the show is a pretty good example of that. Because there's some of my personal work in it and Kim's and Thurston's, everybody's, but it's really about this sense of community, and walking through it is really a trip. If you spend a couple hours there, you go down all these different alleyways, and there are lots of points where it connects obviously with Sonic Youth, and there are points where it doesn't. But it's evocative of a sense of a lot of people doing interesting work over a period of time.

That's why we take interesting bands on the road with us, and why we're always talking up other people's books and records, because we love the idea that we fit in as members of a community, not standing above it. You know, in spite of having this kind of higher-profile visibility than maybe we've deserved compared to our peers, our heart has always been in the underground. That's where our real soul has been, in little clubs with people who are experimenting or in galleries with people who are trying stuff. It has not been about major hit records or hanging out with blue-chip artists, it's been about who's doing something interesting, and that harks right back to the beginnings in New York.

DT: While I have you in this retrospective mood, I wanted to ask about something you said in the '80s, which is, "We don't have some big new statement to make." Twenty-something years later, are you more aware of there being a statement Sonic Youth has made, whether it was intentional or not?

LR: You know, the thing that makes a band magic is that it's four people. It's about a group mind-set, in a way. And for us, if it's anything, it's that. We are all very different people but we have this group mind about what we do, and it unifies what we do. People always ask us, do we have a political agenda or do we have any kind of political interests. And for us the whole thing has always been about trying to have things work on our terms. And it always has worked out that way, and if we have any political message at all, it's got something to do with that. It's like, the thing you can control the most is the thing that's right in front of you, the little group of who you are. And you can set your mind about what you're going to do and what you're going to let sway you and if you're going to sell out or whatever. And things can ripple out from that.

Like I was saying, the culture doesn't begin or end with what we're doing. I think for any group that feels like they've got something special, you're talking about something that lasts for a bright burst, and after that it's all sort of mop-up. In a way I thank our stars that we haven't had a hit single or some crazy burst on the public consciousness, because it would have changed our working methods by default. We've always managed to do what we do and bring enough people along with us to keep our trip going.

DT: Actually, I wasn't thinking of the band making a political statement so much as a sonic one, like, here's a whole world of stuff you can do that no one else was even trying.

LR: Sure. Sure, and we're still mining that world. We're still discovering new tunings and playing; we're still finding that six strings and an amplifier, there's fodder for a lifetime's worth of exploration there. We always say the electric guitar is limitless in its potential, you know? It's not the only perfect instrument, but it's perfect in a lot of ways. There are so many things you can do to it. I love playing acoustic guitar, but what we do with electric guitars is just unlimited.

THE BELIEVER

JOHNNY MARR

"It is difficult to find people who understand the profound meaning of the 'pop sound.'"

—Arthur Russell

Halfway though "Paint a Vulgar Picture"—a midtempo meditation on pop music and pop life on the Smiths' final album, 1987's *Strangeways, Here We Come*—Johnny Marr doesn't burst into a solo so much as drift into one by a strange inertia. The fact that it was, four years in, his first true lead on record says much about the way Marr, born in 1963, was able to innovate without repeating the pub-rock conventions that per-

PHOTO BY JON SHARD; COURTESY OF JOE MOSS

vaded his youth in Manchester, England. Marr opens the tune with chiming chords that are soon undercut by Morrissey's Wildean lyrics, flippant on the surface but fatalistic as a penniless French exile. "At the record company meeting, on their hands a dead star," the singer begins, before quickly swerving off topic into the longing of "No, they cannot hurt you, my darling. They cannot touch you now." In this apparent contrast, pure Smiths, music fandom is like any other obsessive love, and when it finally happens Marr's solo is languid, detached, almost whistled, and utterly suited to the gloom around it. "The guitar is the one area where I can demonstrate what I feel when I say emotion, beauty, melancholy," Marr says. "If you could cross all of those—and poignant too, I would use that word every day."

Like Morrissey, Marr had a singles fixation that held the 45 as an artifact unrivaled by cock-rock spectacle. As a guitarist he yearned to be Bert Jansch instead of Jimi Hendrix, to chisel melodically as opposed to blowing away crowds with aggression. Among his other (not necessarily) "horribly unfashionable" models were Nils Lofgren and Nile Rodgers—just a couple he mentions in a 1997 article in *The Guitar Magazine*—as well as James Williamson, James Honeyman-Scott, and Robert Quine. These influences helped make Marr a conundrum in the hairy '80s, a vaunted axeman whose ability to move from the slow-picked lull of "Ring Around the Fountain" to the *wah* panic of "The Queen Is Dead" to the Madchester highlife of "The Draize Train" confused a literal-minded press. ("Anyone with half an ear could listen to The Smiths records and hear hard guitars, distorted guitars, backwards guitars, slide guitars, acoustics, Nashville tunings, open tunings," Marr lamented in that same piece. "Yet every time I opened a music paper it said, 'Johnny Marr—jingle jangle.'") The asexual, acarnivorous Stephen Patrick Morrissey attracted most of the attention during the band's prime, but in the genre-bending millennial world, Marr's dexterity became ever timelier.

Upon his defection from the Smiths in 1987, Marr drew the attention of the Pretenders, Talking Heads, and Bryan Ferry. Those gigs led to sustained collaborations with ex–Joy Division guitarist Bernard Sumner in Electronic, which released three albums of Haçienda club music between 1991 and 1999, and with longtime acquaintance Matt Johnson in the The ("The The became a sanctuary, musically and personally," Johnny says. "From a guitar-playing point of view it was amazing, because Matt wanted me to do absolutely anything that the Smiths hadn't done."). Marr fronted his own Healers on 2003's *Boomslang*, then went back to throwing paint on other bands' canvases with American indie rockers Modest Mouse (beginning 2006) and the UK's Cribs (beginning 2008). Over the years, these compulsive moves also have been fodder for the critics, taken as dalliances rather than resistance to becoming a brand. As part of his self-identified "guitar politics," this refusal to be compartmentalized is one of Marr's strongest inversions of the heroic archetype, no less important than his boredom with the blues.

DAVID TODD: How did punk affect you growing up?

JOHNNY MARR: First off, punk exploded when I was about fourteen, nearly. And I was very involved in music that was out. I was collecting punk singles, whether it was the Nosebleeds, who were a Manchester band, or stuff coming from New York like Patti Smith. I was lucky, because the guys around me were tuned-in sixteen-, seventeen-year-olds, so I was able to discover Blondie, the Dead Boys. Although there was definitely a generation gap, and I was excluded from getting into some clubs. There was a very symbolic event that happened when I tried to see Johnny Thunders, who was my hero for a time, and I was not allowed in. My memory of it is looking up to the cloudy Mancunian skies and swearing revenge on behalf of my generation. [*laughs*]

When I came of age a little bit and got to seventeen, eighteen and was just starting to think about putting the Smiths together, the music that I suppose was called post-punk felt very much like my time. I formed the opinion that punk, for me, was actually not the letter A in the new musical alphabet but in fact was the letter Z in the old alphabet. And I've never changed that opinion.

DT: So you couldn't see yourself doing something like the New York Dolls?

JM: Obviously I loved the Dolls and I loved Johnny Thunders, but there were some songs of theirs that fell into too much of a Chuck Berry vibe, and just purely as a guitar player that was one of the things that was definitely a no-no for me. So it was an interesting thing, because I knew how cool the Dolls were, but they seemed to belong to an older generation.

For some reason the Stooges, and in particular *Raw Power*, clicked with me, and that became my touchstone. That was really because Billy Duffy said that I sounded like James Williamson, and I didn't know who this person was. I had this riff when I was fifteen and he said, "Well, what's that, 'Gimme Danger'?" And I was very defensive like, "No, no. This is my own original genius." [*laughs*] So that was what was going on with me in my teenage years.

As regards punk rock, I almost took it for granted, because it was really just about all the 45s that were available for me, whether it was New York stuff or the better selections out of the UK. See, after the Pistols and Wire and the Buzzcocks, a lot of stuff out of the UK was pretty lame.

DT: So you were into punk as a singles thing, not unlike how you were into '60s music?

JM: Yeah, because it was contemporary pop. And after some of the New York bands got big, like Blondie or Television, there was not a lot of new music coming out that I liked as a guitar player. I knew the Specials were cool, but it wasn't really my thing because it wasn't guitar-based. And by then I had a different agenda; I was already more serious about being a musician. I definitely knew that I was going to be a musician as a lifelong thing.

Luckily, a friend of mine had an older sister who liked Motown, and I started listening to a lot of those singles. And like a lot of people, I got a lot of my information from my heroes, like David Johansen would often mention the Shangri-Las in his interviews, so I started getting into the girl groups and they were like an edgier, white-trash Motown to me. And I loved that. And then "Be My Baby" really opened a lot of doors for me, because I decided that Phil Spector was a god, you know. And then bubbling along-side all of that, everyone I knew loved the Rolling Stones in their mid-'70s incarnation, and because I had this appreciation of the 45 as an almost mystical object, I started to collect the Rolling Stones 45s. So that's what was going on with me around about '77, '78.

DT: I was going to ask about Phil Spector, because it seems like you were interested in him and Rolling Stones manager/producer Andrew Loog Old-ham from early on.

JM: I had this idea that the coolest thing to be would be a cross between Phil Spector and Andrew Loog Oldham and Brian Jones or Keith Richards. And I stuck with that until the Smiths started to have some success. You know, one of the great things about having Andrew Oldham as a hero was that he promoted the idea of fandom as a special relationship that goes beyond admiration to almost fetishism. And I only ever really found one person I had that in common with, and that was Morrissey, you know. That was a very important part of our relationship. Much is made of the differences between Morrissey and me, but I always said that as with a lot of my friendships, the things that run really deep, that were really important to me, I have in common with these people. And without Andrew Oldham, the Smiths probably wouldn't have existed.

These people I mentioned—Phil Spector, Andrew Oldham, [songwriting duo] Leiber and Stoller to an extent—were very carefully chosen as a counterbalance to guitar culture. I ran out of people to like from guitar culture, because there wasn't a lot of thinking going on. It seemed the only aspiration was to sweat and rock out, which I had a little bit, but I also wanted to be slightly poetic, you know. I had enough guitar culture in my heart but I needed something else in my head.

DT: Did guitar culture pick up for you with the post-punk people from '78 on? It seems like they might've been more to your liking.

JM: Well, in truth I was fairly precocious, I guess, because I related to most good modern guitar players as rivals as much as with admiration. And that was before I was even making records. It was a kind of a yardstick, really, a bar to raise yourself by. John McGeoch, for example. Keith Levene. When I heard Keith Levene, I wanted to kill him as much as to shake his hand. [*laughs*] So I liked him.

DT: Do you think you were in a transitional generation for guitar players in a sense?

JM: Yeah. Well, one of the things about the time I came out of—let's call it post-punk—was that art became very reductive and fashion became very reductive. And when that happens, it can sometimes be great. So, to be specific, Chuck Berry riffs were thrown out, R&B and "*ka-jinka-jinka-jink*" riffs were thrown out. Now, that was really saying something, because you're getting rid of thirty percent of guitar playing right there. Long solos were thrown out, obviously, but unlike with punk, distortion was thrown out too. So you had no Chuck Berry licks—which includes your Steve Jones licks—no R&B rhythm playing, no distortion, no lengthy solos, no blues, no bending unless you were kind of out of tune or being aggressive, unless you were no wave. So what you were left with was a skinny white, very pure guitar aesthetic, which you could also apply to the clothes. The clothes were very unadorned and stark, not necessarily because the times were stark, but because the style was reduced. Reduced, reduced, reduced, reduced. And you know, you were either left with Edwyn Collins or some of the new wave guitar players or no wave guitar players, right. I mean, Richard Lloyd, who I loved and still love, was probably too elaborate for this—so beautiful, though, which he is. A better example of what you were left with was David Byrne. And there was a space that I fit right into that was playing the Rickenbacker and arpeggios, because that way you got to be melodic, which I was obviously interested in, and harmonic, which I was interested in. Basically, you could either be scratchy/twitchy/funk or you could be avant-garde. Or in my case you could utilize the great things that you picked up from being a folk guitar player.

I've said it before, but pretty much what I was doing with the Smiths was really like what was going on in my head, you know. My mind was on Andrew Oldham and Phil Spector, my heart was in all kinds of guitar culture, my fingers and my hands were concerned with folk music, and my equipment was from the Patti Smith Group. That's what was going on with my senses.

DT: Is the folk tradition where those arpeggios you played came from?

JM: They came from folk guitar players like Bert Jansch, because I was into Bert Jansch particularly. I was often compared to Richard Thompson when I first came out, but I think it was mostly because Richard Thompson was more well known. And before that, in my early teens, Rory Gallagher was my guy. I picked up a lot of principles from him.

DT: It's funny, because I can see the connections to the guitarists you mention, but your playing still sounds a lot different from theirs.

JM: Yeah. You're right, I can talk about a lot of guitar players, whether it's Bert Jansch or George Harrison or Rowland S. Howard. But I've always felt that I can admire people but my own guitar playing is pretty much hermetically sealed. In a way it may just be that I'm too lazy to appropriate anybody else's style. I was never interested in working out a Jimmy Page lick, or anyone's lick with the exception of Bert Jansch, because I'm fairly impatient and I think subconsciously I don't like the idea that I would be aware of regurgitation in any way. It always seemed like planespotting or trainspotting, listening to people's guitar parts and then working them out.

DT: Another thing that seemed to set you apart was coming at the music from the angle of the whole song, rather than the guitar part.

JM: Well, I did, because of this thing that used to happen to me when I would hear a pop single. I would want to hear it twenty-five times, and then go and tell somebody about it, which is what my mother still does to this day. It's probably in all honesty the first memory I have, of her and one of my aunts having an Everly Brothers single, "Walk Right Back," and I watched them stand by the record player and play it thirteen or fourteen times and analyze it. And I'd never seen that done before and it kind of taught me to do it. It was a fascinating, fascinating experience. I would have been six or seven when it happened, and I understood it.

So looking at a song, I had these dual passions. One was for the guitar and all aspects of the guitar, which has never diminished to this day. But when I would hear the right pop single—whether it was "All the Young Dudes," or particularly "Metal Guru," "Telegram Sam," "Drive-In Saturday," stuff that's got dramatic chord changes—I would find it transcendent. And once you've had that experience, you can't pretend it never happened. It was so powerful that when I play the guitar I'm still trying to emulate that. I'm not trying to emulate the little portion assigned to the guitar, I'm trying to play the whole record. Yeah, the whole thing. Which expanded my guitar to being like a one-man band approach, really. That's partly why I play melodies inside chords.

One of the best objects that I've ever come across, I got when we did the "Dashboard" video for Modest Mouse. I'm only in it for a split second, but I'm playing a guitar that is a record deck with a guitar neck on it. That was the device I've been looking for all my life. That's what I'm trying to do, using the guitar as a record player.

DT: I understand that as a symbol, but in practical terms, how do you go about working in a collaboration like Modest Mouse? Do you have a set process?

JM: Well, the process is that I make sure I've got the guitar plugged in and ready to go the first time I hear the song and then I warn people that I'm going to completely overplay, because I feel like my initial impression is the most objective and possibly the most inspired. I've learned to not worry about making mistakes or hitting bad notes or whatever in the pursuit of some sort of thing.

DT: You have to be assertive?

JM: Well, I think I was a little shy in the past on a couple of things, but no matter what you've got to do, it needs to be appropriate, because you start taking yourself out of the realm of being a real musician if you start showboating. You have to stick to that code of doing what's right for the song. I only had to grasp that concept once at the age of fourteen, fifteen—and, again, that was flying against the things that my friends liked, because they were all digging Ritchie Blackmore and I was like, "Well, actually John Lennon's a good rhythm guitar player on 'I Should've Known Better.'" [*laughs*] I think it's something I learned out of what I call guitar politics. Because one of the things that my generation of guitar players were concerned with was how inappropriate toward music guitar culture had become before punk rock. You know, the music was coming a very poor second to that cock-rock shit, really. And, you know, from what I hear it was one of the things that people noticed about me when I first came out, that I was playing I guess fairly interesting guitar parts but without belaboring the playing too much. There were some guitar politics that I had to avoid.

But looking at what I've done as a kind of overview, as a person I started feeling like I tore up a map, so to speak, in '85, when we decided to produce the second Smiths record ourselves, which in effect meant I did it. I used to read these books about the Kinks and the Stones, and I actually stopped reading them because what was going on in my own life was more dramatic, seriously. Because of the crazy stuff that was going on around the Smiths with no management, it was like a very powerful rudderless boat, all over the place. And it kind of made the music what it was, but nevertheless, probably at nineteen or twenty I realized, "OK, it's time to get the torchlight out, because you are actually on your own path. You are going to need that fucking torch, because it's not very clear," you know? But now I see that path was OK. As an adult, I feel that was an interesting way of living. I feel very fortunate to have done that. It was a little scary, but it was great.

Maybe someone in the future will be looking to forge out "the wrong thing" as a guitar player, to go play with different bands and all of that, and they'll be compared to me, because people have not been able to compare me to anyone. And I know what I've done frustrates some people, in some quarters. It gets dismissed rather than, you know . . .

DT: Right, rather than being seen as purposeful. I think one thing that's overlooked is that you were working with other people from the beginning.

JM: See, it does start before the Smiths, and it's difficult for people to get their heads around that, but I was as serious about what I was doing before the Smiths as I was in the Smiths and as I am now. The first time I collaborated with anyone was in 1983, with Bernard Sumner, and that was before the Smiths' first album came out. When we were making our second record I collaborated with Billy Bragg, and then when we were making our third record it was Kirsty MacColl, and then when we were doing our last record I did the Brian Ferry thing. Then there was this idea when the Smiths split up, like, I went out like some jock musician for hire, which is very simplistic and actually completely incorrect. The truth of the matter is that I've always felt very fortunate to be able to make records with my friends and make a contribution to interesting groups. And when I had access to that world, I wasn't going to turn down the opportunity just because some prick at the *NME* thought it was bad form. That's nonsense. I'm a guitar player. I play the guitar, you know? I like the idea that Beck might be down at the studio and seeing if I could improve something that he's got. I'll always continue to do that.

I suppose I'm sensitive to being criticized for that, because I've been criticized quite loudly for it. But the more opposition I got to playing with different bands the more it screamed narrow-mindedness to me. It made me think that rock music is actually quite reactionary.

DT: Do you think there was a particular continuity among the bands you've worked with? It seems like for one thing all of them are hard to pigeonhole, individually.

JM: Yeah. I think that, luckily for me, I've been asked to join bands that I really loved. And I think the short answer is that I like music that's kind of heady. And heady music is less easy to categorize, really, not so easy to frame. And I think one of the problems I had with the Smiths at the end musically is that we very much framed ourselves. Possibly, if we had not been successful we might have been another band that you can't quite categorize, [but] because we became our own thing, you categorized it by saying it's a Smiths thing. And we maybe invented our own thing, which is great, but I couldn't see a way that we could live outside of that frame and I was too young to stay in there forever.

DT: The audience and media seemed to frame you too.

JM: I agree. I mean, I think the other members of the band would have been really happy to stay there, and they might be smarter than me—maybe they know something I don't. But I always have to follow things other than just my rational mind, for better or worse, really.

DT: Working with strong personalities, was that another factor in your choices?

JM: Well, I think one thing that I've learned over the years about the people I've worked with is that they say quite a lot about me, you know. And I don't think I'm cut out to work with anybody who isn't intense, because that's what makes me tick. One of the things that happened with the Smiths and the sort of success we had—when you become sort of vaguely a caricature—is that I think I was a little tired of the assumption that I was a party-going rock 'n' roller, although I think that's probably changed now. But, you know, I'm not afraid of intensity myself. I'm only really interested in serious partnerships with people who are interesting and have something to say. So whether it's Isaac [Brock] or Matt Johnson, I like heavy people.

DT: Speaking of Isaac Brock, one of the things that put your career in perspective for me was the tour you did with Modest Mouse in 2008, a stadium tour where you were opening for a band that came out around the same time as the Smiths, R.E.M. I was wondering if it ever crossed your mind, the idea of which side of that coin you'd prefer to be on at that point.

JM: Sure. It did cross my mind, in that I feel thankful that I'm doing unexpected things and that what I do and what I'm about to do is still something of an unknown quantity, even to me. I see that as a blessing, and I'm old enough now to know that there's definitely a pattern here, you know what I mean? Being somewhat of a free agent is in my nature, and I'm happy to be that way.

DT: So you do see a pattern?

JM: It all makes total sense to me. The way I play guitar, I can't really put my finger on ultimately how it all comes about musically. But the way I follow a path or career trajectory does make sense to me.

DT: There is something you said earlier I wanted to go back to. You were talking about how what you had in common with your collaborators were usually the things that were most important to you. It seems like what you and Morrissey had in common, what made the Smiths unique, was a regard for pop music as something important and worthwhile.

JM: Yeah, well, one of the things that Morrissey and I shared is that feeling of transcendence outside of your regular senses brought on by a combination of owning a record, the sound of the record, the sound of the voice, the message in it, what that band meant to you, being in the room with the lights out playing it on your own . . .

DT: And it's unusual to make a connection like that?

JM: It is unusual to find the other guy, because that's a very personal thing. And I can verbalize that now. To an extent I'm a good communicator—I've learned to be that way as I got older—but not at eighteen I wasn't. I was a little nutty in a way. But it was unusual to find the one being the key and one being the lock, who both understood that through all their differences. And then because we did have that, I then come across people sometimes who are able to see that. Because this thing existed. I know what you're talking about, and we kind of crystallized it in the band really. People talk about the tensions in the Smiths, but it wasn't like we were sitting there seething and arguing with each other. The tensions that were emerging were just very deep infatuation and love and admiration. You know, if people sat in the room with us, they would definitely feel a vibe. They would feel totally vibed out, because the two of us had this insane connection, you know? And I think that's the quickest and the easiest way of putting it, this insane connection.

But that experience I'm describing is like—I know it's not unique to me—but it's weird when you encounter a world other than the one that engages your regular senses, that is both mysterious and familiar at the same time. And I accept that that's mystical and I'm really happy to have that. If that makes me a mystical person, I'm cool with that.

DT: I don't know if it makes you mystical necessarily, it just seems like a certain kind of . . .

JM: Idealism.

DT: Yeah. But I don't think the music could've been the same without it. Do you?

JM: I don't know whether I'm answering your question, but I think that enough people liked the music and regard it so highly that I can accept it is good to other people. And without extemporizing, which is a little unpalatable to me, that belief in pop music and us being able to realize those musical ambitions in songs and lyrics and slide parts did make the music as good as people say it is. Now if the question is, did that make us important, right, then I doubt it, because I now think—I wasn't always of this opinion—but I now think the reason the music has this magic is purely because of the high emotion that was around when it was written and when it was recorded and when it was performed. Because as well as the melodies and the riffs, there is a kind of high mania, or there was a feeling that was high and manic and elated and neurotic once we were all in the same room at the same time, for whatever reasons. And I think it's in the feeling of the music. It's in the tempos, it's in the string arrangements. There's a sort of gothic intensity in there. I was playing the sound of my feelings, so it was pretty intense. And you can go, "Oh, would this track have been better with different reverbs?" Well, yeah, it might have. But there's a very high level of frantic emotion in it.

DT: Yes, that definitely answers my question. As a listener, that investment comes across. But I should point out that when I use the term "important" I don't mean in the way that Live Aid was important, just in the sense that pop music itself is intrinsically valuable. I could see from your expression that you were wary of that other implication.

JM: Yeah, I take it when you say "important" it's like a big fucking serious idea. A serious and noble idea.

DT: Well, it is, but more in the sense of what you said about the 45 as a kind of powerful talisman that doesn't need to be done with pretension or anything like that, that making pop music is just a virtuous thing to do with your life.

JM: No, absolutely. It wasn't arrogance or ambition that made me want that band to be great. Maybe it was like a young kind of arrogance or idealism, and I've still got it. I'm only here for a certain amount of time on this planet, so what I aspire to be is great and do great things—but it's the work that I want to be great, you know. I don't want people to say I'm great; I want to do great work and I want to do stuff that is like the greats, like my generation's version of the Who. It was useful for me, and scary, when I was compared to, say, Pete Townshend. I remember very clearly going into the writing of *The Queen Is Dead* thinking, "Oh, shit," right? Because I have to be that great. And that's probably why I started drinking so much brandy and taking lots of drugs; it's the old corny Charlie Parker trap, isn't it, because that's what I knew those people to do. But I knew as sure as shit that I had to get to some very precarious place to make something that wasn't just *easy*. And that was a very clear predicament.

I'm not someone who mythologizes in hindsight, but I remember after the second album we were lorded as being great, and frankly I felt that the people who were saying this, God bless them, that their idea of great and my idea of great were probably quite different. I was thinking, "Shit, man, if you think the bar is there, me and Morrissey know the bar is really way higher," because we had this insane mystical belief in it, and we were like, "Holy fuck, here we go." And it's certainly easier to do that in an iconic band with three people working with you every day, but in my own way as a solo guy now, or whatever it is I am, that's what I'm trying to do. I'm trying to do that as a guitar player.

(18)

PURPLE SPARKLE

J MASCIS

PHOTO BY TIMOTHY HERZOG; COURTESY OF SUB-POP RECORDS

J Mascis changed my perspective on rock guitar with a single solo on an otherwise nondescript Dinosaur Jr. bootleg. The song was "Bulbs of Passion," and about two minutes in, right after laughing into the mike at one of his own mistakes, he launches into a sequence that at first sounds like another tour through classic-rock yawns. But instead of sliding into cliché, J attacks the old boxes with reckless abandon, sending a furious, spiraling scream of unpacked feeling out of the three Marshall stacks that forever loom behind him like an indie Stonehenge. With a gasp, the entire audience is raised like a sharply bent string, only to drop in slow motion as

J lowers them to pitch, out of breath, like they've just done the fucking wave or something. And then of course J goes back into his half-there vocals as if he hadn't just declared, um, I'm about a million times more intense than I appear, and I'm, um, able to kinda . . . remind you how it feels to have complete, um, you know, emotional, um, ah . . . access . . . when I'm working through these leads on my, uh . . . Jazzmaster?

J Mascis isn't known for his banter—his Tobey Maguire laugh and comic timing notwithstanding—but it doesn't matter. He says it when he plays, and all those tacky colors and Claymation covers are just a mask for his vast depth, for after all, J is the one who feels the pain of everyone before he feels nothing, to paraphrase the most accurate lyric of a numb but raging generation. It was always clear that the wheels were turning under that mop of greying hair, no matter how detached he came off in Michael Azerrad's indie bible *Our Band Could Be Your Life*. That sado-Mascis who fired Dino bassist Lou Barlow in an act of muted class warfare, that's just cover for the high-lonesome J who sang, "You're not going to get me through this, are you?" The Uma Thurman–longer who bleated his way through *The Year Punk Broke*, just a guise for the J who travels the world to see Mata Amritanandamayi ("Ammachi"), a contemporary saint known for hugging.

On the factual side, there are so many connections between Joseph Donald Mascis Jr. and other tuned-in musicians of his time that one would think old Robert Johnson hit the crossroads in Amherst, Massachusetts, in December 1965. J is the one who took the counterintelligence of Sonic Youth, the fury of the Birthday Party, the high warble of Neil Young, and the dynamic pummel of late-Ozzy Sabbath, and mixed them into a ferocious blend of underground Zen, which he in turn handed off to Nirvana, who Starbucks'd it like a good Seattle enterprise should. It was J who was mates with Kevin Shields, connecting My Bloody Valentine to their American counterparts by virtue of something more than a shared preference for offset guitars. It was J who played possibly the best-ever cover of the Stooges' "Loose" with his post-Dinosaur group, the Fog. And yes, as is widely acknowledged it was J who reinvigorated lead guitar in the lo-fi 1980s.

As a guitarist, J plays like a first-generation skate punk, one who has no preexisting knowledge of what happens when you get that much air that fast.

Sure, he uses a lot of notes, but just when you think he's about to hit some spooge-rock crescendo he switches up, disappearing into deeper purple. His songs are full of singular moments like the soul-damaged opening of "Little Fury Things" and the counterpoint trumpet of "I'm Insane" and the sledge-hammering chorus of "Ammaring," the devastating reverb of "No Bones" and the blistering sludge of "Turnip Farm." When the reunited Dinosaur blazed through "Almost Ready" on *The Late Show* a few years back, J really did seem like a remnant from another time when epic soloists stomped on their Big Muffs.

DAVID TODD: When you think of guitar players these days, are there people you still find interesting?

J MASCIS: Oh yeah, a lot of people. I like the guy in Big Brother. Do you remember his name?

DT: Big Brother?

JM: You know, Janis Joplin's band.

DT: James Gurley?

JM: Yeah, he seemed pretty out there. And, I mean, Rory Gallagher. Mick Taylor. I really liked the Stones early on, that era with him. I liked his solos, you know, because he didn't seem to fit into the Stones but he made them better musically, like the contrast of these fluid leads going on within their music. I also liked Fast Eddie [Clarke] from Motörhead, Bones [Tony Roberts] from Discharge.

You know, I tried stealing things from some of those people, but I couldn't do it exactly right so it came out sounding like me. I guess that's good, that might've helped in getting a more original sound. Like, I know guitarists that can play every song by anyone else, but then they don't have their own sound.

DT: What other guitarists did you try to steal from?

JM: When I was starting, Greg Sage from the Wipers and Ron Asheton from the Stooges.

DT: You did some shows with Ron Asheton, right?

JM: Yeah. I felt like "the apprentice" or something, learning how the songs were really played. It was pretty cool.

DT: Are there contemporary guitarists you like?

JM: I like Elise [Elisa Ambrogio] from Magik Markers. She's brutal on the guitar, you know. Her playing doesn't sound anything like classic rock; there's no basis in rock, but it's got a lot of energy. That's interesting to me. I like Awesome Derek [Stanton]; I guess he learned how to play from Scott Asheton. He definitely has a Stooge style.

DT: You must hear a lot of free folk up there in Western Mass.

JM: Yeah, I get to see a lot of that around here. I just saw Richard Thompson recently, he was still awesome.

DT: Was that a solo show?

JM: Yeah. I prefer him solo.

DT: I liked your version of "I Misunderstood" on the Thompson tribute album.

JM: Yeah, that one I was really into. I asked if I could be on the record and do the song, you know, 'cause I had seen him play it live, and then when the record came out it didn't sound the same to me. I thought it was weird how it could be so much heavier acoustic than when Mitchell Froom put all these stupid keyboards on it in the studio. [*laughs*] So I did it more the way I heard it, and I liked how it came out. I guess Richard Thompson liked that one too.

DT: How was it for you going from playing electric with Dinosaur Jr. to doing solo acoustic shows?

JM: It was really hard to fill up the space, you know, just sitting there alone, without amps. It was nerve-racking.

DT: On *Martin + Me* (1996) you seemed pretty casual.

JM: No, it's 'cause I was drinking that I could talk onstage. [*laughs*] That was a period when I was drinking, and I didn't really drink before that or haven't really since.

You know, Richard Thompson is chatty, telling jokes and stuff. I can never think of anything to say. I want the show to be over, or the silence is too deafening. I just get freaked out. Like with the electric guitar, you step on the Electric Mistress and you don't have to play for a while. You just sit there with the noise. But you always have to play on the acoustic; there's no sustain or anything. There's just a lot more silence to fill.

DT: Where do you think you are in your guitar development? Have you peaked yet?

JM: I think I peaked immediately. [*laughs*] And just kinda went down from there. Because when I first started playing, my mind didn't have any ruts in it, so I could come up with more interesting things.

DT: What about in terms of songwriting?

JM: It's hard for me to say. I'd like to think I'm getting better. At the very beginning, I realized I put a million parts in every song. I grew out of that, I guess. As you get more confident, you can play less and feel better about it. You know, back then I was just bored and wanted everything to change all the time. I was afraid to bore myself or other people.

DT: On the second Dinosaur Jr. album, songs like "Sludgefeast" have a lot of parts but they fit together well.

JM: Yeah. That album is where we formed our own sound as a band. We put out the first record pretty quick, so it's all these kind of stabs at different sounds. But then we did a B-side for a single after the first album, "Bulbs of Passion," and that was the first time I felt like we had come together. I was really into the Birthday Party when we started; that was my favorite band at the time. But whatever I was playing didn't sound like them—I was just playing whatever came out. It sounded more like our own thing than pieces of other people's things. Just the whole concept felt better.

DT: What about the solo on "Bulbs of Passion," were you happy with that?

JM: I dunno. I remember liking the solos on *You're Living All over Me*. But I don't specifically remember "Bulbs of Passion."

DT: That's a song where the solo is a section itself; there's a whole part built around it.

JM: Yeah.

DT: You have others like that. I guess "Say the Word" would be the extreme version.

JM: Which song is that?

DT: "Say the Word," on *Free So Free* [2002, with the Fog]. . . . J?

JM: Man, I'm drawing a blank. What number is it, do you know?

DT: It's second-to-last.

JM: Can you sing a few bars?

DT: I can't sing that to you. "Alone" is another one with a long solo—I was curious as to how much of a part of the song you considered a solo to be.

In "Can't We Move This," for example, the opening solo sets up the whole feel.

JM: Well, the solos are kind of an immediate way to express myself. Whatever solo ends up on the song I guess adds whatever emotion I had at the time. So in the songs then, I just leave space for solos and sometimes I'll leave a lot of room and then see how long the solo lasts and, you know, maybe edit the rest of the song shorter than the solo section. I try to give myself enough room to see what happens.

DT: So "Say the Word," you remember it now?

JM: Yeah.

DT: That could be . . .

JM: Just an excuse to have a long solo, I guess. I don't hear that many bands that seem to be into soloing these days, like in a way that seems interesting.

DT: When it comes to songwriters, did you have particular influences like you did on guitar?

JM: I don't know if I think about it like "songwriters." When I think of songwriters, I think of James Taylor or something. It sounds pretentious to me.

DT: I mean like Brian Wilson, not a guitar player. Gram Parsons. Why is that pretentious?

JM: I just think about the bands and songs I like—it's all kinda one big thing. It's hard to separate songwriting and guitar playing. But I guess if I think of songwriting, it's more like Sabbath. There are these parts you stick together and that's a song, and I like that. That's the way they construct songs, throwing different riffs together and seeing if they fit.

Yeah, Sabbath was a big influence, how they would go through different textures. Like "Thrill of It All," the way it cut from a heavy part to an acoustic part, that was the first loud-to-quiet thing a lot of indie rock bands used as a formula. It seemed for me that started there. I just really liked the drama of it.

DT: Writing-wise, your albums with the Fog seem to have more overt themes than the ones with Dinosaur Jr.; they were more entered into the world in some way.

JM: Yeah, I guess I was feeling a little better about everything. I wasn't as hopeless as I'd been the past.

DT: You mean personally?

JM: Yeah, I mean, I'd been depressed most of my life to that point, I guess. [*laughs*] And probably the time of [Dinosaur Jr.'s] *Without a Sound*, like, that album was my lowest period. And a lot of people don't like that record and so in that way, yeah, I don't know if you make your best music when you're most depressed. I guess there's this idea of being more romantically depressed when you're younger, but that phase was over for me by then. Because I had money and stuff, you know, I'd achieved some success, but then when you realize that doesn't help, it's a more serious kind of depression. Because a lot of people think, "Oh, if I had money, life would be better." And I was realizing that wasn't the case.

DT: Did you actually have diagnosed depression?

JM: Oh, no. I mean, I wouldn't ever go to see anyone, but who knows.

DT: What got you out of that?

JM: It took a lot of effort. I was really trying to get help from people, and just kinda searching for a . . . I don't know. I was just making an effort to get out of it, I guess.

DT: As a title, *Free So Free* seems to reflect that.

JM: Yeah. I just kinda realized there was "freedom" or "free" in all the songs. After a while it was funny, like, "Oh, I guess it's a concept album." [*laughs*]

DT: If you ever made a concept album, freedom seems like the kind of thing it'd be about.

JM: Yeah. I read something I wrote about Deep Wound, my hardcore band. And it's like, "We're this band that stands for freedom." [*laughs*] I was like writing that when I was fifteen.

DT: One of your solo projects I liked was *Sing + Chant for Amma* (2005). How did that come about?

JM: Well, that's one thing that helped me get out of being depressed. I saw this lady Ammachi around the time I was most bummed out. And, you know, she tours every year and hugs people and that's her main thing, but she has charities all over the world, and she's just 24/7 helping people. And I just got more into it over the years, and there's a lot of singing at her get-togethers, so I started singing the Indian chants, you know. I couldn't totally relate to those, so I started writing some of my own stuff in that same vein, the call-and-response stuff they sing. After a while I had enough songs [and] I just made the record, and, you know, sometimes I'd play it at her gatherings.

DT: How did you get introduced to Ammachi?

JM: Someone told me to check it out and I was like, "All right." And then every year I kind of got more into it. The main thing was that I felt like I wasn't wasting my time if I was around her. Any other time, it's a good question whether I'm wasting my time or not, doing whatever. So that's a good feeling on its own.

DT: That one song "Heavy Metal Ai Giri Nandini" is based on a pretty metal-sounding hymn. It's got some hard-core imagery.

JM: Yeah, it's [the Hindu goddess] Kali, she wears a necklace of human heads. Male heads. [*laughs*] That's pretty metal.

DT: A lot of your lyrics on *Sing + Chant* didn't seem far off from your usual ones, like "I got lost again / I tried everything / Couldn't find my way / You seemed miles away." It seemed like you kept the same motifs but switched the situations. Is that accurate at all?

JM: It sounds good, I don't know. [*laughs*] It's also, you know, there's such a wide variety of people at Amma's gatherings and I was trying to make music palatable to that scene. I mean, the Indians, they don't understand a lot of Western music. Even a drum set is too much. So with the record I was trying to make something so I could communicate with other people and they could somehow grasp it. It was an interesting thing to do; it was kinda trial and error, you know. 'Cause I'd do something [harder] and people were like, "Whoa!" And I was like, "All right, don't do that." [*laughs*]

DT: That sounds much different from how I would imagine you'd write for an American rock audience. Do you think you could ever try to communicate with them like that?

JM: I don't know, I'm not sure about that. For America, I have no idea what people want, I'm just out to try to entertain myself—that's the only gauge I can have. You know, it's too big a world to try to please people, really. I've never gotten anything from that, and it's never really been my way. I always just did what I wanted and hoped for the people to catch up to it.

DT: It might be cool to bring some of that in. Rock people don't usually try too hard to communicate, it's usually more of a stance like what you just described.

JM: Oh, I'm sure it's all seeped in somewhere. But I don't know specifically how.

DT: Actually, I wanted to ask you about the persona you have as this super-laconic type. Is that ever tiresome to you, or do you not mind it, or do you not care?

JM: You know, it's all of the above at different points.

DT: Do you feel like it holds you back?

JM: Yeah, sure. I remember doing some blues jam and people were like, "Oh, I didn't know you could play like guitar like that." People think you can only do the one thing that they know you do.

DT: One of the other things you did a while ago was Allison Anders's film *Gas Food Lodging*, which you scored and appeared in.

JM: I just thought it was cool being in a movie. Just for shits and giggles, to see how it works. And to realize that I'm definitely not an actor. [*laughs*]

DT: Maybe. You know who you reminded me of in your film appearances, a little bit, was Peter Sellers.

JM: Oh, cool. I remember hearing on that other movie I was in, *Grace of My Heart*, that Martin Scorsese was into my performance or something. I was like, "All right." That was pretty funny.

DT: Did you like doing that soundtrack?

JM: Oh yeah, soundtracks are good. They're easy to me somehow. 'Cause there's some scene and you just watch it and the music kinda writes itself. You know, it's easier than trying to just pull music out of the air.

DT: Has anyone else asked you to do one?

JM: Not lately, no. That's another thing with my reputation where they don't think you can do it. You know, I hear soundtracks by what's-his-face, the Oingo Boingo guy [Danny Elfman] and I'm like, "That's terrible music, how did he get . . . ?" [*laughs*] I feel like I could do music I like better.

DT: *Gas Food Lodging* came out in 1992. Over at the other end of the grunge-era spectrum, Dinosaur Jr. played Lollapalooza in 1993.

JM: Yeah, that was the low point. It was our worst tour ever. It was just horrible, everything about it. That was when I finally felt that I had given in. The record company was like, "You have to do this for blah blah blah . . ." and I knew it was a bad idea, and I just did it anyway. And it was a bad idea—you know, it pretty much made [drummer] Murph [Emmett "Patrick" Murphy] go insane.

DT: When did you go on?

JM: Like three o'clock in the afternoon, and in every town it was the hottest day of the year. It was just misery. And, yeah, you do play in front of maybe a million people in the course of a summer, and then you end up selling like *ten more records*, you know. They're like, "Oh, you'll sell all these records," and we proved that theory doesn't work.

I thought it was interesting how we played the Lollapalooza in Chicago a few years ago, and it recreated the exact hell that I remembered. You know, it was 106 degrees, complete misery. I was like, "Wow, it's wild."

DT: In some ways you're seen as being from that time period, the late '80s–early '90s, Lollapalooza and SST Records and all that. Are you comfortable with that, being put in with the bands in the *Our Band* book like the Butthole Surfers and Mission of Burma and Fugazi?

JM: Mostly, you know. We were definitely into a lot of those bands and wanted to live the SST dream. I mean, we're part of the end of SST, but I guess we're still a part of it. SST kind of made us, the Minutemen, Meat Puppets.

DT: What about your guitar contemporaries like Kevin Shields, the guys from Sonic Youth, and Chris Brokaw? Do you see yourself in a sort of loose movement with them?

JM: Yeah, I suppose. I'm not sure. Those are definitely friends and I understand where they're coming from. Yeah, a loose movement, that sounds good.

REVEREND SPACEMAN

JASON PIERCE

PHOTO BY KIRSTIE SHANLEY

"Spacemen 3 are better at this carbon monoxide garage trip than a thousand overrated U.S. geetah schmucks." —John Robb, *Sounds*

In the early 1980s, a drone chemist called J. Spaceman (born Jason Pierce, 1965) looked through fuzz-colored glasses into quiet Rugby, England, and found Bo Diddley beats, Cramps sheet feedback, and Staple Singers devotionals. As Spacemen 3, Pierce and partner Sonic Boom (Peter Kember) debuted with 1986's *Sound of Confusion*, covering the 13th Floor Elevators and writing originals that could have been homage. But by the next year's *The Perfect Prescription*, tributes such as "Ode to [Lou Reed's] Street Hassle" seemed quaint after the transporting "Take Me to the Other Side," the album's simple concept—a single trip from ingestion to comedown—crystallizing their maximal/minimal obsessions. For *Playing with Fire* in 1989, the Spacemen traded a few layers of distortion for the processed nuance of "Come Down Softly to My Soul," and on *Dreamweapon* (1990) they showcased their inner La Monte Young. After dividing creatively for *Recurring* (1991), they disbanded, leaving their mystique to grow with posthumous titles like *Taking Drugs to Make Music to Take Drugs To*.

With Kember out fronting Spectrum and E.A.R., Pierce launched his new outfit, Spiritualized, with 1992's glassine *Lazer Guided Melodies*. Moving through 1995's whistling, microtonal *Pure Phase*, he perfected his method of placing resonant lyrics within musical settings that blow up from piano whispers into freak-outs of guitar, orchestration, and reverbed tambourine; this effect is encapsulated in the "Intro" to *Royal Albert Hall* (1998), which starts with a snippet of the standard "Oh Happy Day" before blasting off toward a Sir George Martin crescendo. While many musicians affect an abundance of originality, Pierce was content to let his emerge in modest doses, through reflections of the "alien" inspirations he absorbed. "I bought into that whole myth, the Jerry Lee Lewis side of rock'n'roll," he told Phil Sutcliffe of *Q* in 2001. "Then when I actually attempted it with Spacemen I realized it wasn't in me at all. I haven't got the temperament or the lungpower. So we sat down to play." Fully seated, Pierce took Spiritualized from interstellar voicings to plaintive soul-baring in the first few seconds of *Ladies and Gentlemen We Are Floating in Space* (1997), the record widely considered to be their master-trip. For the seventeen-minute expanse of "Cop Shoot Cop" that closes that album, he pulled even guest pianist Dr. John down the hole in his arm where all the music goes.

Following *Let It Come Down* (2001) and *Amazing Grace* (2003), Pierce was hospitalized in 2005 with double pneumonia, wasting away in intensive care to eighty-four pounds. "One by one, everybody else in the room died," he recalled in the *Observer*. "And I remember thinking, 'Well, somebody's got to get out of here alive.'" Perhaps it was all those "Lords" he'd sung, but he did make it out, only to face the challenge of finishing heavies in progress like "Death Take Your Fiddle" once recovered. Fortunately, an encounter with cinema empath Harmony Korine led to a gig writing incidental music for the director's 2007 film *Mister Lonely*, which set Pierce on his way back to full (deceptive) strength. Named for the hospital's Accident and Emergency ward, Spiritualized's *Songs in A&E* (2008) put Pierce back on the road with his sly humor intact—"the work of the devil," he called the album in the *Guardian*, "with a little guidance from me."

DAVID TODD: I was reading about Harmony Korine, who you describe as this mad visionary who inspired you following your illness. But even though he is known for being wild, Harmony was quoted as calling you "a dreamer . . . a crazy bastard." Are you more similar than it would appear?

JASON PIERCE: We're way similar.

DT: Is that what you think?

JP: Yeah. I think Harmony and me, it's better that we met later in life than earlier in life. I think we would have been a bit more harm to each other.

DT: What do you have in common?

JP: I think when you have a kind of vision for something and you're singular in your devotion to that idea—I think Harmony's really like that. I remember when he was making *Mister Lonely* and saying, "This is it. This is my big film." And when he showed it to me, I was like, "Whoa, *this* is the commercial one? Shit." And I loved him more for that, because there's this total disregard for anything other than what was important in his world, you know. And I think that about a lot of the stuff I do.

DT: What was your experience like in terms of composing for that film? It seems like other people find that liberating.

JP: Yeah, because you don't have to front it, you know. It's something that is almost like a behind-the-scenes thing. And for me, it put me into a place musically that's really hard to get to, which is making music like a child, like when you open a piano for children and they just hit the keys with this weird abandon. And sometimes you have to unlearn everything you know [in order] to do that, and that's really hard to do. So when I went in to make that record, I could abandon my songs and the whole concept of an album as this thing that you produce, and just make pieces of music.

DT: Do you think you can take anything away from that, bring it into your main work?

JP: Yeah, sure. That's what you do with anything in music—you hold onto the great bits as best you can and try and drag them in. See, with music, the greatest bits are the most elusive. You hold on to them and try and drag them forward. And it's a nice idea that you could take all the greatest bits from all the records you've ever made, pull them all together, and make a single great record. But it just doesn't work that way, because it's not about notes and the way you play them. It's about this weird thing that you're after every time. And it doesn't work by just going over the same old path you know, which is kind of weird as well. You think, "Well if that's the path to glory, let's do that again." But it doesn't work.

DT: Even though the new path could be ninety-nine percent the same as the old path.

JP: Yeah, because I think it has to be. The change is slow. I'm very wary of radical change. I'm wary when people are stylistically like this and then suddenly they're like *this*, because generally that's to do with hipness, with whatever's selling. And there's so much music that is made in that way— that's replicated, that's copied. And they say that every copy by its very nature is a dilution. And that's why it's important to push outwards, but in the way that you evolve. It seems like if you make a massive leap—actually I don't think it's a leap; it's just a massive change—it looks as though, "Well, were you on the wrong path before?" The thing is, it's about you as an artist and as a person. My music's always going to be coming from me and I'm not changing radically. I'm not reinventing myself.

As I was saying, though, the great bits of music are elusive, so it's like there are these things that you have to draw into your own world. And I honestly think that what I want to make is records that capture all the beautiful moments in all the records I love, everything from George Mitchell field recordings to Phil Spector to Howlin' Wolf to the Staple Singers. And you can't make records that stylistically capture all that, because it would just be a mess, you know. And so you kind of have to capture the ghosts of these records, these little bits that you can grasp. And it takes time. I don't know why it takes time—maybe I'm not very good at it—but it just takes time to get where I think, "That's it. I've got it there."

DT: Is that what you were doing when you were starting out with Spacemen 3, pulling things in?

JP: For us, it was almost like that thing of distilling something—like, you force it into your world. You force it, and you can get just this tiny element of it. You know, I've said before that if you hit a single chord with enough ferocity and for as long as you can, it can become the single most important chord in your life. And for us it was that kind of thing, distilling Bo Diddley, the way he hit a single chord, alongside the Stooges and a lot of Velvet Underground, in the early days. It all got leveled out.

DT: To me, one of the things that Spacemen 3 did was show how these sources fit together. You could take the drone of La Monte Young and the drone of the Stooges and see where they overlapped.

JP: But again, drag that into our world. Not to try and visit that world, not to copy that world, you know. When we started the Spacemen, there were a lot of bands playing like '60s groups, wearing the clothes and the paisley. And it's important to never go back, you know. To just try to drag everything we loved kicking and screaming to our world. That was the deal, I guess.

I mean, some of it comes through a certain inability. There was no talent there. And I think that's really important. Not in a bad way, even, but it was about being in love with this thing but not being able to copy it, not being able to do anything that was proficient in that way.

DT: You didn't seem to think that acknowledging your inspirations would limit your own identity.

JP: Everybody's always trying to pass off something as their own like it dropped in from outer space, like "Hey, we're the lucky people to deliver it to you." Our music has always been a sign of love as well, you know. We're deeply indebted to Suicide and to all that stuff, and so some of it's like saying, "Thank you. This is where it's coming from." And all the bands I loved at that time like the Cramps and Tav Falco, Alex Chilton, they weren't saying, "This has just arrived today, everybody. Get hip." They said, "Look, if you like this, this is where it's coming from. All the threads are coming together here."

Early on we figured if you put that kind of stuff in, you'd draw people. And I think that was a bit of youthful naïveté on our part, you know. We did a poster that said "Stooges? Velvets? Stones? . . . Spacemen 3," and then put the date and where we played. And we had one person that showed. Because nobody knew Iggy Pop then. I mean, nobody understood it; there was no little section of people who were into that same thing. We used to think we'd draw the fucked-up children and it'd be like this big . . . I really thought I'd look out from the stage and it'd be like Altamont out there, you know. I joke about this all the time and it's so not Altamont out there.

DT: You thought you were going to have a big crowd?

JP: Well, no. Just those kinds of people.

You know, that's why we're deeply in debt to Detroit. It just seems like we arrived here [where the interview took place] and these people came out from the corners of the city. And they were just the right kind of people. I thought, "This is where we should have played."

DT: It's good to be welcomed in Detroit when you're playing with echoes of the MC5 and Stooges, in terms of street cred or whatever. And it's interesting that you pull off playing gospel music as well. That's not easy for a rock band to do.

JP: Yeah. But, again, I think there's something about it that comes from a place of deep love. I love the stuff. I said I make a lot of truth in music, and gospel music just by its very nature is from a place of deep truth, you know. You can't sing the ballad unless you believe, unless you have belief. . . .

But I don't believe. So I can't really play gospel, you know. I can't really move my voice like that. But it still feels right.

DT: Do you think you replace that belief with something else?

JP: I don't think what we do is gospel music in the same way. So I don't think you have to replace it, you know. I've said before that when you walk with Jesus everybody knows what the conversation's about—it has to do with the bigger things, with morality and the way you see what you do. It's a really simple message in that song, you know. So it makes a sense of that song to me where it wouldn't make sense in any other way.

DT: I've heard you use the term "alien" to refer to music you like, and gospel I presume would fit into that. But what exactly do you mean by that term?

JP: When you almost can't imagine the audience. You know, some of those old early Utah Smith records, you can't imagine what the audience is. And America's full of this kind of accidental music that you feel like someone just pressed a button and got this thing that happened. And that's what I love. I think the majority of all music is made outside the industry of music. Whether they're singing in the kitchen or whatever, there's this sense that people make this thing. And a lot of gospel sounds like that—like, you hear Washington Phillips and you go, "Why did he make those records?" you know? "What were they doing?"

DT: I like that, although I think in the US people might know who those audiences are. Like Elvis did gospel albums; it's part of the culture. I don't mean that to be critical, but to say that there's a divide that it's interesting to see someone jump. Because maybe in Spacemen 3 there were songs that were more psychedelic and more gospel, a little more separately, but as you went along they started to merge in a way that could be unexpected. And of course there were other styles mixed in there too.

JP: Yeah, but I didn't invent that kind of thing, you know. I think even Suicide's "Cheree" is like a doo-wop song, isn't it? And there's a lot of Bo Diddley that's like doo-wop, and I think it's all sort of rooted within rock 'n' roll in a weird way. I'm not drawing on anything that isn't within that canon anyway, and it's not a deliberate thing. It's just, when you start to put music together, some things fit. You whistle a tune and you go, "Wow. That's going to go in there." And later you might realize it's more rhythm-and-blues than you wanted it to be, then you try and pull it back and then it goes somewhere else, you know.

See, I don't ever sit down and write. I can't. I wait for songs to get locked in my head, and occasionally I get one that isn't a tune I recognize, and that starts the thing. And then when I go to the studio I just put all those ideas down and then keep working at them until something fits. So they construct themselves over time. But it's not really ever a case of going, "OK, I'll take a little bit of that and mix it with a little country, a pinch of soul." And lyrically it's the same. I try to write lyrics about anything other than what people think I write lyrics about and they wind up coming back to the same things. I say a line and then I try and rewrite it and it doesn't write in any other way other than with the word "Lord" in it, you know. And I try. Lord knows I try. But some things just fit.

The acoustic shows we did were a revelation, because I found I'd play a song and it would be on the chords G and D and then I'd start the next song and I'd be horrified to find that they were the same chords, D and G, played in exactly the same way. I'd think, "Jesus, Jason. Couldn't you have done something a little different there?" But they just go down and they feel right.

DT: Is the idea of an alien quality something you'd want with your own music, how it reaches the listener?

JP: Wow. No. I don't think I ever picture the listener. I just think it's what feels right for me. I've got this needle that goes all the time, like, "that's good," but when it goes *there* it turns into "that's not good." You know, like,

"Suicide's good . . . Suicide's good," and then it leans into other bands that play keyboards and that kind of thing, and my needle won't go across that line. And it's doing that constantly. It snakes around a bit, but it's a rigid set of ground rules. And I make records within that, I guess. They constantly shift until they find a place.

DT: Something I find fascinating about your most recent record is that you wrote the songs before your illness, and they're all on themes that are very grave. It seems like *Songs in A&E* was a lesson in applied songwriting in a way.

JP: Yeah, because you can apply the experience to the songs with hindsight. And people are saying I prophesied my own downfall, like I best be careful what I write about.

But that's hindsight, you know. You can make anything fit.

From where I stood, my experience made it very difficult to get back into working on those songs once I got better, because they were really harrowing. They felt really close to what I'd been through, but only initially, you know. Once I started working with them again I didn't believe that I'd prophesied anything.

DT: But aren't your songs on *A&E* on the same topics a lot of songs are about? Songs often play off these life-and-death issues, but only on a figurative level.

JP: Yeah, because I think they're about bigger things, aren't they? You're quite right about that. I mean, I say I write from a place of truth, but I don't mean the truth that's mundane. It's about asking big questions. I've said before that I don't think I would ever have written a song like "Death Take Your Fiddle" after that event. It would have been a really foolish line to write, almost like writing from a place of something I wanted to gloat about. The fact is, it was written about death as a part of life that makes real sense of life, you know, and life really isn't worth living unless death is close. And I think maybe initially people inferred that the record was about my illness. But over time that will disappear and the record won't be about me at all. It will be about the way people hear those songs and relate to them.

DT: If you tend to come back to the same chords—D and G—how do you know when you've found a combination you can build a song out of?

JP: I'll tell you why. Because like I said, I don't write the songs down, I sing them into a machine. And then somebody else might say "Well, let's work out the chords," and I might say "OK, what are they?" And they go, "D and G." [*laughs*] I go, "Again?" And that's just where I sing, you know. So I don't construct them with any musicality—I'm not at the piano like, "Oh, I need another chord." I'll just go, "Wow. What a beautiful melody I've got in my head," and I'll sit down, I'll sing it six times and then I'll go, "That's it." So they're kind of by accident. That's why I think "Accident and Emergency" was such a great title. The whole of my musical life—maybe the whole of all of my life—seems to be a product of accident or emergency. It's all just falling into the next thing.

DT: And you're open to those accidents.

JP: I think truly great things come from them, you know. You can have all the great plans in the world, you can have this dogmatic view of how you should make a record, and then something could come in that really makes it special. You know, like the breathing, the accordion at the front of "Death Take Your Fiddle" that draws you straight in . . . I couldn't have asked for a better thing to go there. And it was an accident. It was a way of trying to cover up the harrowing nature of that song with children's toys, one of those pipes that twirls around and this accordion. And it just gave it this atmosphere. But it was accidental.

    This last record was written on guitar, written strumming a guitar for the first time I think ever. And because of that, the songs on *A&E* became almost like standards. They became traditional in their form. My voice is louder than the acoustic because that's how you record these things; you don't put the acoustic louder than the voice. And that's how the songs stayed, but I didn't want to make a record that sounded like a traditional record. But I don't think it was a bad place to start.

DT: Eventually, it seems like all your music's going to be transposed onto the guitar one way or another.

JP: Yeah, generally. But like I said, I don't sit and play guitar. I can't think of anything worse than people who put guitars on and then they say, "I've got a song I want to play to you." That's so far away from my image of rock 'n' roll. I'm more like, "I'm going to put on this thing in the corner. I'm going to be making a fucking racket. If you're interested, you can come and have a listen." But I ain't playing these *songs*, you know. I'm doing this thing that's really fucking important.

DT: You were also saying before that you don't often get asked to do interviews like this.

JP: Well, that's because I didn't know if you were you talking about guitars or guitar playing. What are you talking about? [*laughs*]

DT: I hope it's clearer by now. But I guess the big question is, do you think the guitar is still the basis of the music you make, or has it been for the music you have made?

JP: Wow, there's a question. In an odd way, yeah, but in a weird way, I don't write on guitar, and I don't play guitar recreationally at all. I pick up a guitar when I go on a stage, so it purely is like this thing, this tool. But I think whatever music we make, and however it's played, even if it's played on a flute and a banjo, it's still rock 'n' roll, and I still think that the guitar is the core of rock 'n' roll music. And to me, rock 'n' roll isn't about showing a talent; it's not about saying, "Hey, look how fast my fingers can move on this." Rock 'n' roll is about just hitting a chord as loud and as long as you can. And rock 'n' roll is, like, cheap guitars plugged into the electricity, you know—it's this primal thing. And I think the core of that is still, for me, the guitar.

DT: That's a lot of what I was interested in. Another thing would be moving away from focusing on the playing itself toward other things.

JP: Yeah, like talent. The world doesn't need any talent, you know. This music doesn't need talent. It really is about this spirit thing. And as I've been saying, all the best bits of music, the bits that really move you, are the most elusive things, the hardest parts to find. And that's the search, to find them, and it's really hard to do. It takes a lot to get there, to find these little bits. And it's not about the notes you play. You can get fifteen people to play the same fifty notes on the guitar and maybe only one of them will move you in any way. So it's not about the notes and it's not about the way you do it; it's about whatever it is that hangs between the notes, you know.

It's like, when you play an instrument, you might hit the same chord forever, and then one day, a year-and-a-half in, you move a finger and you go, "Whoa, I've got a second chord." And that's how you learn, you know. And then you'll hit those two chords forever. Or then you might learn how to bend a note up. Unless you go to school and learn it all in one hit. But, I mean, what's the point of that, you know? Then you've just got all this knowledge with no way to tame it.

DT: So where do you think talent fits in?

JP: When I say I don't think talent's important, that doesn't mean I don't admire people who are deeply talented. Like, Jack White is a ferocious player. It doesn't matter what he's involved in, he's like a Tasmanian devil in everything he does. And, you know, nobody can deny Hendrix's talent, but I don't think it's important, and I don't think that it's the most important thing in either of their playing. Jack White could excel ten times more in a kind of "looky-here, looky-here" way, but that's not what's important to his world. It's not what's really fundamental to either of their worlds.

We listened to Bo Diddley this morning and I was thinking, "It's astonishing what he's doing, and he's just not changed the chord for two and a half minutes." But it's just on that *thing*, and it's like . . .

I've said all along, it's hard to drop straight into [free-jazz saxophonist] Peter Brötzmann. Sometimes you need bits on the way to understand where you're going, and that's an evolution-of-music thing. Nobody's working in a vacuum. Everybody's hearing stuff, and it's everywhere. You can hear it out there in the streets. It's just the noise of life, and it goes into everything and everybody distills it, you know, and I've said "distill" too many times now, but everybody distills it in their own way and filters it and puts it out.

FURTIVE GESTURES

DAVID PAJO

PHOTO BY SEBASTIAN MLYNARSKI; COURTESY OF DRAG CITY

"I'm the kind of guy who needs his privacy." —David Pajo

Search for David Pajo online and you'll find traces of him at a site called Pink Hollers and at "Pajo's Old Ass Blog." You'll see references to Aerial M, Stereolab, Interpol, Zwan, and the mysterious Evila. Somewhere behind these breaking links is the real David Pajo, a wiry skullfisher who was born in Texas in 1968 and was raised in the indie city of Louisville, who grew up on metal, fell in with local characters including Will Oldham, then began accelerating through identities like a con man on the lam. Responsible for the stinging, aluminum guitar of Slint and the pensive bass of Tortoise, Pajo materialized in various scene-arios from the late 1980s onward, offering a presence that is stridently peripheral and ever evolving. "I can't understand these bands who have one sound and stick with it for the rest of their lives," he explained to *Penny Black Music* in 2008. "It's not like I have some sort of disorder or something, but I definitely feel the need to do something I haven't done before like every day."

Slint's first album, *Tweez* (1989), was recorded by Steve Albini, but instead of reflecting the aggression of Albini's own band Big Black, it was defined by a listless intensity, a moodiness that takes "Ron" into lurching rhythms, "Nan Ding" to gentle riffs, "Pat" through math-rock problems. Certainly, Pajo was abandoning the rock template in the flanged "Carol," but his real genius was in taking the usual devices and defamiliarizing them: using a heavy riff as a break instead of the main motif, masking doom chords within tempo changes, widening the space between repetitions, mixing up the techniques and effects . . . on *Tweez*, the old-school tools are there, only repurposed. Much of this inventiveness stemmed from a harsh reassessment a young shredder faced circa 1986–87 as his hardcore band Squirrel Bait morphed into its legendary offshoot: "I remember feeling so proud when I figured out all these fancy arpeggios," Pajo recalled in the *A. V. Club*. "[Drummer] Britt [Walford] would just point at me and laugh in my face." By the time they got to 1991's much-lauded *Spiderland*, Pajo and Slint had such full command of their *In Cold Blood* Americana that each of the album's six tracks is draining even to listen to as they wring the life out of it—witness "Don, Aman," a mini horror flick sung by Brian McMahan as if making an elocution in open court. What Slint was doing wasn't as direct as grunge—punk + heavy rock—it was weightier and darker, a conundrum to the band themselves, even, fourteen years later when they reconvened for a few command performances. As Pajo attested to Mark Rowland of *Penny Black Music*, "When we put all the parts together I couldn't work out where the mystery came from. I don't know how it happens."

Pajo's comfort with ambiguity made him the perfect augmentation for the Chicago-based Tortoise, a band that didn't even have a guitarist for its first album and wanted him on (second) bass. As with Slint, Tortoise was the sound of something in the air, a working-out process when rock had nowhere to go besides "post-" iterations that were more encompassing. Instead of Slint's SST fare, blues and twang, Tortoise looked into Krautrock and electronica, dub and jazz, all of which it did up with a kind of classicist grandeur. Like *Spiderland*, their *Millions Now Living Will Never Die* (1996) has been rhapsodized so fully it would do no good to pile more praise on the heap. The important thing is that for a multi-instrumentalist, multistylist like Pajo, Tortoise was a perfect loose fit; he didn't have to do much besides be himself.

Of course, being himself meant Pajo would eventually have to leave Tortoise to concentrate on exactly that. "I'm really good at collaborating," he observed in *Nude as the News* circa 2002. "And it's kind of like I lost my own identity. That's why I started M." Beginning with *As Performed By . . .* in 1997, this collection of solo pseudonyms—including Aerial M and Papa M—developed his troubadour side in the vein of old friend Bonnie "Prince" Billy. Like any reasonable ex–metal kid, Pajo allowed himself the occasional relapse, such as Dead Child, the band of Louisville vets whose 2008 *Attack* finally gave him a chance to show off all that woodshedding he'd turned his jean-jacket on years before.

DAVID TODD: It seems like there's so much pressure on musicians to find a vehicle that works commercially and then stay with it. Is this something you consciously avoided?

DAVID PAJO: It was intentional, at a young age, to not repeat myself. That doesn't mean I couldn't develop an idea across a series of records. I've just always admired artists who surprised me with each new release, for better or worse. The first seven Mekons records are a good example of that.

There will always be a thread that connects the various sounds, and that's what I'm most interested in. I suppose one way of figuring out who the fuck I am is by looking at how that thread exposes itself.

DT: Have you ever actually looked for that thread among the work you've done?

DP: I played different instruments on some albums, so it might be difficult to pinpoint. Also, my level of involvement varies from band to band. My solo music often involves me playing all the instruments, engineering, recording, mixing, mastering, and assembling artwork. But a band like Zwan, for example, was based around one person's vision and I didn't contribute much. Then there were true collaborations, like Slint and Tortoise.

I guess I've always been in multiple bands simultaneously. I was playing drums in the hardcore band Solution Unknown at the same time I was playing guitar with Slint—two very different sounds. Louisvillians used to refer to me as the "band whore."

I think there are concepts that are consistent in my career: make records that get better as they go on, do what thou wilt, don't repeat yourself, less is best, keep it simple, stupid, etc.

DT: Are you concerned that you'll always be judged by your past?

DP: It's unavoidable. Lemmy could form a pop band but he'd always be the guy from Motörhead, and not the guy from Hawkwind.

It used to bug me, living in the shadow of Tortoise and Slint. But I think at this point I've managed to discern myself as an autonomous freakozawa and appreciate the graces of those shadows.

DT: You once said, "The Papa M manifesto is simple: divided we stand." What does that mean?

DP: It's a play on words as well as a worldview. Instead of "united we stand, divided we fall," why not "divided we stand"? Individuals together and distinct.

DT: I was wondering if that had anything to do with all the name changes you've undergone as a solo artist.

DP: It was just a way to delineate time periods. I'm not good at remembering years, but I know the difference between Aerial M and Papa M. Whenever a change in attitude or approach occurred I had to determine whether it justified a name change or not.

I always thought that every aspect of a band should always be in a state of evolution and tuning, and that includes the name of the band.

DT: Another musician who's similarly evolving is your collaborator Will Oldham—is that a Louisville thing, by the way? If it's not, what is it about Louisville that's so "indie," then?

DP: That term "indie" kinda turns my stomach, but I think I know what you're getting at.

People don't seem to realize that Louisville always had an amazing music scene—absolutely God-like bands that you'll never hear. I'm talking about mid-to-late '70s punk rock bands. There were key players back then who would go to NYC and come back with all these records. We had an art school in the '70s, and punk bands became an extension of that. We also had a DC-style hardcore band that opened for Minor Threat and every great band in the early '80s. To this day, if you ask Ian MacKaye about local heroes Malignant Growth, he'll shake his head and say they were the greatest fucking band on the planet.

And he's not being dramatic. It's true!

DT: What about the wider scene at that time—Touch and Go, Drag City, AmRep, all those labels and bands—how do you see that now?

DP: That moment was massive and it's truly undocumented. I think it's a crime that Touch and Go were left out of that *American Hardcore* documentary, for example. But that's what I like about the Midwest: we're a secret society.

DT: Has your opinion of those bands changed much?

DP: Yes, a lot of bands just don't age very well. Jesus Lizard still rules, and Royal Trux. The Cows. Void. I won't name the bands that deserve to be forgotten.

DT: It seems like that period was when rock music was arguably the most polarized it's ever been between independent and mainstream. Did that limit the ambition of the musicians you knew?

DP: Definitely. There was more integrity playing with a blues band from the West End than playing a big club in Berlin to thousands of people. I usually

left bands once they started to get popular, only because I couldn't compre-
hend that level of being in a band. There were too many chefs in the kitchen
and it didn't seem tangible.

Now that I've had more experience and I understand the chain of events
that goes into a mainstream band, it doesn't faze me anymore. Especially
after touring with Dead Child, I've decided that I'm too old to be sleeping
on floors after a show. There's a comfort level that bigger bands are allowed,
and I think it's a good lifestyle for musicians who want to be around for the
long haul.

DT: You broke out with Slint, which to outsiders seemed to present a new
sound without a lot of context. Was there a buildup for the band that we
didn't see?

DP: Among band members, definitely. We were into groups that are well
known now but were pretty obscure back then, in the mid-'80s, especially in
Louisville, Kentucky: Hüsker Dü, Big Black, Sonic Youth, Dinosaur Jr., Meat
Puppets, Minutemen. When bands around us were getting louder and more
extreme, we decided to get quieter and more vulnerable. We took from the
above-mentioned bands but also took in the old-time country and Delta
blues that we were most excited about.

DT: What about thrash and metal?

DP: Britt Walford and I were in a thrash/metal/weirdo band called Maurice. Our last song became the first Slint song. When we broke up, Britt and
I started Slint with Ethan Buckler of King Kong, and the bass player and
singer went on to form Kinghorse—I don't think they were down with our
wimpy, clean-guitar, Minutemen-influenced songs!

DT: Is that sound you described something you were consciously going for,
or did it come about naturally?

DP: Our only agenda, as I remember it, was to do something different. In
1986, I had a long talk with Ethan Buckler about how fucking awful all the

new music was and how we wanted to do something unlike anything else. Like all my favorite music, it was born out of frustration. At least for myself.

A lot of it was just about interplay between the melodic instruments. We were trying to express a mood, I guess. Something hazy and dark. Our focus was nonspecific.

I always thought that we had round edges, as opposed to the hard edges of conventional rock. We were going for a bass sound that sounded like the low notes on a piano.

I imagined that the only people who would like us in the future would be the same people who owned Victrolas. I remember saying that to Britt over twenty years ago!

DT: With Slint, you played a lot of arpeggiated lines on songs like "Breadcrumb Trail," as opposed to heavier riffs like on "Pam." Where did that come from?

DP: I was really into that style. I think it developed from a couple different sources. The Meat Puppets were doing it at that point. Sonic Youth a bit. [Philip Glass's] *Mishima* soundtrack was a huge influence on my guitar playing in those days. In fact, Philip Glass had a big impact on me in general, and he made a career out of arpeggios.

DT: "Glenn" combines one of those with a recurring riff—how did those parts fit together?

DP: Our method of songwriting was the same method we used playing in punk bands: someone brings in a riff and we all hammer it into a song. The main difference was that we were shooting for something more organic. Since none of us were particularly good at improvising, we had to plot out every single movement to give the illusion that it was loose and natural.

Also, we didn't want to repeat ourselves from song to song. That is, we didn't find a sound and then hone it to perfection, like the Fall or the Ramones, for example. Each song was different from the one previous.

On the vinyl for the EP [*Slint*, 1994], both "Glenn" and "Rhoda" have a drawing that represents the song. "Glenn" has a three-lined triangle on it, which is perfect, because all the repetitions and arrangements are based on multiples of three.

DT: After Slint, how did you wind up joining Tortoise?

DP: It's pretty common these days to look for a wide range of music in obscure places, but I think all of us musicians—especially the midwestern contingent—had been doing it since we were kids. By the early '90s, with the start of alternative music becoming defined as a style, I was so disappointed with all current music—I despised grunge—and the first Tortoise record and Stereolab's *Transient Random-Noise Bursts* were the only two current albums that excited me. So naturally it was a dream come true to eventually join both bands.

DT: Did you have much of a dub or electronic sensibility going into those bands?

DP: I didn't know much about Krautrock before I joined Tortoise. Living and playing with those guys really opened my brain to some sounds I'd never heard before.
My background was in Slint, of whom they were fans.

DT: With Tortoise you were playing bass. Is that different with Tortoise than with other bands?

DP: It's not too dissimilar. But the main difference is that there were usually two basses going at once. Doug McCombs was a true bass player and had lockdown on the low end. I played the bass more like a guitar, playing higher melodies, chords, and whatnot. I always saw the bass as an extension of the guitar.

DT: It's not easy to tell who's doing what on *Millions*.

DP: That was always part of the charm for me. It wasn't a gimmick to switch instruments; that's how they wrote songs. You just added ideas to songs using whatever instrument you felt like playing. At a typical Tortoise concert in the mid-'90s I would play bass, guitar, drums, Rhodes [piano], and marimba, probably some other stuff I don't even remember now.

DT: What was the process like with Tortoise for "Glass Museum"?

DP: "Glass Museum" isn't a typical Tortoise song—I wrote that when we were rehearsing in a barn out in the Vermont countryside. It started life as Slint-esque song and became a Slint-esque Tortoise song. I originally wanted it to be different from what it became, but I still think it turned out cool.

DT: If you didn't like "indie" too much, what did you make of the term "post-rock"?

DP: It was like nails on a chalkboard for such a long time. I still think it's a vague, broad term, at least for those early bands that got lumped into it. You know, Can never called themselves a Krautrock band.

Nowadays if a band gets described as post-rock or shoegaze, my eyes glaze over and start to cross.

DT: I felt the term could be useful in leading audiences to expect something other than an old-fashioned rock show, if nothing else. Was that something Tortoise had to deal with?

DP: Tortoise was always well received as a live band, despite some early shows that some dolts thought were boring. Tortoise had roots in punk rock, and I always respected that about them. But they are just as engaging in a theater atmosphere as a filthy club. They are a bass-heavy, uber-rhythmic band—it's acceptable to miss the subtleties and enjoy the grooves.

I've never been in a band that had it as hard as Dead Child!

DT: There's one last thing I wanted to ask you about, which is the fasting and cleansing I've heard you're into. Is that something that affects your music?

DP: Binging and purging is all part of the bigger picture. Although as you get older you naturally get less interested in extremes and more interested in balance. I'm trying to unencumber myself from the past, at least those fragments of the past that persist as obstacles. Cleaning out the physical pipes kind of forces me to clean house emotionally as well.

The goal has always been to contact someplace pure and irrational inside of me.

21

THE JOY OF DESPAIR

KIM DEAL AND KELLEY DEAL

KIM DEAL

T he Breeders began as a leap of faith for twins Kim and Kelley Deal (born June 10, 1961, in Dayton, Ohio) while still in their teens. After mastering what she calls the "Neil Young easy guitar" book, compulsively songwriting Kim pulled harmonizing Kelley along as a duo in their hometown's dives. Together they charmed the shit-kickers with Hank Williams and Everly Brothers covers, crooning originals such as "Do You Love Me Now?" that moved the pregnant girls next door to tears. Though talented (for sure) and focused (enough), the pair were unable to find a rhythm section willing to go coed in a land where the wankers wore their spandex high. After graduation, they put the dream on hold and trudged into adulthood: Kelley defied her party demons with a high-security tech job at Hughes Aircraft, while Kim hit the college circuit.

With Kelley in L.A., newlywed Kim relocated to Boston in 1986, where she answered an ad for a bass player that led her to singer/guitarist Charles Thompson (a.k.a. Black Francis, a.k.a. Frank Black) and guitarist Joey Santiago, and a whirlwind ride that began with the Pixies' 1987 EP *Come On Pilgrim*. Over the seven years of their original lifespan, the Pixies grew into one of the most inventive groups ever, while on a personal level they grew apart (but not too far apart to reunite in 2004 as a touring entity). For Kim, the problem wasn't the punky, surfy, nearly perfect Thompson creations the band was doing; rather, it was her own stockpile of infectious tunes they weren't. As irrepressible as she appeared in the band's press, there was always more to Kim than the "Ms. John Soda" alias she adopted for their early recordings, a complementary figure content to bide her time in the background. Her bass lines throbbed "like the Cure," she recalls, "like keyboard, *do-do-do-do*, where they would never stop." Her background vocals oozed charisma, and the rare tracks she cowrote, like "Gigantic," took their place among the band's best. "I'm a rhythm guitar player," Kim says, meaning at her essence. "I can't play lead and I can't play bass either. I was always a songwriter." As the Pixies wound down, she began moonlighting with the equally stunted Tanya Donelly of Throwing Muses, working up songs such as "Doe" and "Lime House," which their mutual label, 4AD, jumped on. With 1990's *Pod* the Breeders were back—minus Kelley, stuck at her day job like a kid inside with a summer cold.

"We were a band like a guitar-based band," Kim said in a 1994 Breeders promo. This was made clear by the high-pitched stitchings, grungy jangling, angling solos, and classic distortion Kim and Tanya layered all over that first release. Coming to her senses in time to serve as third guitarist for the Breeders' *Safari* EP in 1992, Kelley took over lead duties when Donelly left to form Belly. The fact that Kelley had never really played lead guitar—or any guitar, for that matter—didn't slow her down much. By their breakthrough *Last Splash* in 1993 she was pulling splintering harmonics ("New Year"), off-kilter slide ("No Aloha"), blunt Stoogery ("S.O.S."), and descending snarks ("Flipside") out of her bag of tricks. "I would rather listen to a bad player than someone who plays stock blues riffs," Kim told the *Guardian* in 2002. "And Kelley is so musical. She creates new parts; most guitarists just repeat everything they've ever heard." Coming out of the Frankocracy of the Pixies, Kim did most of the writing and singing in the Breeders, leaving Kelley—who's released two albums of her own originals to date—to serve as her interpreter. But when asked by the *Dallas Observer* if that reflected anything about the group's pecking order, Kelley replied, "It's Kim's and my band, but I let her think it's her band. And she probably lets me think it's our band. It's a total mindfuck."

The Breeders toured hard in support of *Last Splash* hits "Cannonball" and "Saints" until burning out on the road. They went on hiatus as of 1994, leaving Kim to release the garage rock *Pacer* with her group the Amps the next year. Describing herself in the *Guardian* as "obsessed with sound," Kim also continued cultivating tones that were darker and shiftier than the Breeders' "summer is ready" rep, as evidenced by the dreamy Bible-smoking of "The She" and the bass wriggling of "Put on a Side" on their 2002 come-back CD, *Title TK*. "I saw Brownsville Station, [Ted] Nugent, Stevie Ray Vaughan, Black Oak Arkansas," Kim says, describing a musical childhood she's lucky to have survived. "But it's weird—if I was talking about guitar I liked, I would probably mention other instrumentalists like Nat King Cole's piano playing or Sarah Vaughan's voice." On the Breeders' latest CD, *Mountain Battles* (2008), Kim quietly picks and croons "Here No More" like an old country ballad, happy to use the guitar as a vehicle for making music as opposed to hockey-arena spectacle.

DAVID TODD: So who are the guitarists you've liked over the years?

KIM DEAL: I like Thurston Moore.

DT: Are there others?

KIM: Let me think . . . [*laughs*] I like Willie Nelson. He plays a really good guitar. There's a jazzy sensibility to him, not exactly jazzy but really nice—I mean, the bass lines he plays at the same time he's doing a melody line.

But what is it about him? I like his *tone*. There's some kind of sadness to it. The texture is good, and, again, the lines played together—and Thurston too, you know; in a lot of ways he's got a couple of things going on at once. Maybe he doesn't look at it like that; maybe he's just looking at one melody that has a dissonant thing that forms itself as a second part. I like that kind of complicated thing, but the thing I don't like . . .

You know, I remember when Van Halen first came out. The first album was exciting, but I was never a huge Eddie Van Halen fan, there was so much *diddlee-diddlee-diddlee-diddlee-bleeee!* There was a lot of busy work just for the sake of being busy, and that never moved me. When somebody sounds like they could be either doing scales or the lead, like, "I'm not sure, is he doing rudiments right now? Or is this a good melody line that moves me?" You know, because a really simple guitar line can be moving.

I'm not one of the people who like shredding, up-high things. I do have a nostalgia for Lynyrd Skynyrd and some Zeppelin; I like the Allman Brothers too, and Joe Walsh. But, you know, Neil Young had those long leads but they never came off like that. "Cinnamon Girl," I think Kelley counted how many times he hit that one note and it was like twenty-one times or something. And she counted how many times he hit that note—not how many seconds the lead was, but how many times he hit that one note in a row. So it doesn't have to be complicated to be good, you know.

So . . . who else is a good guitar player?

I like Jimi Hendrix's playing.

DT: What do you think is the difference between Hendrix and the people who overplayed?

KIM: I guess if he had a rhythm guitar player in the band he might've turned into that kind of *diddlee-diddlee-diddleeooooh*. But since he was responsible for the rhythm a lot of the time, if he left it too long it would've dropped completely out. The way Hendrix was playing, in the [Band of] Gypsys or whatever band he was in, I think a lot of the grooves, he had a big solid part in them. With Hendrix, his guitar would be part of the groove.

DT: His solos always have those rhythm moments thrown in.

KIM: And he's doing two things at once again, isn't he? I like two things at once, I guess.

DT: What about your philosophy for the guitar with the Breeders?

KIM: I think of the songs. Yeah, the guitar was always an instrument for songwriting, that's all. Because I usually had the burden of getting the song up and keeping it moving. A lot of times if I quit playing the whole thing stopped. Not because I'm so brilliant [*laughs*], but because it was my song and I was the one who knew how it went.

DT: I see that when you perform. The bar chords you're playing are pushing things.

KIM: Yeah.

DT: Kelley might sit back on a section or two but you're always going.

KIM: Exactly.

DT: Don't tell her I put it that way.

KIM: [*laughs*] Oh yeah, you know, one of the great things with Kelley was that she was really malleable at first, because she didn't have any preconceptions. Same thing with Joe, it was easy to say, "Hey, try this!" And they'd totally do it; they'd be like, "Whee! Who cares?" But as I noticed with Kelley, it's getting to where I can't even suggest she's not a great guitar player now. I mean, she's fine, whatever . . .

My point being that they . . . yeah, forget my point, I'll just get in trouble if I say anything else.

[*laughs*] My point is, I wish they would stay like that, you know! They don't stay like that! They become a little more stubborn.

DT: But there is a trade-off there, don't you think? They might lose one thing as they gain another.

KIM: Yeah, I like that. See, I bet somebody would come up with some great things in a song because they didn't have those limitations where they think of themselves as a guitar player. If they think of themselves as a great guitar player, they're always going to have to play something that sounds good rudimentarily, or rudimentally. [*laughs*]

You know what I find interesting? Joe Santiago—in the '80s, the Pixies were in [drummer] David [Lovering]'s garage and we were working on a song, and we were like, "Oh, this will be the section for the lead," you know? And we all kind of looked at Joe, and then we started the song again. And then here comes the section, and the three of us are playing—we're rhythm, even Charles is rhythm now, right—and we're looking at Joe, and Joe gets really nervous, and he looks at us, and then he gets embarrassed, right, and then he bends over and he goes, "*Whrrr-whrr-whrr-whrr-whrr!*" and he's just joking around, and it sounds fucking fantastic, you know? And everybody's like, "Oh my God, do that! No, for real, do that exactly!"

That becomes the "Vamos" lead. He goes, "*Whrrr-whrr-whrr*," but that's the reason why. So it is interesting that it's not only about the guitar player but it's about who you have in the room, a group of people with a shared feeling, a moment in time that allows the guitar player to play something different. It doesn't have to be about the best melody line ever to have a good guitar part come up.

But I guess the point is to be able to look at music like that, to have a sense of humor about it. To be confident that you don't have to rock somebody's socks off, you don't have to show that you have chops at every moment. You know, have you ever seen a band and you don't know if they're good or bad because they're so loud you can't actually hear them? And usually they're not very good, because they're not doing the hard part, which is actually coming up with something effectively in your face and confident and scary; they're just obliterating the audience by sound. It's like looking at somebody on steroids. It doesn't mean that band is dangerous or exciting at all. It usually means the opposite: if they're too loud they're usually not going to be very brave in their music.

DT: I suppose the exceptions are rare, the guitarists who know everything . . .

KIM: And they can throw it away?

DT: Yeah.

KIM: Yeah, exactly. Which is probably the hardest thing to do, where you actually do know everything and then ignore it all. Yeah, I just never learned it all because I never wanted to. I always wanted to make sure I wasn't ever going *diddlee-diddlee-diddlee-diddlee*. If somebody asked me, "Hey, play something on this song," I didn't want to go, "OK, what's it in?" "A." "OK." *Diddlee-diddlee-diddlee-diddlee*. That would be a nightmare. But a lot of people think that is what a good guitar player should do. They think that's the only thing a good guitar player should do. And to me, that is a nightmare. That is *the* nightmare.

DT: I have to say, even if you don't play that way for real, you're the best air-guitar shredder I've ever seen.

KIM: Oh yeah, I know 'em all. Classic rock, right here in Dayton. The Schenker brothers, they were big. Michael and Rudolph. UFO. That's what I grew up on. So I know a lot of guitar, and I can't tell you how many times I've been at a concert, a little show around here or at Hara Arena, where I almost felt sick to my stomach by the guitar solo that was happening. It was almost as bad as the drum solo that was ready to come up. So it's not really what one can do with the guitar, it's the damage one can do. [*laughs*] I mean, I actually like the sound of a guitar. I like it, there's a lot of good it can do. The guitar can be a force for good, too.

DT: Are all these things why you lean toward playing the acoustic so much?

KIM: I didn't always have an electric, you know. When you have an electric you need cords and an amplifier—you have to know about gear. But acoustic, I knew how to do that because my dad had an acoustic guitar in the room. Eventually, I got an electric.

DT: But even recently you play the acoustic a lot, sometimes like an electric with a distortion pedal.

KIM: Oh yeah, it just sounds badass! I like an acoustic because again I don't really like shreddy, high-pitched stuff, I like the *boomsh!*, you know, a big and thick sound. And I think the acoustic is hugely big and thick. And I've got it to the point where I can control it pretty well, so I can play it like a wave, ride it like this *beast*! [*laughs*] But you know, the challenge is to never let that gallop out of control.

DT: Are you ever tempted to play more lead guitar?

KIM: I would love to do it on somebody else's song. I think I'd be good at it. But, again, if it's my song, literally, a lot of times if I'm not driving it the song will stop.

DT: Do you ever play lead on your own, just at home?

KIM: Not lead, no. For songwriting, sure, I play all the time. Or not even for songwriting, I'll pick the guitar up and just play around with it, totally. But always with the hope that I'll come up with something.

DT: Are you also inclined toward keeping things simple songwriting-wise? I don't mean simple as a negative, but a song like "Here No More," that's the antithesis of the band playing so loud you can't hear them.

KIM: Oh, it is simple. That's something built like it could be done anytime, anywhere.

Yeah, I like that stuff. If it's done well, the simple stuff can be really good. And it's really hard to do actually, super-simple stuff. That's why I think "Here No More" was so successful for me, because it really is hard for me to do that. I'm trying to get better at that.

It is funny, though—I mentioned that I like Willie Nelson and certain things because they've got this stately, somber effect to them. And I've said a couple of times that that *diddlee-diddlee-diddlee* stuff, I'm not really inclined to like. So it does make sense that I would typically not tend to sit down to write *diddlee-diddlee-diddlee*. Yeah.

DT: What do you think that means in songwriting terms? Are there equivalents to those guitar clichés?

KIM: You know, being from Ohio and being from the country music area here—I don't know where it comes from—but I have a problem with singing something four times over and over again for a chorus. Now, I've done it before, and I can do it as a backup singer with Charles, doing his things, like, "I've been tired, I've been tired," singing that for the big chorus. But I've gotta tell you, I'm not really good at writing a song like that. And I think people respond to that, and if you don't do it they get like, "Why are you fucking wasting our time? Give us this chorus where we can sing the thing over and over again!" [*laughs*]

I'm not better than anybody, but if I'm the one standing there, I feel a little stupid doing that. I'm not a natural frontperson anyway—I do enjoy singing but I'm not a good singer, I can't hold vibrato or anything, and I don't want to. I never wanted to be the frontperson, I just wanted to be in a band. So if I stand in front of people with a guitar, and I wrote a song—first of all, it has to mean something to me, OK? My relationship to what I'm doing has to be real or I feel embarrassed. And it's hard for me to stand there and do four things in a row, because it really doesn't mean much. Even though it's fun to sing. I enjoy songs like that, but, jeez, I don't know why people think I have to do that.

DT: I understand all that, although I'm surprised to hear you never felt comfortable as a frontperson.

KIM: I did more when I was drinking, you know? [*laughs*] Now it's just hard to stand up when I'm not drunk. It was always hard. Joe and I were always like that, whereas David Lovering, he's a magician. He's an entertainer. Charles is the same way. I swear to God, he should be in the opera. He loves to be onstage. Joe and I are just like, "Oh, this is so embarrassing"—not embarrassing, but awkward, you know.

Joe says there are two kinds of frontmen: the preacher and the karate instructor. Elvis was karate. Anthony Kiedis, karate. Charles, preacher. U2, preacher. They're either the preacher or they're the karate instructor.

DT: Which are you?

KIM: Oh God, I don't know. I don't think the frontperson decides. I think it's like a nickname, you can't give it to yourself.

DT: Are there other songwriting principles you have besides that "four times" thing?

KIM: I do have a pet peeve. I try not to write middling songs that only work well enough to where, you know, they're gonna need a tambourine and a keyboard to sound good. [*laughs*] I tend to enjoy that—like, Van Morrison does that stuff. I think Bruce Springsteen and Tom Petty, all three write songs like that—and Sheryl Crow and U2—where it all sounds better with a little tambourine and keyboard. Because there's really no beat to it, it's just like, "Hey . . . We're gonna have a good time tonight." And a lot of times I don't know whether I think that's a good song or not.

Like if I did the Tom Petty thing: "He was a good man, loves his mama, *ber-ner-nar-nar, nar-nar-nah*." [*taps a beat*] Just wait . . . he's telling a story, John Cougarish, pretty good . . . [*tap-tap*] "'Cause I'm *freeee*! Free fallin'! 'Cause I'm *freeee*! Free . . . free . . . free . . ." And then there's my problem. You know, the backup singers come in and they do the "Free fallin', fallin' fallin'," and then I get confused. I go, "Did he just write a good song?" If I'm onstage and I'm singing that song, and I'm standing next to some girls or some boys that go, "Free-fallin', fallin', fallin'," I think I'd feel like a *douche*. But to everybody else that's Top 40 successful radio. That *is* success. Glittering, shining, respected. By the industry and by the people. That is gold-standard stuff right there. Everywhere.

DT: That's very well put. The only thing left is to call Joe Santiago, ask him if Tom Petty's a kicker or a preacher.

KIM: A kicker! [*laughs*] Not a kicker! A karate master.

DT: I thought Elvis was kung-fu.

KIM: No, it's *kara-tay*, dude. He actually *took* karate. He actually *did* karate.

DT: What I notice is that your songs are moodier overall, for lack of a better word, than people associate them with being.

KIM: Our stuff is moody? I like that.

DT: Me too. But it seems like the Breeders are associated with this up-tempo, bright sound, but I found going back over your albums that a lot of the songs were darker in some way.

KIM: You know, I did see this review of *Mountain Battles*, people were saying how depressing it was, like, "God, I wish you would get happy again." I was thinking, "I'm not any less happy." It seemed weird. And it's really hard to write a song that's just happy. You know, "Divine Hammer," talking about the hammer, I'm making fun of the whole Peter, Paul and Mary genre of folk music. But it sounds happy.

DT: It has a hook and a catchy guitar line.

KIM: Mmm-hmm.

DT: But a lot of your other songs have slower tempos and use an organ or other instrumentation, like "No Way."

KIM: Yeah.

DT: Is there anything you have in mind with those?

KIM: I don't know. It does seem to be like that. I feel like I do do that. Like, "Spark" is moody and weird—and that's another thing, we're supposed to be being weird for the sake of being weird. [*laughs*] Oh my God, if only! Like I could stop it!

You know, when we did "Cannonball," it starts with my brother's harmonica mike plugged into the Marshall and me going, "*Ah-huh-ah-huh-ah-huh.*" I never thought that would get on the radio. And it is funny, because out of everybody in the *world* who was doing something to get on the radio and then who needs to be hated because she was mainstream, it's like, that's *not me*. But it's funny that for a lot of people I am that person. And that's really true. And I can spend all that time in the Pixies and all that time afterwards in the Breeders, but, you know, that *one song* on the radio . . .

DT: Is that frustrating?

KIM: No, it's not. It's weird. I might think the same thing about someone else, actually . . . although I don't know if I would, because I'd probably know the band before they had a hit. Because I like music, I wouldn't just know the person from one song.

DT: Partly it was that time, the early '90s.

KIM: What d'you mean?

DT: If you had a hit then, it was held against you.

KIM: It's true! I agree, but there was a reason why, because there were those heavy metal assholes who would do anything for a hit. I mean, they were acting like idiots just to get on the radio. "I'm too sexy for my shirt"—there were really idiotic things going on.

DT: I'm not saying this because it would get on the radio, but one thing it seems like you could do is a quieter, country-style album. That music seems to come naturally for you.

KIM: You know, it does. I think Kelley and I have known that we could do that for a long time, even back when we were playing the Ground Round. And you know, nobody would play with me then, not in Dayton, because I was a girl. It was like, literally, it just was not done. You know Blondie, they were laughed at here. I remember specifically people thinking Blondie was a joke. There was so much [Dan] Fogelberg and Loggins & Messina, so much Ovation guitar. There were so many dudes and they were all singer-songwriters. And no rock band would play with me. So I finally called up Charles and his friend Joe—because I had just gotten to town when I saw their ad; I was in Boston for like a week. With the Pixies, I finally got to be in a rock band. You know, there's a drummer in the room, it's, like, real. It was so exciting. It was never even possible in Dayton.

Anyway, I think the idea of doing a quiet acoustic set with Kelley reminds me too much of doing four sets a night at Joe's Fish House. The idea of doing a country record with Kelley, it's like, "I guess so, when we *die*. When we're close to *dying*, I'll do that again."

DT: I'm not trying to force it on you.

Kim: No! Somebody asked us to do it and we've been talking about doing it.

DT: It does seem like it's in your DNA.

Kim: Yeah. We've done it a lot.

DT: You harmonize well together.

Kim: Yeah, sisters. With family, it's always nice. I think so too.

I am getting really sentimental now. A couple of things I'm doing sound like the early '70s, like "Goodtime Charlie's got the blues," that kind of thing, "The train they call New Orleans in the city." And also George Jones, when the country-ish guys, the jailhouse guys were doing romantic songs, sexy, tinted-sunglasses songs with sideburns and hair, Charlie Rich and that. Yeah, I'm kind of doing some things like that, but I'm turning them into more like a Velvet Underground thing, I hope. Because I'm not able to pull them off like that.

KELLEY DEAL

Born eleven minutes ahead of her twin, Kelley Deal at least tried to be the dutiful older sibling who played it straight, first by pursuing a career in computer science and later by struggling against the temptations that came with the Breeders' commercial peak. A 1994 heroin arrest led to a stint in rehab—and for the Breeders, an extended break—but she bounced back as leader of her own Kelley Deal 6000, whose *Go to the Sugar Altar* (1996) and *Boom! Boom! Boom!* (1997) were filled with power-pop sketches, Lynchian moods, and fucked-up love songs. ("You've got to make sure that you're flexible and unprofessional enough to deviate from the plan," Kelley said in the documentary *The Real Deal.* "And to know that when you deviate from the plan, it's just opportunities.") Before the Breeders reconvened in 2002, she also duetted with Kris Kristofferson on a version of "Angel Flying Too Close to the Ground" and covered Pantera's "Fucking Hostile" for the *Free the West Memphis 3* benefit CD. But perhaps the best reflection of her unique vision was the weirdo group she put together with singer Sebastian Bach, Frog Jimmy Flemion, and Smashing Pumpkin Jimmy Chamberlin, an experiment that somehow worked on *The Last Hard Men* (1998).

Like her sister, the hoarder Kelley has proved that it's never wise to underestimate what she has in storage. "A thick fabric doesn't necessarily mean you used a heavy-weight yarn," Kelley wrote in *Bags That Rock*, her 2008 book on, yes, knitting. "Some yarns are sturdy enough to stand on their own. Others need nothing more than to be knitted with smallish needles."

DAVID TODD: You've said that the roadies are always more skilled guitar players than you.

KELLEY DEAL: Oh yeah.

DT: So what was it like when you were first starting out, coming right out of a regular job and going public with your playing so quickly?

KELLEY: Oddly enough it has to do with this idea of . . . my mother was an early childhood education teacher, and she had this idea of play and learning, that it was really important to the joy that came from that, and how music is joyful and it's playing and it's having a great time, you know. But because of this other idea that only certain people could do music, were allowed somehow to do it—and maybe it's because I learned guitar so late in life—I always felt like I didn't belong, that I shouldn't be holding a guitar. Like I was always going to be found out. And I really kind of thought, you know, "Fuck you. I can play what I want on this here. And it's music. If it's communicating something for me then it's music." And so when I started doing the Kelley Deal 6000—again, I thought I had no right to. You know, I had just learned how to play guitar, basically. My sister was famous; why they even knew my name is because I looked like her. But I really was like, "Well, fuck you." Not in a mean way, but kind of taking charge of it. "Yeah, that's right. I don't know what I'm doing. And I'm gonna have fun being weird about it." I was championing the idea that nobody could own it. You couldn't own music or the joy of it or the right to play it in any way.

DT: Privately, were you self-conscious?

KELLEY: Oh yeah. I don't know if you've seen the "Safari" video that we did.

It's kind of an homage to the "Paranoid" video by Sabbath, done like that. And that day I got off of work—I was working at Litton Computer Services, I think—we were supposed to meet downtown at a warehouse here in Dayton, and Josephine Wiggs was there, and Tanya Donelly, she was in town, and Jon Mattock from Spacemen 3. And I had my suit on, because I thought it was weird to change, like, "Wait, let me get my rock outfit on." I couldn't seem so dishonest somehow.

So . . . that was the day I learned bar chords. The day of the video. Because on "Safari"—did I play on that at all in the studio? I don't think so, 'cause that was recorded in England . . . No. So it was weird. You know, you can imagine. And I'm sure the people setting up, I'm sure everybody knew how to play guitar. And I'm going [*moves hands slowly*]. [*laughs*]

DT: But you played music growing up?

KELLEY: Yeah. Kim and I were in this thing since we were fifteen or sixteen.

DT: And in your cubicle years, did you still think of yourself as a music person?

KELLEY: A music *person*, yeah.

DT: Slash musician?

KELLEY: No, not really.

DT: Hadn't crossed over yet.

KELLEY: Correct. Still have not. [*laughs*]

DT: What I'm getting to is, you've said that people tend to see your situation as a good story, one sister being brought into the band by the other out of the blue. But you had some things to start with.

KELLEY: Yeah. And actually my first instrument was drums. I was a drummer first, 'cause of Karen Carpenter.

DT: Did you take lessons?

KELLEY: Oh yeah, from third grade on to probably sixteen. When I just started smoking too much pot, you know. Got into the wrong music. [*laughs*]

DT: I find some other things you were bringing in interesting too, like you mentioned the idea of joy. Because in the early '90s there weren't a lot of people who were making what you'd call joyful music.

KELLEY: Right. It was considered very uncool.

DT: Well, in the Breeders' case it was cool, and that's part of what makes them unique. But what do you think of that, the role of joy in music for you?

KELLEY: There's no other reason to . . . how do I even describe it? I mean, even when I'm doing something super bleak it's the joy of the bleakness I like. I mean, that's so silly to talk about, but there's not a better word that describes it to me other than joy, the joy of that despair, which seems really pompous and bullshitty, but it's *true*. Because why else would you be alive, you know? Why put up with all the other shit? Maybe religious people talk about it more in terms of "faith," but I'm very secular when it comes to all that stuff. I get a lot of joy out of making music with others. I enjoy *that*. I guess I'm just not very disciplined, but I'm not good at practicing, you know; I'd rather sit and play right now and just investigate songs: "Ooh, I wonder where he's going. Ooh, listen, he went there; I wouldn't have done that." You know? It's like having a conversation, an emotional conversation, without all the necessity for words.

DT: You said something about that before, where the words fit into the music for you. Is that not something you're drawn to?

KELLEY: I don't know . . . When I listen to a song, very few of the words actually speak to me, but, like, the shit behind the song, all the nonverbal communication, is what actually speaks to me more. And that could come from lots of different instrumentations, although it happens to be the guitar most of the time. But you know, when you think about something like a Hank Williams song with the "whip-por-will," just having that word in a song, I mean, that's good, but there's a lot of other stuff that I don't like.

Oh, the "Hallelujah" song, when Leonard Cohen talks about the minor fall, the major lift . . . yeah, that's a really neat use of words too. But most often the words don't do anything for me. Like, maybe your favorite song is Santo & Johnny's "Sleep Walk," and there ain't no words on that.

DT: So it's more about what the song evokes for you.

KELLEY: Totally. Whatever emotion is being evoked, versus being told something. But I think a lot of people are like that.

You know, I've been thinking about songs and songwriting, and although I appreciate well-written songs—I can appreciate the artistry that is "presented" with a well-written song, and that's people like, you know, Elton John—but being well written has nothing to do with whether or not I like the song. It has absolutely nothing to do with whether it speaks to me in any way—emotionally, intellectually—other than as some interesting sound waves just going through my head. It's like when you look at art. You can look at a piece of art and you can say, "Wow, that really looks like a tree. Damn, that's amazing!" And that's all that it evokes is, "What a craftsman." And not to diminish the skill and the hours that went into that, but it doesn't hit me in any way. But then you can have something like a Rothko—which is demeaning to him, I'm sure there's a lot of skill in that even though it looks like somebody just went *tchht!*—where you just think, "*Wow.*" And it actually speaks to you in some way, and you're looking at it emotionally or physically and you're not looking at it like, "That really looks like a leaf. How'd he do that?" So songwriting to me is kind of like that.

I know I'm not writing "songs." Not real songs. I know that. But nor do I want to. And there are some songs I've written that have a verse, then a little bridge thing, then it goes back to the chorus. I do that, but it's because that's what that one song is. It helps the message, whatever that is. But my favorite stuff has very little to do with song *writing*, you know?

DT: With the Kelley Deal 6000, a song like "Canyon" seems pretty . . .

KELLEY: Straightforward? Yeah, exactly. Because it's a "song," not a feeling.

DT: But then a lot of the others on your solo albums, and on the Breeders albums, are more evocative, so to speak. This is something that also came up with Kim, that even on *Last Splash* there are songs with different complexions.

KELLEY: I think that *Last Splash* was so defined by songs like "Cannonball" and "Divine Hammer" and "Saints," which are all classic, poppy—not that Saints is a "pop" song necessarily, but it's a rock song, and it has a repeatable chorus thing—and then "Drivin' on 9," which is a cover song. But other than those four . . . "Mad Lucas" is like this complete fucking dirge, and "Roi" has this reprise that's just craziness, and "New Year" starts out really slow and then gets hard-rocky, but it's not a pop song. So there are a lot of non-pop songs on it, it's just that it's defined by the ones that were. And so when people listen to records like *Mountain Battles*, they go, "I like their old stuff." I'm like, "Man, did you ever hear anything other than the 'Cannonball'?" Because *Mountain Battles* is not out of the spectrum of our stuff at all.

DT: Are these things we've been talking about the reasons why you asked Dave Shouse to produce *Go to the Sugar Altar*? He had a rich, moody sound with the Grifters.

KELLEY: You know, there was one particular Grifters EP called *Eureka* I just . . . it was in the summer, and I find that there's something about the summer—there are certain things that I relate to, and this is all about mood, whether it's books or music. I remember reading [Marguerite Duras's] *The Lover* back in the '80s, it was really hot and muggy, and I just remember that book, all this *sensuality* and *foreign* stuff, and I don't actually remember anything that happens in the book but I remember, you know, the feeling of it. And the same thing with the *Eureka* EP, all this wonderful music, and I remember, like, it was hot and I was having to clean out a storage shed, and there was a lot of sweating, something about it being hot and sweaty, and I just remember I loved how that made me feel. All that . . . whatever it was.

DT: That sort of swampy, barroom feel?

KELLEY: I do like that. I do. But it bothers me if you go too far. If you go too far that way it becomes something else, just fully clocked into white man's blues. You know, you gotta be careful. Especially coming from Ohio, where every band on a Friday night at the bar, they're all doing the blues.

DT: The blues seems to be the dividing line for guitarists.

KELLEY: Yeah. I try to stay away from it. But I can't help it sometimes!

DT: But whether you consider yourself a blues person . . .

KELLEY: Oh, good God, no! No. And I think part of it is, like, authenticity— like, I would never be a hip-hop singer. I couldn't just a take a whole ethnicity and put it on like an outfit.

DT: In addition to joy, the other thing you mentioned that I wanted to come back to was play. And when you referred to the joy of despair, I found that interesting, because you might hear someone like Nick Cave say the same thing, but he might not pursue it with the same tone you have. That also seems important to what makes your music unique, because for so many guitarists, even though what they're doing is "playing" it seems so . . .

KELLEY: Rigid and particular, yeah. Oh yeah.

DT: It seems like the idea of play alone would've singled you out in the music scene, even if you had come in with a Berklee degree in guitar.

KELLEY: Right. Yeah, and it's not just the Berklee school of "jam," it's also those ready-mades that everybody seems to be able to do. I don't know . . . I don't know why you'd ever want to play anything that's already been played. It just baffles the mind. Why on earth would you sit down and learn the lead to "Stairway to Heaven"? I honestly would rather take a bullet to my head. I just think it's pointless and not in a way of "Ah, it's already been done," but, I mean, literally it makes me *hurt* to think about doing that. It just is, like, *repulsive.*

I went to a guitar store recently and there was this motherfucker there doing bullshit stuff—and, I mean, he was good too, he sucked so hard, so well, and it makes me physically ill to hear that shit. I would rather hear a cat walk across a piano. It's crazy how that is. But I wish I could play that badly. I feel like if I could, I would have more right to complain about that kind of music. It's one of those things where you've got, "Oh here's Picasso," who obviously can draw a leaf just like a leaf, but who has gone above and beyond that, and, you know, that must be very hard. To be able to play like that and then choose not to. To reject it and then move on. That is something that I will never have to worry about, because I will never play like that. But I don't know which guitarists are like Picasso, because those people you never hear play these musoids of [*guitar wailing*]. I don't know who can actually make those horrible sounds and purposely chooses not to, somebody who's a critically acclaimed sound dude on guitar. Whereas I know that Picasso can, because I remember seeing some of it. I remember thinking, "Oh, I didn't know he could actually do all that." It never occurred to me that he went that route and then went another way.

THE RADIANT GUITARIST

JOHN FRUSCIANTE

The original Red Hot Chili Peppers—with its founding guitarist, the vital Hillel Slovak—crossed P. Funk bottoms with Gang of Four tops, blasting out of L.A. chanting "Get Up and Jump" in cock socks. After three records and Slovak's lamentable passing, a second Peppers emerged in 1989 with teenaged John Frusciante (born 1970), who in addition to his Zappa chops wrote tunes so sweet even rap-prone vocalist Anthony Keidis began to croon. Following *Mother's Milk* in 1989, the band went big time with 1991's *Blood Sugar Sex Magik*, with hits such as "Under the Bridge" that inspired millions of now-faded asterisk tattoos. Despite the apparent pleasure of playing alongside bassist Flea in his favorite band, the news came out in 1992 that Frusciante had quit the Chili Peppers in mid-tour, leaving their manager to "just tell them I went crazy."

Frusciante reemerged in 1994 with a whole new freaky styley of his own called *Niandra Lades and Usually Just a T-Shirt*, two hypothetically separate albums recorded straight from the psyche to four-track. Of the seven million who picked up *Blood Sugar*, only 15,000 followed the cowriter of "Breaking the Girl" down this solo path; what they found was a chilling, intimate self-portrait in the tradition of Syd Barrett and Skip Spence, a slashing dream of a weekend in which everything is lost but music. From the opening count-off of "As Can Be," Fusciante's guitar pulls the listener down a PVC tube, into a mood further fogged in "My Smile Is a Rifle," then smashed by the piano in "Curtains." Further in, "Untitled #8" has the teetering quality of being on the edge of something—of how much one can healthily pack into a piece of music, of what a song is, of a rare, unfiltered inspiration. It didn't hurt that Frusciante was a masterful guitarist, but it helped that you could feel him, as he admits in this interview, taking all the theory he'd learned and "throwing everything out the window," as if the album was the act of hurling. Even the prettiest instrumentals, like "Untitled #2," are warped by backward guitar, the disc's signature, often harrowing effect.

Though released at the height of Frusciante's well-publicized heroin addiction, *Niandra* was recorded with *Blood Sugar*–period lucidity. Thus, it seems he didn't need to be losing his grasp to make the record, but perhaps he did to put it out, because the rest of the music scene was so rational that his utterly free, reckless vision was likely to come off as damaged by comparison (as it later did, when 1997's *Smile from the Streets You Hold*, as he says, "freaked people out"). Since rejoining the Peppers in 1998 and/or leaving them again eleven years later, Frusciante has been unfailingly productive, releasing six solo albums in 2004 alone, but he never made anything as striking as *Niandra* again. Yet despite its minority place in his body of work, it is the one record that only John Frusciante could've made—that is, in the most molecular, shit-coming-together-in-time-and-space way—because it's more than a record, really; it's like one of those sci-fi movies in which an entire being is trapped in a sheet of plastic.

Reportedly, Frusciante wanted to release *Niandra* as the work of a fictional acid casualty from the 1960s, but casualty or not, he's the one of few contemporaries who could have held his own in that "golden age" of guitar, who could've taken a chorus on Mingus and Dolphy's "So Long Eric" or carved a solo into Kraftwerk's "Autobahn." A hard-core phase-goer, he's a walking encyclopedia of obscure chords and harmony theory, with a need for newness he applies to projects ranging from the afro beat of his stint with Swahili Blonde to the Public Image Ltd. revisitations of side group Ataxia. Few musicians have gone from more-is-more to less-is-more and then all the way back, but John Frusciante has, and will surely make the rounds again.

DAVID TODD: I've heard you talk about guitar "antiheroes"—what do you mean by that?

JOHN FRUSCIANTE: Well, I grew up dedicated to the guitar, so I studied all the flashy players when I was kid. And I think I grew up with a misconception—which is pretty normal for a person who plays any instrument, but especially the guitar—where the physical action that's taking place on the instrument seems to count for something more than it should. It's such a complex thing, making music, and I feel like when flashy guitar players get really good, a lot of the time they lose sight of the fact that really slow notes and really simple notes, just because they fall in strange places, can create various types of space with the other instruments. People have the tricks that they do—they have their little techniques and riffs—and they forget about trying to shape music into something that depicts an energetic picture, a picture in sound that arouses all these feelings inside you. With the flashy guitar players it becomes more about demonstrating something.

So, you know, I lost interest in that as a teenager, and I became fascinated by people like the guitarist from the B-52's, [Ricky Wilson]. I started to find more meaning in people who played simpler, because these people seemed to have a better grasp on the complexities of *that*, you know. A lot of people who are really good technically don't give that same kind of care to each note. People fall into patterns at fast speeds, when really to have a clear musical thought—the kind of musical thought that makes a melody work—our brains just can't think that fast. At a certain point, you're going on automatic. When it comes down to it, when I hear somebody playing really fast, to my mind it doesn't sound complicated at all, and what somebody like Matthew Ashman in Bow Wow Wow or Bernard Sumner in Joy Division is doing sounds complex, because each note pulls you in a different direction.

I like all kinds of guitar players, but it's people like the ones I just mentioned whose playing really amazes me, and it's because of their ideas, it's because of what they *thought*. It's because they approached the instrument differently than anybody else. It's people like Keith Levene from Public Image and Daniel Ash in Bauhaus who are exploring the possibilities of what you can do with the guitar, whereas other people seem like they're just exploring what you can physically do, and that serves no interest to me anymore. It did when I was fifteen [*laughs*], but not anymore. Not since I was twenty-one years old.

DT: What happened when you were twenty-one?

JF: That was when I first started to really find myself as a guitar player, because a lot of things happened to me on the same day, and a lot of them had to do with me as a human being and my philosophy switching poles. I went through this change as a person, and I went through a musical change too. Obviously I'd been moving towards it, but I remember clearly the main part happened in like one day, you know?

DT: What were you listening to then?

JF: Tom Verlaine. I remember listening to [Television's] *Marquee Moon* and being dazzled by it. What he did with a sort of jaggedy guitar sound, the amount of beauty and expressiveness that came out of it, was really exciting for me. It made me remember that none of those things that are happening in the physical dimension mean anything, whether it's what kind of guitar you play or how your amp's set up. It's just ideas, you know, emotion. I'd grown up thinking, "Well, a guitar player should be a good balance between technique and emotion," and I just realized, that's ridiculous. It's *only* emotion, it's *only* color. It's not half physically what you're doing that's important and half the musical idea, it's *only* the musical idea, you know? And it took me like eight years of being really devoted to the guitar to realize that.

[*laughs*] I kind of knew it when I started and then I gradually forgot it, and then when I realized it again, it hit me like a ton of bricks.

DT: It seems like at least some of the people you're talking about asked musical questions that were effectively left unanswered. Is that what you had in mind with Ataxia, picking up where someone left off?

JF: Yeah. We all loved Public Image and we felt like their music pointed to so many possibilities. And sometimes I'm amazed with that, when one band or guitar player points toward a style in the same way that, to me, Jimi Hendrix's playing pointed at certain possibilities. And I'm shocked that people don't run with these things. We've had so many people trying to imitate Jimi Hendrix, but I don't understand why people don't build upon these ideas that seem to be such revolutionary new places for music to go.

DT: Ataxia was also a way of getting into something of your own, I assume.

JF: With the Ataxia records, our starting point was Public Image, like, "Let's do something based on bass lines and exploratory guitar and exploratory drums." And it was just a simple idea based on the musical elements of one particular group, but we were able to do something original with it, because it was just a sort of door into the infinite for us. It wasn't like we were covering their songs—they opened a certain door and we walked through that door and then played with it in our own way, you know? Whereas someone like Eric Clapton came up with a style in the '60s based on blues music, and people are still walking through that door. Plenty of people walked through it in the '60s and '70s, and people are still doing it, but with somebody like Keith Levene . . . nobody walked through that door. Keith Levene said, "Here, this is a new way to look at infinity," and nobody went through it.

A lot of people don't even *notice* that somebody opened up a door for them. Their minds are so focused on doing something that's cool, or on trying to look like they're not trying too hard. Musicians so often put themselves in these holes when there's so much to explore from the past.

DT: Is it good when people combine these schools of playing, in your view? Even if it's rare?

JF: It's cool when you have these guys who do stuff that's pretty hard to play but it still has that quality where there's great care to each note. I put Curt [Kirkwood] from the Meat Puppets in that category. He'll do a lot of faster, fancy stuff, but each note has meaning, so he's different than somebody you think of as flashy. Vini Reilly [of the Durutti Column] is another one; he has amazing harmonic concepts and each one changes the meaning of what's beneath it.

But I was gonna say, even though I have these feelings, I love all kinds of guitar players. And I should point out that there's nothing in particular that's better about simplicity for its own sake. I really like progressive rock, but to me that's not about blazing through things but trying to be inventive and trying to approach music from a new standpoint. Things like King Crimson and Genesis, that kind of music isn't just fancy; you don't get the impression somebody is trying to impress you so much as they're trying to explore musical ideas that you can't explore unless you have the technique.

DT: In general, the antihero types may be more instinct driven, with less theory than someone like you. Do you think that period when you were twenty-one was when your instinct and theory came together?

JF: Yeah. At the time I thought it was because I wasn't thinking too much in terms of theory anymore, but I *was*, it was just that it was so . . . like the point of my first solo record, in my mind I was just throwing everything out the window. I was throwing all theory and technique out. But then after that, when I hadn't played guitar much for about four years, my playing felt quite different. Without that technique I didn't know how to twist it as well.

I don't have an extensive background in theory, but the amount of it that I've learned I've applied, so I have a vocabulary of melodic and rhythmic relationships. And that's all theory is, it's symbols to help you identify those relationships. To some degree, somebody can perceive them just by playing the guitar a lot and seeing them in terms of shapes on the neck. But I notice that with those people, a lot of the time they have to fiddle around for a while to find a part. If guitar players don't know the modes, for instance, it takes them a while to figure out which notes they can play, whereas somebody who's practiced those scales knows immediately what notes apply. So for me theory has always opened things up to where I can walk into a room and just by hearing something I know exactly where to go on the guitar. I have a better time playing because I have a variety of colors to bring to the table.

To me, it kind of makes sense that so many people end up resorting to the physical part of guitar playing. People want to do something that they can conceive of, you know? Like, "Oh, I'll practice scales all day and I'll be able to play really fast and impress people." It's a real cut-and-dried, straight-ahead way to learn something. But when you start really boggling your mind with what can make something that's as simple as a Beatles song—when you actually examine it lyrically, rhythmically, and melodically, and chordally—something very complex, in some way an understanding of that is less intimidating, you know? To me, the only thing that makes music not intimidating is the ability to take it apart.

DT: I know what you mean when you say that you haven't studied theory extensively, but compared to most rock musicians you break things down easily. And although it's obvious how much of your playing comes from an internal place, does this theoretical knowledge ever lead you toward more of a formalist approach?

JF: No, for me to enjoy making music, it has to generate an excitement in me, and form in itself doesn't generate any excitement to me. For instance, I don't feel that the way to make the most free music is through music that has no limitations, like if you don't establish a tempo and you don't establish a key. I feel like a lot of the time the music that can be the freest is the music that has a lot of limitations put upon it. All kinds of music from sonatas to acid house to drum and bass have real strict parameters, and for some reason that encourages originality rather than stifles it. So for me, working in a pop group like the Chili Peppers, working basically with the pop song format, I did everything I could to try to infiltrate that with musical ideas that were exciting to me, you know? But that's lost its interest for me at this point. It's been a couple years now that I just don't have any interest in writing those kinds of songs. I feel like I did some interesting things within those parameters, but I have more interest in exploring different things.

DT: Just to clarify, when you infiltrate that pop song format, as you put it, does that create any meaning—say, by having the music hit the audience differently?

JF: No, no, no. There are certain chord progressions I like that modulate in a certain way, or there are beats I like where certain drums fall in certain hits, but it's not as if they have any value on their own. The beat itself could be played really badly, that modulation could be terrible sounding—it's all about the person who's doing it. My knowledge of these things comes from the fact that I'm a person who likes to understand things, and because I'm obsessive, you know? [*laughs*] But my knowledge of those things doesn't have any musical value; my music is what it is because I'm who I am and I've lived life the way I've lived it. My sense of melody is my sense of melody.

Even when I realized those things when I was twenty-one, it's not as if I was thinking about them while I was playing. But I came up with drastically different types of musical ideas because of them. I mean, it's not luck that I make up a good guitar part, because I've got enough combinations of symbols and musical ideas swimming around in my head to where parts can be generated by referring to those things. And those coordinates where a word meets a musical moment, and the word meets the note, and those two things meet the rhythm that the word falls on, that's where the real meaning comes from. I just think it's short-sighted to think, "The note he played is the note he played." That note he played is different based on where it falls in the space of what's going on around it.

DT: That makes sense. I thought it was one of the strengths of your music that you're able to do so much with technique without giving up an intuitive, emotional approach.

JF: Well, but what do you mean by emotional, though? Like, if you're saying that there's something else besides emotion that's going into the music . . . how is any of it not emotional?

DT: I suppose it's all emotional on some level, but what I mean is like what you were saying before about the ideas of a musician, the way his or her thoughts come through. "Musical ideas" might be the term you used.

JF: I just call it "organizing sound," you know? That's the essential quality of music: you take sound and then organize it with your mind.

DT: But, I mean, the word "organizing" seems more conscious than imagining or creating, for instance. And that's not a bad thing, in my opinion.

JF: But that organization, would you even be doing it if it weren't your emotions behind it? I'm not saying emotions like somebody crying or somebody laughing, but that intuitive sense that tells you, "This note means something." And I think that's an emotional response, because you feel that the note that goes here does make sense, and you feel that the one that goes there doesn't. It's not overt emotion, but I feel like that's an emotional response.

But what are you talking about where you're saying that with music there could be something other than emotion driving it? Because I can't think of anything where I don't feel like the person was not really excited to be exploring whatever they were exploring, and that's emotion.

DT: Well, I've heard you say that you can understand the way musicians think by listening to their music.

JF: Yeah.

DT: That's what I'm talking about. I know you might say that's because you understand music well enough that you can recognize their choices. But even for a nonmusician it seems like as the person goes about organizing sound, you get glimpses into their point of view. You get their perspective, basically.

It's like what you said before about Public Image Ltd. You were saying that, as a musician, you found what they did to be interesting?

JF: Yeah.

DT: So my question is, for the people who wouldn't claim to understand music in a theoretical sense, what was so alienating about them, then? PiL had the same lead singer as the Sex Pistols and a lot of people went through that door, so to speak, but as you pointed out, so few went through PiL's. To me, that has something to do with what they were doing formally, like in the Sex Pistols the attitude was punk but the music was closer to old-fashioned rock, whereas in PiL the music was more challenging to the audience even though, at least on the surface, the lead singer had toned himself down. Just as I see it, that's most likely because of how PiL infiltrated pop forms with songs like "Death Disco," but either way, something was rubbing people the wrong way, right?

JF: Yeah, something definitely was. A lot of people hated them. They're one of those groups that you might have one friend you play it for who thinks it's the greatest, and then you play it for another friend who's like, "Oh please, don't ever play that around me." [*laughs*] It was always that way with Captain Beefheart; some people connect with [that music] right away and other people it really bothers them.

But I don't think musicians should even think about those kinds of reactions. I think people should just go in whatever direction interests them. I think it's a shame to do things based on whether people will follow them.

DT: Is it possible to ignore those things though, in an absolute sense? Has that been your experience?

JF: It's like you might have a situation in a band where one person can't play in odd time signatures or something, so you just don't do that with them. Like, I think in a lot of ways, in the Chili Peppers it was these four very different people and each person could do something that the others could relate to, so the end result was that what we did was comprehensible to a lot of people. But that was also in the context of this band entity, but for me, just as an individual, I really like exploring a lot of possibilities from a lot of angles. You know, I've made tons of music that I haven't even released. I've gone through phases that people don't even know about, because I like trying to push music in different directions. And I feel like people who were able to do that like Miles Davis or David Bowie, who could completely transform themselves before the public eye and who weren't worried about people's expectations, that's really the goal. And for a lot of people it's hard to do that.

DT: Sure, I see your point on that. And by the way, you'll have to take my word for it that I wasn't trying to provoke you with that question about emotion.

JF: No, I didn't think you were arguing with me. I didn't want you to think I was arguing with you. I was just having a discussion. I was trying to redefine emotion, because when a lot of people say emotion they mean these formulaic ways that you can trigger people with music. But my point was that even with someone like Iannis Xenakis, it's still emotion that's going into his music. It's because he was excited and had a sense behind making the precise choices that he made. I don't think that could be anything but an emotional decision. So yeah, I feel like I know what you mean but I've just been expressing it in a different way.

DT: OK, I have a more straightforward question for you. I know you've covered Lou Reed's "Ride into the Sun," and I remember when I first heard the original version, with Steve Howe on guitar, I thought it sounded like you.

JF: That's not the original, though. He did the original in the Velvet Underground.

DT: I mean the version on Lou Reed's first solo album.

JF: Yeah, that's the first proper release of the song. [*laughs*]

DT: Well, anyway. You've covered a lot of songs, but I was wondering if that one was significant for you.

JF: My dad had *Fragile* on the shelf when I was a kid, so I was listening to Yes when I was like seven years old, so I heard Steve Howe and I liked him. And yeah, I love his playing on the first Lou Reed solo album. But for some reason, the chord progression that "Ride into the Sun" is based on is very meaningful to me. There's something about the tonality of that song that I identify with a great deal. I have no idea why, but there are certain basic chord progressions that have been used thousands of times, and it's completely your interpretation of them that counts—it never sounds like the same song, you know? I feel like at various times in my life, especially when I haven't been making music, I see clearly that it's my job as a musician to explore the possibilities inherent in certain chord progressions or harmonic climates, and that's a really limited way to be thinking, which is probably why I've thought that way more when I wasn't making music than when I was. [*laughs*] So there are certain things that I've explored more than others, and that's definitely one. But I don't really like . . . I don't know what else I can say about it. It's a song that I relate to a lot.

DT: My other random question is about *Niandra Lades*. I've heard that you've somewhat disavowed that album—is that true?

JF: No, I think that's a brilliant album. I never would've said anything like that. I did let my second album go out of print. And it's not because I don't like it, it was just that it freaked people out so much, and at the time I had a vision of myself making more records, so I wanted to start fresh. I didn't want people to be scared of me. [*laughs*] Now, it doesn't make any difference to me what people think, but I still wouldn't release something just to release it, you know? I'd only release something if I was ready to let go of it.

Those first couple of solo records, they were such a natural thing, and they were so meaningful to me and my friends when I made them. I did them with the mind-set, "I'm not going to release this music," and it was just shocking in both cases how much my feeling about them changed as a result of letting them into other people's consciousnesses. Gradually, after twenty years of making music in the public, I've settled into a healthy relationship with things so I know how to not let people step on what I've done. Like with my last record, I released it a while after it was done, because I was enjoying sitting around with my friends listening to it. I didn't want to let go of that, and then when it seemed like that had run its course, it was time to let other people have it.

But you know, it happens to a lot of people; like Captain Beefheart, he went into some crazy direction for a while where he made these really lame, straight, commercial records, and I remember the quote was that he was tired of scaring people, you know? And it's unfortunate, but that's part of being a human being. I don't think that artists should be led by public opinion; I feel like it should be our duty to express what there is to express. But it's something I wrestle with, because the difference between making music for yourself and making music for the purpose of releasing it is that an audience adds this level of intensity, this live-or-die feeling that you wouldn't have if you were sitting around in your bedroom. But I think that in general, if you think of music as a living entity, the things that should be motivating it and making it grow—if what we want is for music as an art form to grow—should always be internal enough to deal with your own relationship to the creative force of the universe, and it shouldn't have anything to do with what people are going to think of it.

DT: If somebody else said to me that music should deal with your relationship to the creative force of the universe, I might not be as quick to believe them. But I think *Niandra* delivers on that.

JF: Well, my experience of making that record was pretty cosmic, you know? A lot of crazy shit happened to me during the making of that record, and psychically, some of those things were really uncanny and incomprehensible and supernatural—I heard my cat talk in my head during one song while I was playing the guitar solo! [*laughs*] But, you know, that album was a lot of fun to make. Everything was so automatic, just one take, with no thought whatsoever being given toward "Is this good?" It was just a pure representation of that time of my life and how I was living. There was no purpose to the music, there was no goal. And so I feel like it had some of the most inventive things that I ever did just because I just had no guard up. The music was just the pure music of life.

I think there are rare times in a recording artist's life when they really drive ahead and make music clearly to make it. And it's just magical. It's really . . . you know, I'm in awe of that album. I've been accused of that before, of not liking it, but honestly I think I probably like it more than the people who like it do. [*laughs*] It means a real lot to me, but at the same time, I was able to do it because of those circumstances.

DT: OK, this is the last one I have for you, and it goes back to the idea of those guitar traditions. I'm not asking you to categorize yourself, but if there are these two main schools of guitar players as we've been talking about them—the virtuoso approach and the post-punk approach, to use reductive terms—do you think of yourself as fitting into one more than the other?

JF: I definitely don't have any interest in aligning myself with a certain type of guitar player. But it is something I think about, and basically, I think of myself as somebody who put the same amount of time into guitar playing as a guy like Steve Vai would, but I used that time completely differently, in order to have a good grasp of a wide variety of musical colors, many of which I perceived through the study of people who played with very little technique but whose brains were nimble, whose brains in terms of creativity were exactly where you'd want to be. I studied those players and I applied them, so that while I was capable of doing something more based in the basic tradition—you know, I had that finger strength where I can play like a "guitar hero" or something—but instead of using my ability that way, I tried to do something that was more based in the approaches of people who had less technique. And I tried to make mine a cohesive style, because like I say, a lot of these people just sort of stumbled on what they did without knowing what they were doing, and they had no control over it, which is what I like about it, but then I was able to come upon that and say, "Well, what if I crossed Bernard Sumner's approach with Jimmy Page's," you know? "What if Jimmy Page tried to play like Bernard Sumner?" [*laughs*] "How could I play in a rhythmic style but with no blues?"

So yeah, I think that I'm kind of a learned guitar player who didn't have any interest in learning along the same lines as a lot of other people do. I was more interested in studying people like Fugazi and Bow Wow Wow.

PSYCHEDELIC SOUND FREAK

MICHIO KURIHARA

Translated by Eric Ozawa

orn in Tokyo in 1961, psych-master Michio Kurihara spent more than two decades blowing Pacific solos over the acid rock of White Heaven and the acid folk of Ghost before finally releasing his first solo album in 2005. "I had many informal requests over the years, but I politely declined them," Kurihara says. In fact, it wasn't until Pedal Records suggested that such an outing would actually benefit his regular ensembles that he took the plunge. Pedal "had absolutely no idea what kind of album I might come up with," he reported to J. Hakan Dedeoglu of *Bant Dergi*, and their (lack of) expectations turned out to be right. With *Sunset Notes*, Kurihara delivers something far greater than the usual guitar player's solo outing, that being a truly singular impression of his Gibson SG at the sonic magic hour. His "Time to Go" is a surreal Fripp-and-Eno waltz, "Do Deep-Sea Fish Dream of Electric Moles?" a hazy power march, "Twilight Mystery of a Russian Cowboy" pure macaroni-Western thematizing . . . and yet somehow all of this fits together, as if part of some fully realized tradition the listener never encountered before. When Kurihara rides his EBow into the abrupt dream stop of "Boat of Courage," it only makes the point that there is still much to him left uncaptured at the album's closing.

From his early days with bands like Onna and YBO2 on through to later projects like the Stars, Kurihara has been known for blistering reanimations of 1960s icon John Cipollina of Quicksilver Messenger Service. But he has spent almost equal time airbrushing quieter landscapes behind vocalist Ai Aso and dream-pop duo Damon & Naomi. Whether he's screaming or whispering, a certain imprint remains, presented without the faintest need to impress, performed without ever hitting a wrong note. "There's an emotional core to all of those different styles," Damon Krukowski told the *Austin Chronicle*. "I've heard him say in interviews that he's not a technical player, but he's so skilled. I think what he means is that he doesn't play for technique's sake. . . . The playing comes out of an emotional core." As a pejorative we call musicians of Kurihara's type journeymen, but he takes that term literally, as a way of heading forward, with one experience informing another. "I've learnt so much from [Damon & Naomi]," Kurihara told Dedeoglu with his usual modesty. "They've helped me move from being somewhat introverted to becoming more positive and more ready to open my heart to the external world. And that change is reflected in no minor way on my solo album."

Among Kurihara's projects worth seeking out is *Rainbow*, his 2007 collaboration with the heavy rocks of Boris, in which he melts whatever faces are left intact by the trio's primary guitarist, diminutive sound assassin Wata. In "Sweet No. 1," Kurihara unleashes one of his patented Quicksilver flashbacks; in the title track he wields a gnarly tremolo. Basically, he destroys on the album with parts that bore into the listener's brain like surgical instruments designed in America by Gibson and Fender but copied in Japan by Tokai and Greco.

DAVID TODD: In addition to having your own style, you're known for being responsive to whoever you're playing with. How do you approach a new collaboration?

MICHIO KURIHARA: For each band, I strive to play in a way that matches the overall sound and atmospheric balance, including all the songs and instruments. It may sound obvious, but the first thing I do is listen closely, then it's almost like we have a conversation back and forth through the sound. But it's not as if I consciously calculate my performance; the other members of the band and I trust each other, and the sound we produce comes out of that trust.

The fact is, I'm not some studio musician who has the technical versatility to handle any kind of song. I just play what I'm able to play.

As to why I've adopted this approach, no matter what kind of band I play with, it's important to me that we work together to become as balanced as possible. I think that's the greatest pleasure I feel, when the performers and the song become an organic whole.

It's a real pleasure when a good ensemble is born.

DT: When you listen closely, what do you focus on first?

MK: If I had to put words to it, I'd say that I enter into what's called in Buddhism the state of "no mind." When I'm composing, it's like I'm transforming the feelings that well up spontaneously inside me into sound. It's almost like a mental image. I feel that the sounds I'm creating are reflecting memories, the subtle movements of my mind, and nature, which is very important to me.

DT: Are you conscious of changes in your playing from one band to another?

MK: I think that my approach and tone change based on each band's particular features: the overall volume, the singer's voice, singing style. Also, each band naturally has its own distinct sonic world, which draws out different elements of the sounds within me. Often something one of my collaborators plays inspires me to play some phrase I could never have thought up. If that chemical reaction happens for each of the performers, we're able to play music that only our band can create.

Each band I've played with had its own style of expression, its own ideas, but the members often had a lot in common, like musical taste, for example. Because of this, the members more or less shared a musical lingua franca. In that sense, a lot of this collaboration was easy for me to handle. So I think that, generally speaking, no matter what band I play in my basic style has been the same.

DT: How did the process of fitting in go with a band like Boris? They seemed to have a different sonic palette than you were accustomed to.

MK: That started when they offered me the chance to collaborate on an album. Before then, I was acquainted with the members of Boris since I had played in concerts with them when I was with the Stars and when YBO2 got back together. When he was a student, the band leader, Atsuo [Mizuno], had been a fan of YBO2, so the fact that I was an original member of YBO2 probably played a role in their offer.

I felt that the basic recording they'd made had already taken a few steps toward my style, like they had already set up everything so that I could play freely. So the recording was very easy, and as a result I feel that we were able to make an album that brought out our distinctive characteristics. Maybe because of the difference in frequency ranges between Boris's sound and the sound I create, we were able to make an interesting ensemble.

Performing with them live I could feel the unique texture of this huge wall of sound that was different from other bands I've played with. However, the sound never hurt my ears. The feeling wasn't harsh; it was like being wrapped up in sound. It was something that I have a real musical affinity for.

Since I wasn't used to their so-called hardcore or heavy metal style, it took me a lot of time to adapt to it. I went on tour with them, playing over a hundred concerts, so we ended up being able to come together naturally.

DT: In 2007 you toured on a double bill with Boris and Damon & Naomi. How was it playing in both bands every night?

MK: To be honest, when we first had that conversation, I thought, "That's impossible." The two bands are totally polar opposites.

First, we got both bands together and played for a total of around three hours to see if it was possible for me to maintain my concentration for that long, and to see how well I was able to switch back and forth between the two sensibilities.

The thing that was especially difficult was the difference in volume.

With Damon & Naomi, I normally use a Fender Deluxe Reverb with slightly less than 20-watt output, so the volume scale is around "2." In comparison, with Boris I use two Fender Twin Reverbs, each with a 100-watt output. If you add up the outputs for Boris's amp setup, you get an average output of 1,500 watts! So you need at least as much as I use to create a sound with that arrangement.

If, for example, I damaged my ears during a sound check for Boris, I wouldn't be able to play Damon & Naomi's more tranquil style. Because of this, I started wearing earplugs, which ended up solving the problem. Up to that point, I hadn't worn earplugs because I didn't like them.

As for the problem of changing sensibilities between the two performances, it would've been much easier if my body had a gain switch like the amps. [*laughs*] To a certain extent, I think I was able to deal with the switch in sensibility by changing which guitars I used between the sets. Boris doesn't use normal tuning—each string is three notes lower than usual, and the sixth string is an A♯—so in order to match everyone else, I had to change guitars.

Finally, in order to maintain my concentration, I ended up thinking of the whole thing in my mind as a single continuous show with peaks and lulls. Thinking of it that way was somewhat successful.

In any case, it was really exciting to tour around with both bands, and have the opportunity to have a lot of people come hear us. Also, I was sincerely happy that the fans of both bands responded more positively than I expected.

I learned a lot from this experience, but in the end I think for a long tour I'd prefer to be able to concentrate on a single band.

DT: If you were switching guitars in those shows, do you mean you were playing something other than an SG?

MK: With Damon & Naomi I used the Gibson SG. With Boris I use an SG Custom copy model made in Japan by Greco.

Before, I used the Gibson as my main guitar and the Greco as my sub-guitar, but last year, during my tour with Boris, the Gibson copy's "ringing" started to improve. It's just like a living thing. Compared with the Gibson's distinctive sound, the attack on the Greco is not as intense, and the sound is a little bit thicker, so it matches the ensemble well.

I'm going to continue playing these two guitars in the future.

DT: What makes the SG so important for you?

MK: Everything about it suits my tastes: the mahogany body has a uniquely clean sound; it's good for matching the fuzz tone; it's lightweight; the thin body gives it a dry sound with a strong attack; it's easy to play. The shape seems perfectly beautiful. As I said, the ringing on my Greco has clearly gotten better since I first started playing it—maybe it's important that I've been playing it continuously with love.

DT: Obviously one of the best-known SG players from the '60s was John Cipollina, who is often cited as an influence on your playing. Can you talk about what you think of him?

MK: The phrasing and the expressive power of John Cipollina's music are just amazing. His sound has a wonderful gloss and glamour to it. His playing is especially wonderful on his first album, *Quicksilver Messenger Service*. That's why it's an honor to be compared to him, though at the same time I feel about overwhelmed by the comparison.

Of course, I respect his guitar work, and so naturally I was also influenced by him. I think that his sense of sound was more important than his playing style itself. I've never tried to copy his performances, but I've listened to his music so much that I probably absorbed some part of that sense. I think that it became the sustenance for my own style. However, this isn't limited to Cipollina. There are a lot of other guitarists I love: Leigh Stephens of Blue Cheer, Robby Krieger of the Doors, Lee Underwood, who played with Tim Buckley.

DT: In addition to those American or '60s musicians, what has affected you from within Japanese music and culture, or from today?

MK: There are very many excellent musicians here now. The ones I've been influenced by are mainly the ones I've played with. But outside of that category, I'd say [composers] Akira Ifukube and Isao Tomita. I heard Akira Ikufube's music from the time I was a child through the famous scores he did for monster movies like *Godzilla*. His compositions mix the indigenous plaintive melodies that remind you of Japanese folk music—the music of the Ainu, the aborigines of Japan—with Western-style melodies. It's interesting because his music had a fairly experimental technique for the time, considering that it was composed in the 1950s as sound effects for film images.

Of course, he has some wonderful orchestral pieces too, but if I had to divide his work into commercial work and artistic, I'd have to say that I'm more attached to his film scores. I hear a similar sound in the work of Tomita, particularly his music before he started working with a synthesizer. I especially love the theme song he did for the documentary show from the '60s called *Shin-Nihon-Kikou* ["New Japan Travel Journal"], in which they traveled around the country looking for new primitive landscapes.

The works I mentioned were all orchestral pieces. Maybe one of the reasons that I took to classical music so naturally was that I had already been enjoying that style of music in the monster movies and TV shows I had been watching from my childhood.

DT: You were exposed to quite a bit of traditional classical music growing up, right?

MK: Under the influence of my brother, who is two years older, I listened to a lot of classical music when I was a child. I think I listened to classical music the way other people listen to pop or rock music, which in those days I couldn't really understand. It wasn't until later on that I was able to appreciate rock.

The composers I liked were from the so-called late romantic period, such as [Alexander Porfiryevich] Borodin and [Bedrich] Smetana. I was interested in works that were easy to understand, with a lyrical melody and worldview. I especially liked the form of the symphonic poem. For example, in Smetana's "Vltava" ["The Moldau"], the composer adds depictions of scenes with simple phrases in each part. As I listened, I pictured scenes that I had never seen before. In my child mind, I thought, "Wow, this is what music can do."

When I made my solo album, many people were kind enough to point out that my album shared a lot in common with the symphonic poem. Actually, at the time I wasn't aware of it. I think that rather than being influenced by musical theory, it's more likely that I was unconsciously influenced by that sensibility.

DT: I wanted to ask you about how you conceived your solo album, because it does seem more like a meditation than the usual guitar player's solo record.

MK: Since I started with an image of the sound I wanted to express, my feeling was that I just happened to have a guitar as my instrument to make it a reality. Depending on the situation, I played bass, organ, or synthesizer. Even though I basically can't play keyboards, I'd rather play what I'm able to, however amateurishly, to keep up the consistency as I transform the sounds from my head into music. So in a certain sense the album has a different feel from a so-called guitar album.

DT: How would you describe that image of sound you had in mind?

MK: At first, what I wanted to do was to make an album that had a liberating sonic world. That's how it started. . . .

Let me explain how the title ended up being *Sunset Notes*.

The recording took place in November 2004 during my short tour with Damon & Naomi in America. I had the chance during our stay to go to

Walden Pond on the outskirts of Boston, and I got to see a beautiful sunset there.

The ticket I got as I was entering the park read "Admission Until Sunset." This easy-going spirit that led them to write "Until Sunset" instead of a specific time seemed to be the influence of the writer-thinker-naturalist who had built his cabin there, Henry David Thoreau. . . . Or maybe this is normal in America? While it was just a chance occurrence, this event was a big inspiration for me in developing my concept for the album.

Sunset has been my favorite time of the day since childhood . . . before sunset, the orange light that you can stare straight at . . . after sunset, the short period in which the color of the sky keeps changing moment by moment. For me, sunset is an image that seems to symbolize nostalgia, beauty, and things that are lonely but warm. Even if the sunset gives me a feeling of loneliness, it's absolutely not a negative feeling. I remember my childhood awareness that "for there to be a sunrise tomorrow, the sun had to take a brief rest."

Because of all this, I decided to try to construct an expansive world of sound around the song "Yuugure" ["Twilight"] that I had loved in my childhood, a world in which hope and nostalgia could coexist.

DT: How did you go from that idea to putting the album together?

MK: When I started making the album, the songs were created around those elements like the setting sun, evening cicadas, the sea, the stars. I wanted to make an album that would feel like the fables I read when I was little.

For each song I had a concrete image in my mind. I thought that the setting for each song should express something like the feeling of a season. For example, each season has its own feeling in the air, its own smell in the wind, its own temperature. I wanted the listener's five senses—sight, sound, touch, taste, and smell—working to activate their imagination.

I think it's amazing if you're able to take what has touched the five senses and transform those unique sensations into sound. I'm not sure if I've been able to do that one hundred percent yet, but if someone listening to my solo album is able to glean a few bits and pieces of the sensations that touched my heart—the scenery and atmosphere of my childhood memories that were starting to be forgotten—then I'll be very happy.

DT: Did you also have a specific idea of what you wanted in a musical sense?

MK: I didn't have any particular model for the album. While I was creating it, I didn't dare listen to any other music, because I wanted to have a neutral background in which I could create sound out of the sensations inside me. The images took shape gradually as each song was put together, and I was able to construct a sonic world that contained the things that were important to me. You could say that the album found its form very naturally.

DT: Could you talk about developing a song such as "Time to Go," which opens the album?

MK: "Time to Go" was the first song I created. It seemed like it came really naturally in a short time. My image for it was "a simple sound that was expansive, warm and positive." Something like the feeling in childhood when your father buys you a present and you open the box.

Once this song was finished, I felt that the whole feeling for the solo album had been decided.

DT: What about "Pendulum on a G-String ~ The Last Cicada"? That seems like one of the cornerstones.

MK: One evening, I happened to hear a cicada call by a lake near my home. There was something special about the lyrical beauty of the sadness of the cicada's song that I loved. This experience was the origin of the idea for the song.

In the larval stage, Japanese cicadas live underground for five to six years, then in the summer of the last year, they hatch, and sing continuously for two weeks in the trees. At the end of this process, their lives are over. Because of this, the cicadas are considered a symbol for Buddhist ideas about mortality and sadness of life. In any case, what I wanted to express in this song was the lyricism of this sense of mortality, substituting human life for the life of the cicada.

The tuning for this song was D-G-D-G-A-D. At first, I was strumming the guitar in this tuning, and certain repeating riffs came to me, followed by the main melody. Little by little, as I felt my way around the image I described, the song developed.

In the first half of the song, I was only playing the main melody on the third string. That's why the title is "Pendulum on a G-String."

For the quiet double-EBow part in the final section, I wanted to create a requiem for the cicada singing itself to exhaustion. When the next part, "Canon in 'C,'" floats in, I wanted to create an image of the chorus of cicadas echoing in the mountains, a symbol of the cycle of life repeating itself for eternity.

In most of the other songs I wanted to express a worldview in which a sense of the evanescence of life and the pain and hope coexist, ending in a kind of liberation.

DT: Did making a solo album reveal anything to you?

MK: What I discovered was the fun of songwriting. For me, the process of seeing the raw materials turn into a living thing was exciting. I'd had similar experiences with other bands, but this was the first time I'd been working from my own initiative. When the album was finished it felt like a part of my body.

To commemorate the release of the album, I had the chance to play a solo concert. There were around two covers, but I was surprised that I was able to put together a concert of only my own music. I'm sure that that sort of thing is perfectly normal for other artists, but for me it would have been unthinkable before that point in my career. What made me happiest was that I could feel the audience listening intently and enjoying the music. It was an unforgettably moving experience. The fact that I was able to create this album and perform this way has of course added to my confidence as an artist.

DT: You mentioned the EBow a moment ago. Could you talk about that and other effects that are essential to your sound?

MK: I've been using the EBow a lot since I started playing with Damon & Naomi—for example, in the live version of the song "Eye of the Storm." I think that an important element of the trio's expressive method is these arrangements centered around the drone of the EBow and the acoustic guitar and harmonium. When the ensemble came together, I remember the way the harmony of the song and the sound of each instrument melted together made me happy.

Since then, the EBow has been an important tool for me. I use it so frequently because it's a fitting way to express the "sense of a wide open landscape" that I see in my mind.

Aside from the EBow, there's the reverb that comes with the Fender amp that's also important to me. Also, there's the old tape echo and the Japanese Shin-ei fuzz [box].

These are the basic elements that I mix and match.

DT: This is a wide-open question to close with, but I was wondering if you could talk about your tone as a guitarist. What do you think you're aiming for?

MK: That's difficult to explain. If I were forced to describe it, I'd say that my tone has been built up slowly from the accumulation of all my experiences as a musician. And all of my experiences, all of the music I've listened to, the scenery I've seen, are reflected in it.

Of course, in order for this tone to be reborn as actual sound, I go through trial and error with the equipment, but those tools are there, finally, to make it easier to transform the sound inside me into actual sound. In the end, the sound is what emerges from my fingers and my heart.

The guitar is an instrument with great depth, so I'd like to work on refining its expressiveness. I feel that for me that kind of expressiveness is making progress little by little. The distance between the instrument and me is shrinking somewhat.

The sound now is pretty close to the sound I've had in my head.

FENNESZ + NOT-FENNESZ

CHRISTIAN FENNESZ

PHOTO BY MARIA ZIEGELBOECK; COURTESY OF FENNESZ.COM

hristian Fennesz started out in bands of the Sonic Youth/My Bloody Valentine variety in his native Vienna in the late 1980s. Not long after, exposure to emerging techno, ambient, and drum and bass styles began to stretch him from his shoegaze roots. In 1995 he opened his debut, *Instrument,* with rippling guitar that could still have come from an extreme Sonic Youth improv, but one underscored by swipes of melody and electronic beats that suggest a deeper change has taken place. By the second track, these guitar effects are further processed among distant synthesizers, and by the end of the EP, the sampled strings are entwined with sampled everything else to a level of Cronenbergian synthesis, the lab results coming back "Fennesz + Not-Fennesz" as if straight out of the fusion scene in *The Fly*. The effect of *Instrument* is one of a shifting plane, the listener oscillating between hearing a given song as either guitar music or electronica, wondering which elements—Fender, Apple, studio, human—are the organic ones and which the artificial. But there is more to Fennesz, who records under his surname, than trickery. Fennesz does rock, as he explains herein, by shifting the genre's basis to the pure power of speakers pushing air.

Fennesz followed *Instrument* with the free-form *Hotel Paral.lel* (1997) and the glitchy *Plus Forty Seven* (1999), then arrived at his pivotal album, *Endless Summer* (2001), which starts dismantling with its Beach Boys–evoking title. Leading off with digital crackling, "Made in Hong Kong" pulsates like those early experiments, but in the second/title track an acoustic guitar introduces a new type of folky, melodic progression shared by other pieces like "Shisheido." As with everything else, melody for Fennesz is never simple, something to hum along with; rather, it's buried and exhumed, detected, hunted for, lost. "What I try to do when I'm playing is to hide a melody behind a sound wall, as though there was a thick curtain between melody and the listener," he explained to *Digimag* in 2006. "I leave it up to the latter to try and push the curtain aside." Though warmer than previous releases, *Endless Summer* is like all of his projects in that what's important isn't the dominant theme, but the contrasts that keep things in play. To paraphrase to a line from his favorite film, Chris Marker's *Sans Soleil* (1983), there is still much black in Fennesz's photo of 1960s California, a Manson family lighting a fire as the sun goes down over Surf City.

It's tempting to hype Fennesz, born in Austria in 1962, as a future for the guitar by showing how it can be used in electronic styles. But the most contemporary aspect of his work is simply the stance he takes, that of the lone musician looking up at Western civilization as a vast billboard of impressions he's faced with recording. "I'm always fascinated by pop music, but not as it stands now," he said in *Tiny Mix Tapes*. "I'm more interested in what's behind it. It's some kind of meta-reality. . . . I try to capture this kind of magic." For 2004's *Venice*, he turns his gaze on a city that exists in a state of perpetual ruin as the waters rise around it. Instead of regarding this decay as a resident or even as an Austrian, he refracts it through the lens of his sec-

ond hometown, Paris, in songs titled "Château Rouge" and "City of Light."
Fennesz finds equal resonance in his remix-like covers of iconic pieces by
(again) the Beach Boys and the Rolling Stones. On 1998's *Plays* single, the
Stones' "Paint It Black" is so strikingly reduced that, for royalty purposes,
even their Verve-suing lawyers ruled it an original work.

DAVID TODD: You once said you worked through all the classic rock styles.
What do you think those were?

CHRISTIAN FENNESZ: Well, I meant that I've had to deal with the clichés of the
guitar, and that I had to overcome this struggle to find it interesting again.
When I was playing in the late '80s or early '90s, the guitar didn't make sense
any more. Everything sounded like a cliché. It took a long time for me to
come back and pick it up, you know. It was a difficult process.

DT: Was that process one of stripping things down?

CF: I did strip down, yes, because when I played in bands in the '80s and '90s
I was one of those [*mimes guitar wailing*]. [*laughs*] No, not really. I played
quite noisy stuff, but, yeah, as a real guitar player. And it didn't lead me
anywhere, you know. I was more interested in sound than playing, and I
had this desire to do something completely different. It became an ideal for
me that I could just strip the guitar down and throw away all the stuff that
you don't need and focus on something like just one tone, but do something
with this one tone on the computer, for example. I began working on this
tone using software.

DT: And then you saw how the guitar could fit into that?

CF: Yes. It was like a breakthrough at one point, that I wanted to get back to
the traditional guitar playing as part of it. But I was still trying to keep the
guitar as minimal as possible. You have to get rid of the cliché—that's the
most difficult thing. I still know guitarists I really admire, they make great
electronic music but when you play with them they start playing all this shit:
[*mimes guitar wailing*]. They still have that, you know.

DT: Was the image of the guitar hero the same where you grew up as it is here in the US?

CF: It was exactly the same. The discotheques in the late '70 and early '80s where they had all those air guitar players . . .

DT: Nowadays, do you ever find yourself on stage and almost lapsing into those old moves?

CF: [*laughs*] Well, there's always a tendency. You have to be in control.

DT: I don't think I've heard a solo on any of your albums.

CF: Not on mine. Actually, there's a track by Yellow Magic Orchestra where I play a solo. It doesn't sound like a solo, but it is.

DT: So basically, the music idea came to you before the guitar idea?

CF: When I started releasing my own stuff as a solo artist it was the music first, and that was the first idea. Then I realized, "OK, the guitar is still my main instrument; maybe I should use it." But obviously I'm a guitarist first, and then secondly I've tried to explore new sound possibilities using electronics, always using the guitar as the main sound source. I think that's kind of my style.

DT: Your work seems to suggest that it's not necessarily the guitar that's the issue, it's the music.

CF: Exactly. It's not important what the music's made with, you know. Of course it is, but it's not the first thing. First there's the idea of the track.

DT: In some ways, that sounds like a producer's perspective, but would you say you lean toward the songwriter approach of having a specific voice?

CF: Absolutely. Yes, I mean, even if I'm supposed to be an electronic musician, I try to have some personal style. I'm really searching for my own language. Because in the early techno days, there was this tendency of not having a personality behind the music, or having the label present it. I was never interested in that, because I was always thinking that if I do something, it's so much of me, you know. I don't want to hide anything.

DT: Do you think you're coming from an overlap in a sense between the early techno world and experimental rock?

CF: Yeah. That was a very strange time in Vienna; there were many people starting with electronic music who had a rock history. It was not such a conscious cutoff, as people are always asking me, it was a development, natural. You know, in the late '80s, early '90s, it was hopeless to be from Austria and in a rock band. You could do something completely weird like improvising or noise, or you could copy something that had been done before, and I immediately realized I was not going to waste any energy on any of that. Using electronics was the only way to produce something of quality.

DT: Language-wise, how much did you take from techno?

CF: There was a time when techno production techniques were fascinating to me, certain programs or sequencers. And of course, I've been influenced by that sound or philosophy. But, for example, I've never made a track that's only synthesizers. There was always some kind of acoustic element; even if it's synthesizer, I recorded it in a room. The element of the room is important for me.

DT: You have a few tracks with a dance foundation.

CF: A little bit. There was a time when I liked to do that, but it doesn't work for me now. There are people who do it perfectly well—like, Aphex Twin is fantastic. But that's his style. I think I'll keep on doing my guitar stuff.

DT: In terms of the naturalistic side of the guitar, are there techniques you tend to use?

CF: I hit a lot of B chords, and D minor. And I'm always using the F major chord. That must be the Neil Young in me.

DT: Other people I've interviewed for this book also mentioned the key of B.

CF: B is great. Each time I like a track that I hear on the radio or on a record, it's always in B. I could make a mix of all B songs. Maybe that's my personal key. I think everybody has his chord or key, that's how they're grounded. That's probably mine.

DT: So in essence your idea is to play some traditional chord sequences and melodies along with using the guitar as a sound source?

CF: I'm interested in all of those different approaches. Sometimes I play acoustic guitar and I want to keep it like it is. And sometimes I go wild with my distortion pedals and then do something more with it on the computer. You know, the center of the song can be completely different as well. Sometimes it's just a quality of the texture of the sound that can be used as the main component of the track. But then it can be almost like a traditional song, the chords or the melody. It's always different. Sometimes it's just atmosphere.

DT: When you're working in electronic modes, do you have things that are similar to pop elements like a chord change?

CF: Yeah, I think I do have those things, also in the more ambient context. They're not so obvious but they're still there, you know. For example, in this track "Endless Summer," there is of course the guitar-chord thing— A, F major, and D minor—and then suddenly it goes down five tones and becomes really slow. I think that's a nice "chord change," you know? And this is something that I've been trying quite a long time to find. I'm kind of proud of that one.

DT: You once said you were interested in the fine line between academic and pop music. Do you still feel that way?

CF: I do, yes. I'm interested in walking this line because both worlds are fascinating, I think. Also, I don't want to give up [on], I wouldn't say the academic approach, but the research approach, so I'm always trying to find new technologies. And also I'm not retro but I like old Fender guitars. And it's important for me to have all those collaborations with improvisers to keep the musician in me alive. At the same time I'm always looking forward to going back into the studio and working alone on the computer. I need all those different work circumstances. It keeps me awake somehow. I don't know if it's good for other artists, but for me that's the way to go.

DT: The *Instrument* EP, was that your first formal release?

CF: Yes. There were smaller things before it, but that was the first international release.

DT: Were you still working out your style as you made that?

CF: Exactly. I was trying to find a way to combine samplers and computers with traditional guitar playing. *Instrument* was almost a techno/drum and bass–sounding record but using a lot of guitar samples—even if they don't sound so obvious, there's a lot of guitar. Yeah, that was my first try.

DT: Were you listening to a lot of techno/drum and bass at that time?

CF: Well, at that time I listened to a lot of ambient music like Main/Robert Hampson and Peter Rehberg, who used to DJ in a club called the Blue Box. Through him I learned about ambient music from the '60s, '70s, and '80s and got really inspired.

DT: Were you hoping that *Instrument* would establish a context for other things you could do later?

CF: Yeah, that was the point. It was the bridge to what I'm doing now. And I think if I would have left the guitar out I wouldn't have gone very far; I would have been stuck. I mean, strangely enough, the guitar was my first instrument but it was also a way to get out of what I knew. It gave me more flexibility, and I was faster with it.

DT: From *Instrument* on, you've said that the albums that you make as Fennesz are your primary statements, as opposed to remixes or collaborations with people such as Ryuichi Sakamoto and Mike Patton. Do you have a sense of how you're developing from one main album to another?

CF: I don't have a master plan or something like that. But they fit together, yes. I think you can hear that one person made the records; there's a certain style even if [the albums] are on different themes. But I haven't yet reached what I wanted to reach, and there are still so many things for me to explore, even if I couldn't tell you right now what they are. When the time is right I always know what to do, but, yeah, most of the time I really don't know. It's more an instinct thing, but it keeps me going. If I know a hundred percent what I'm doing, there's no mystery anymore.

DT: For the individual albums, do you start with very specific ideas?

CF: Well, I don't have a concept at first, but there is a different color to every album that may turn into a concept after a while. Maybe all the tracks are in a certain mood or I use certain techniques. I try to have something like a scene for each album, yes.

DT: For me, the reception of *Endless Summer*—where it was regarded as this evocation of older pop images like the Beach Boys, who had an album with the same title—raises this notion of the audience or media grafting a message onto a work. I'm not talking about a critical reception, but more like a conceptual reception.

CF: I was OK with that. There were so many different interpretations, and for me that was actually great, because I left some space for that, as an intention. What I was particularly interested in at the time were those hidden little memories.

DT: Do you mean your memories or . . .?

CF: Anybody's memories, you know. *Endless Summer* has such a name . . .

DT: You were playing off people's associations?

CF: Yeah. And with the track titles, it was almost too much. But that was my intention, to really push hard in that direction.

DT: What about your version of "Don't Talk (Put Your Head on my Shoulder)" on the *Plays* single, which was an actual song by the Beach Boys? Were you concerned that could come off as a deliberate dismantling?

CF: I didn't really try to explain that, because I thought it wasn't going to lead anywhere. I always thought it would take a little time for some people to understand what I was doing. Some people never will; they aren't even trying. But I have enormous respect for the original song. I didn't want to destroy it, not at all. I didn't sample anything in my version; I really played it again, like a cover.

The song was released on this label Mego, and it was their idea to make a single of cover versions. At this time it was just my favorite song. I was listening to it all the time, so I thought, "I'm trying this."

DT: I wasn't suggesting that you were trying to destroy the song, just that your version might make people rethink a few things.

CF: But there was a very natural approach behind it. It's very natural for me to experiment with things that have been here already. Maybe that's a little influenced by being Austrian. You know, when you grow up in Austria you get educated with classical music like Mozart, Beethoven, Berg, Schoenberg. It was normal back then. And this doesn't really influence me directly, but it's always there. So maybe that's why there was a scene in Vienna that had no problem doing those weird things, you know.

DT: Ultimately, what approach do you think you took to "Don't Talk"?

CF: It's difficult to say. The song has something about it that was like a hypertext, you know. Call it hypertext, call it atmosphere, my goal was to catch this somehow. I think you can find this anywhere—if you take photography, for example. If I take a picture of a flower, it looks like shit. But a really good photographer can create something out of it.

DT: Going back to *Endless Summer*, do you think the audience was ready for something like that at the time it came out?

CF: I think [they were ready for] something like that, because I remember at that time it was cool to make extremely abstract electronic music. And I got bored with that. So I was trying to bring back melodies, you know.

DT: I take it that was also a process, finding the right level of melody?

CF: Exactly. You should never be too obvious, I think. The melody has to be a little bit blurred or hidden, and then it's working better. But the difficult thing is to find the right technique for that. I have some approaches but they're never universal, and I'm never working on only one type of material. But with melody I find that it's always better to bring stuff out as you need it. Find the essence that way.

I was always interested in pop music, you know. I liked the pop approach of having a four-minute song with a hook line and a good melody, but I didn't want to do it like that. I wanted to use techniques from the avantgarde. So a very simple explanation could be this: I was trying to create a mixture of pop music and experimental music.

DT: In the conventional songwriting process, there's a separation between the writing and the recording phase. But your work seems to stretch out the process, where you're writing through the editing phase when you're putting the tracks together. So in addition to the initial creative moment, there's a lot of sculpting involved as well.

CF: Yes, I know what you mean. It is a little bit like that. It's interesting, because most of the material is collected while I'm improvising. I just record everything, so that stuff comes from a very impulsive, emotional process. And then the actual composition is maybe only happening while I'm editing everything, and the postproduction process is actually somehow in the composition as well. It takes both approaches, a very clear and analytic process and a very emotional process. It is something like that.

DT: To me, that alters the notion of the moment or the impulse a song captures. Is that a reception you're comfortable with?

CF: Actually, yes. It kind of covers everything I like, you know. It's great to have both aspects.

DT: One reason I bring this up is because it seems like you get asked about emotion a lot.

CF: They do ask me about that, yeah.

DT: I guess it can be confusing, the way you present it. Like I've heard you say that *Endless Summer* was a collection of love songs.

CF: In a way it was. It's a very romantic record for electronic music. And yes, almost every pop song is a love song, and it's a very pop album, for me anyway. It doesn't have to be played with a lot of strength and power in a rock way.

DT: You just need an emotional core for yourself.

CF: Sometimes I'm waiting years until this arrives. And then suddenly I have a name for a piece and I can move on. And I think the sculpting process can also lead to a very emotional result. For me, the music has to touch me in a way at some point; I have to feel it. And sometimes it doesn't do anything for a long time, but then I polish it here and change little things there, and suddenly it touches me. And then it all happens during the editing.

DT: Ultimately, I suppose it's hard to get around the listener's preference for a clear meaning.

CF: I know, but it's too obvious for me. I have always been so much more passionate for, for example, movies where things weren't so clear and you had to search. For me there was the work of Chris Marker; there's one movie of his which has been an enormous influence called *Sans Soleil.* He works a lot on memories also—he's always hiding things. He really knows how to do it.

I remember in the beginning it looked like it was really difficult for people to get into my music and actually hear any kind of melody because it was so disturbed by the noises around it, and I think this really has changed. It seems like the climate has changed. People are more open to listening to disturbing sounds, and to finding something behind them. But that was something I was always trying to do, hiding the memories a little.

DT: I wanted to ask at least a little about the gear you use. Is the specific guitar you're using still as important for you as it is for most players?

CF: I realized after all these years that even if I just use the guitar as a sound source most of the time, it's still good to have a proper sound source. A well-recorded, good-sounding guitar gives you a better result in the end than a cheap one, you know. If you have a cheap one for certain reasons, it's fine, but . . . like on this track "Rivers of Sand" [on *Venice*], it's really a well-recorded guitar sample that I used. It's a Stratocaster played in a room, recorded with a nice microphone.

DT: Were you making a point about that by listing your recording gear in the liner notes of the *On a Desolate Shore* single? It's the only thing you mentioned there.

CF: I had to say something on that and [Touch label founder] Jon [Wozencroft] said, "Come on, just describe what you're using."

DT: So you told him the model number of your amp.

CF: Yes. [*laughs*] I enjoy reading things like that, because I'm interested in gear, you know, so I thought maybe it could be interesting for other people as well.

DT: It was to me, but I would imagine people ask you more about the software and patches you use, things like that.

CF: Many do, yes.

DT: Or your effects in general. I know you use some commercial products like the Memory Man, but what's this mysterious black box you have?

CF: That's my main effect. I have a custom-built distortion box that a very, very weird guy from Germany built for me. He made three: one for some Swiss musician I don't know, one for Kraftwerk, and one for me. He actually phoned me up and he said, "Hey, I have something for you." And then he came in with his car from Germany and he had all this stuff like old Telefunken preamps that are really fantastic.

DT: And what is this box like?

CF: It's just . . . it looks like Satan. It's amazing. First, he built it in this ancient measurement kind of box, you know—it was, like, super-heavy, and the battery was built from a special metal; it would go for two months or something. It's actually really dangerous; it started to smoke once. And I was traveling with this. I mean, it looked like a bomb. But then I got it built into a more proper kind of container.

But, yeah, it's an amazing distortion box. It's quite random, but if you play with it it's got all these variations.

DT: What are your main devices on the laptop side?

CF: Well, what I use is this Max/MSP patch written by a friend of mine that's like an instrument; you have to play it like an instrument. So what I have is a bank of all my sounds, and when I play live I kind of have to reconstruct tracks, but I keep it quite open and I improvise a lot. Sometimes I try to come close to what I did on the album, but then there's also the guitar live, so it's really free. And sometimes I just stop everything and play a few chords, or come in with another sound or something, mix things together, record the guitar and in real time do something with those sounds. It's more about getting a great mix of those different things together while I'm playing; it's not so much about recreating tracks. But it's quite intense actually. It's not easy.

DT: You have to be conscious and be sort of free?

CF: It's like that, yeah. I'm very tired afterwards.

DT: That's like what we were talking about earlier, a kind of dual-creative process.

CF: Well, for me it's the best way to work, but it's really hard, you know. But at the same time, I think I have to give something to the audience. It's simple: they paid, and I get paid. I don't want to rip off anyone. It's also fascinating when it works. It's very, very satisfying. I could do it much more easily; I could use prerecorded stuff and play guitar on top of it. But, again, I do both and that's the challenge.

DT: I've heard you say that it's not your job to make electronic shows more interesting, which is fair enough, but on the other hand, did you have to work to find a way to present your music live?

CF: I did try so many things; I worked with visual arts and all that, and it still is a problem. I think I'm getting better with it. It's still not perfect, but I am trying hard not to be sitting on stage and staring at the screen.

DT: I read an interview on this topic where you said, "I rock, believe me!"

CF: I said that?

DT: Yeah.

CF: Oh, God.

DT: Well, to be honest, I think the interviewer was goading you.

CF: I remember. I said that because the guy was asking me about laptop performances and I had to convince him that I'm not just reading my e-mails.

DT: I wondered how you defined rock as you do it.

CF: To me it has a lot to do with volume on stage, the visceral impact of the music. I don't want to sit in a gallery and make ambient sound; I want a lot of sub-bass and noise. There has to be a moment of almost ecstasy, a hypnotic feeling, you know. I mean, it's what I want when I go see a concert. And I think when I have good shows people are feeling that.

When I play live, I don't care so much about how to make the perfect transition from point A to point B. It's more of the physical impact of the sound. Because when you play with a laptop and a guitar there's not much stagecraft, you know. The only thing that I have is the music and the sound, so volume is essential for me. If people give me a bad sound system with not enough power, I have a problem.

(25)

BLACK WOLF, WHITE WOLF

BEN CHASNY

Ben Chasny is in many ways a terminus for all the guitar that came before him. A voracious listener, collaborator, whiskey sipper, gunslinger at high noon, Chasny is adept in the millennial art of referencing everything from Keiji Haino to Nikki Sudden, but always with his own distinct style. (It's not until you actually meet him at a restaurant in San Francisco called Popol Vuh that you realize his claims of digesting those cosmic Krautrockers weren't metaphorical.) His primary project, Six Organs of Admittance, blends alt-tuned fingerpicking with lysergic leads, absorbing reedy vocals, bells, and stray buzzes into dream ragas such as "Redefinition of Being." Among myriad other endeavors, Chasny composed a score for *Empty the Sun* (2009), a novel by L.A.-based writer Joseph Mattson, which makes sense given how his songs unfold like great narratives of a river, or *the* river he imagines in his sun/moon subconscious. With restless Zen, he looks into this stream and finds new motifs playable on his two good picking fingers.

Like a lot of outsiders, Chasny was born on the outside of Eureka, California, in 1974. Nourished by record-buying trips to Amoeba Music in Berkeley, he started out with locals Plague Lounge, then emerged solo in 1998 with *Six Organs of Admittance*, released on his own Pavilion label in a run of four hundred. *Six Organs'* droning "Race for Vishnu" and epic "Sum of All Heaven" set a course into dilating East/West flashes charted over twenty-plus outings as Six Organs, including *Dust & Chimes* (1999), *The Manifestation* (2000), and *Compathía* (2003). "For a long time, I couldn't figure out how to put the two things together," Chasny reflected in *PopMatters* in 2006. "I was doing the finger-picked music, but I was also listening to a lot of noise, psychedelia, whatever you want to call it. . . . Then when I started to do the first recordings for Six Organs they started to fit together in a way that made sense." This logic may have been crystalized with that year's *The Sun Awakens*, which builds through elegant themes ("Torn by Wolves") and "out" electricities ("Attar") to a hypnotic, twenty-four-minute meditation ("River of Transfiguration"). Ever shifting, Chasny followed up by heading into whatever taboos remained, such as the standard tuning of 2007's *Shelter from the Ash* and the concise songcrafting of 2011's *Asleep on the Floodplain*, just two of his five releases since moving to the relative major label of Drag City. As he explained to *Visitation Rites* in 2008: "I started just wanting to release sort of mystery records from Northern California. As the years passed, the mystery began to dissolve but my sense of the greater world took over, so it was a fair trade."

Although he claimed in a 2006 interview with Leigh Van der Werff to be "a little busy, no busier than anyone else," Chasny has found time over the years for gigs with raucous pysch-rockers Comets on Fire, Rangda (with Sir Richard Bishop), Badgerlore, August Born, and Current 93, as well as for posting mixtapes at TheQuietus.com and writing the odd late-night dispatch for *Arthur*. His current project 200 Years joins him with Elisa Ambrogio, the Magik Markers wild card who might be the closest thing out there these days to the kind of Rudolph Grey freeist who once blew a young Chasny's mind.

DAVID TODD: The last time I saw you perform, you had a drum kit onstage but no one ever played it. It seemed to suggest that when it comes to Six Organs, you leave the door open to whoever might come in.

BEN CHASNY: I was going to have Ian [Wadley] play drums, but that particular night he just didn't make it. But yeah, it's pretty open in general, and I hate telling people what to do. I'm horrible at giving directions, so I try to ask people that I trust.

Usually there's a certain sound that they have. I know, "Well, Noel [Harmonson] plays drums that sound like Popol Vuh, so in this song I won't have to tell him to do that." They're always just friends and it's always based around whoever is around.

DT: So it's not exactly a band but it's . . .

BC: . . . kind of.

Sometimes they don't even know the material. People hate me for that, especially when the Comets on Fire guys play with Six Organs. Before a tour, I don't practice at all, because I want everything to be really nervous and on edge. I think it's fun to throw everyone in a situation.

DT: Does that include yourself?

BC: It depends. We did a tour with this guy Alex Nielsen, and I was really excited because he was one of the first drummers I have played with in Six Organs that wasn't afraid to go somewhere I hadn't already been. He would do something different and it would be like, "Oh, you want to go over there.

That's really good." It seems like everyone wants to be reverent toward the project, but for me, then it just always sounds the same.

DT: The Six Organs albums often have conceptual titles like *For Octavio Paz* [2004]. Are these ideas important for you?

BC: Usually I just set up times to record, and the record becomes more of a snapshot of what I'm thinking at the time. Sometimes I sketch out ideas beforehand, but usually I don't get going until I know that there's a deadline coming up and then I sort of consolidate all the ideas at the time. But I always think about what the record is going to sound like from beginning to end before I start writing songs. For each individual record, it's supposed to be of one piece.

DT: How specific do those ideas get?

BC: They're pretty specific, but it always just ends up sounding like Six Organs. The record I did with Corsano [2005's *School of the Flower*], it just had this great vibe. I thought, "It's going to sound like Alice Coltrane and Pharoah Sanders," and then it ended up sounding like Six Organs. And then the record after that, *The Sun Awakens*, I was like, "Well, this is going to be one long drone, the entire record." I was going to have a sine wave that just built. And then stuff starts to get written and it ends up sounding like Six Organs. [*laughs*] I can't escape it. The original concepts are usually pretty drastic and then the rest is just how I write, I guess.

DT: You don't seem too impressed with your process.

BC: I am totally lacking in this ingredient that a lot of people have as artists, which is they think they're really good. I'm not trying to be falsely self-effacing, but I see people all the time and they're like, "I'm fucking brilliant," and I'm always worried, like, "What is this that I'm doing?"

That's why I don't release records as Ben Chasny, probably—it's hidden behind that. I didn't even have my name on the first record when I put it out.

DT: When you started Six Organs, did you see it as an underground thing or did you think it could have wider appeal?

BC: It's curious, people always think Six Organs is more popular than it is. Like, if I'm on tour, whether it's promoters or whoever, it seems like Six Organs gets more attention from the press than from people who are actually interested in the music, you know? I mean, I'm not complaining, but when I first started doing Six Organs I thought it was pretty limited. I thought, "I'll send some records to Ajax and Blackjack and then Road Cone in Portland." I thought the entire scope of people who would be interested would be ordering from tiny catalogs. That's what I loved, because I was ordering from those catalogs and that was my life. I wanted to be a part of that.

DT: Is that why you did such small runs of your early LPs?

BC: The limited releases were reflective of how many people were buying the records, for one thing. I made four hundred of the first record and it took me five years to get rid of all four hundred copies. Or it took me, like, three or four years. And then I do love private-press records, so that's another reason, because that's what I like.

DT: It's interesting to me what makes someone aim for that world right from the start. Like, I'm assuming you never wanted to play classic rock.

BC: I don't know. A lot of people would call Comets a classic-rock band.

DT: I was thinking of Six Organs, because that's more of your own thing. Do you think of a band you've been a member of like Comets on Fire the same way, or is the latter more of a liberating project on the side?

BC: It's pretty fun. I've always thought about [Comets on Fire] as, like, the guys who get together and drink some beers after work or something like that.

DT: I've heard you say that, but I was curious as to whether the rest of them saw it that way.

BC: I think so. Yeah, it's generally, like, good times and having fun.

DT: Either way, I just meant that not everyone fits so naturally into the same musical world as you.

BC: Yeah, I know what you're saying. I have no idea why, though. I was just drawn towards a certain thing, and before I knew certain bands or musicians existed, I would imagine that they existed. We would take a car ride down to Berkeley, spend all afternoon trying to find something, and then head back with our load of records, you know, and sometimes it hit the spot and sometimes it didn't. I have no idea where listening to that or wanting to play like that comes from; it just really appealed to me.

You know, one theory on that world is that they're record collectors who started doing music. Someone like Wayne Rogers from Major Stars, he owns Twisted Village in Boston and he is a classic example of the ultimate record collector who started making music that is totally brutal—I mean brutal in good way. I think I was a person who loved records too, who was like, "Well, I want to listen to *this* and *this* at the same time." "I don't have it, I better make it," you know? A lot of Six Organs came out of that.

DT: What were some of the records you wanted to combine?

BC: It's kind of curious. I love music and I was even playing in all these bands, but it wasn't until I was nineteen or twenty that I heard a couple records that I became fanatical about and inspired by at the same time. One of them was by Rudolph Grey, *Mask of Light.* I can't explain it, but I remember listening to it and it cleared [away] everything, even folk music and acoustic finger pickers. My eyes just opened. I remember sitting down in the chair, just being like, "Holy shit." It's a totally "out" record, but the texture in his playing is nonstop. I've heard his style described as "action guitar," and that is a perfect description, because it's not noise guitar, it's *action* guitar. On that record, he's playing with Rashied Ali and a couple of guys from

Borbetomagus on horns, and he's just shredding the fuck out of his guitar, and it totally set me straight. All of a sudden everything made sense—like, electric guitar made sense and acoustic guitar made sense; people like [Leo] Kottke made more sense to me in certain ways, and Bert Jansch. But I also started to listen to more out people after that, getting into Fushitsusha and [Keiji] Haino's *Double Live*—that's another one that rearranged me. So those are the big guys, like, when I was nineteen.

DT: It's interesting that Rudolph Grey opened up the acoustic for you, because he's not known for the acoustic.

BC: He doesn't play acoustic at all, but he just made everything possible. By making everything possible, then so many more things were possible on acoustic guitar. I had listened to noise guitarists before that, but that's the record that split my mind open.

DT: Did you get *Mask of Light* from one of those catalogs?

BC: Yeah. Through Forced Exposure.

DT: What led you to people like Bert Jansch?

BC: I started picking up acoustic guitar around that time as a response against the sort of thing that was popular, because at the time it wasn't popular to be into Bert Jansch.
 Again, that probably had something to do with Forced Exposure too. They were hawking Borbetomagus and Bert Jansch; I mean, those guys knew their shit.

DT: Was it important that you were internalizing these things that were more obscure, in terms of developing a unique sound?

BC: Yeah, because I ended up just playing by myself and practicing a lot, you know. I don't really sit down and practice now, but there was a period where I practiced all day long by myself. No one wanted to hear it up there in Eureka, so I would get stoked on learning things on guitar. That was probably the biggest thing.

DT: Stylistically, were there things from the British players you picked up?

BC: I wasn't into every British person, but with Bert especially, his left hand on the guitar is all hammer-ons and pulloffs, it's just so fucking great. I kind of put [John Fahey and] the American Primitives more in the camp of being concerned with the right hand, the fingerpicking hand, and the dudes across the pond were always doing all those slides and everything, which appealed to me, being more of an electric guitar player.

DT: You identify more as an electric guitar player?

BC: Yeah. I just feel that way because I'm more concentrated on the left hand and soloing.

DT: I guess the conventional wisdom is that soloing is more of an electric guitar thing.

BC: I don't necessarily think of soloing as something for the electric guitar and chords for acoustic, but I tend to play that way. I guess it has to do with the tonality of each instrument.

It's weird, because I can kind of only solo in standard tuning. But when I play acoustic guitar I always play it in alternate tuning, so . . . yes, most of the chord progressions that I write are in an alternate tuning.

DT: Another person from the folk world you've referred to is Richard Thompson. Being a fan of his *Grizzly Man* soundtrack, I wondered why that resonated so strongly for you.

BC: I like things that have themes to them, so whenever you get a soundtrack I like how they present a theme and then develop it. And that record seems like a snapshot, which it was. It's so spacious and it sounds like a snapshot of some people I really like.

Did you see that documentary [*In the Edges: The Grizzly Man Session*]? Fucking amazing. I hate to be a guitar nerd, but when I see Richard Thompson bend behind the nut, a little tear comes down and I'm like, "Don't show anybody that." He's just so fluid and so effortless. It's fucking incredible.

That soundtrack just blew me away with the themes that were going on.

DT: It was fascinating to see Richard Thompson in the Popol Vuh role of providing the sountrack to one of Herzog's films.

BC: That is what I was going to bring up, because I always felt that it was like Richard Thompson doing Popol Vuh, and that's crazy. I don't know if he was conscious of that. I wonder if he even subconsciously went back and recalled Popol Vuh; I don't know. Those are questions I would definitely be curious about, like did he know previous Herzog movies? He must have seen some, so that he could unconsciously take stuff from *Aguirre, the Wrath of God*. You know what I mean? It just fit.

DT: Branching out from Herzog, I was wondering if you were attracted to visionary artists in general. I read your piece "Ten Truths/Untruths" in *Pitchfork*, which by the way was very well written in my opinion in a kind of 3 AM style.

BC: For sure. You can usually tell by the amount of exclamation points that I use in my writing exactly what time it is.

DT: In that piece, you were talking about *Veedon Fleece*, and I was wondering how you relate to Van Morrison or other singer-songwriters who have a mythology in their work.

BC: Well, Van Morrison is one of my favorites, but that's funny you bring up mythology, because on one hand there are these people I love who have built such huge mythologies, but if you were to ask me what I felt about people who built up mythologies, I would say I hate them. You know what I'm saying? Sometimes it's OK if you're not trying to build up a mythology but you can't get away from it—someone like Haino, again, who's such a mythological character in himself. But if any of my contemporaries or people I know try to build a mythology, I'm like, "Ah, come on." It's like there's not a lot of mythology being built around people now unless it is self-mythologizing.

DT: I don't think you do that, but there does seem to be a set of associations you return to.

BC: I guess there are some things I just can't get away from. I think that's part of the challenge, trying to rip yourself away from those things and not be lazy and go back. I don't know if it's lazy or just content. My friends used to make fun of me because for the first five or six records almost every song had this word "sun" in it. I don't know where it comes from, it just sounds right at the time. Usually my brain wants to write a song about something and then I let the words go and I write a whole bunch, and then I come back and carve the song out of it. That's my process.

DT: What do you think you emphasize when carving things out? I notice you don't use a lot of first person.

BC: Yeah. I cross out all the things that are too revealing, or maybe, like, more personal situations that don't fit. Like the song "Shelter from the Ash," it ended up being one verse and a chorus, but that was taken from two pages of lyrics. When I went to record it I was like, "Oh no, no, no, that doesn't work. Don't know how to sing that, that's not working. This is the gem, this one verse. This is what I'm trying to say."

But then again, if you're writing more stream of consciousness then you'll go into stuff you didn't mean to, that you weren't starting with in the first place, you know.

DT: Sure. And I don't think that's a bad thing, anyway, just that it results in more universal imagery.

BC: That's because I want to have something a little more universal that could relate to other things. I guess when you use archetypal imagery it's easier to do that.

DT: The imagery in "River of Transfiguration" might be a good example.

BC: Yeah. Well, when I said "river," I was specifically talking about [Herzog's films] *Aguirre, the Wrath of God* and *Fitzcarraldo*. Going back to Herzog, his rivers are always super muddy and violent, and I was thinking about that, and I was also thinking about the river in *Apocalypse Now*, and the trans-figuration character. I rarely am inspired by movies or anything like that, but I happened to be into both [Herzog and *Apocalypse Now*] at the time.

DT: The transfiguration character, was that from one of those films?

BC: Well, the transfiguration character might have been from John Fahey's *Transfiguration of Blind Joe Death* record. It just tied in with the idea of myth, Fahey's idea of myth, along with the terrible waters of those movies and how those rivers transported and, especially in the case of *Apocalypse Now*, changed the characters.

But also I was tapping into . . . where I grew up, we had a river in our backyard—it was literally in our backyard—and it would flood every winter. We actually had a cement wall built in front of our house so that it wouldn't come in, and one year it actually came into the house. The river moved in. So I think it also draws back on my childhood memories of a very muddy river, you know. It was very specific, but it does have universal implications.

DT: I heard that "River of Transfiguration" was based on a Talking Heads technique.

BC: Yeah. With putting songs together, one of the records that I used as a template for a lot of Six Organs stuff is the Talking Heads' *Remain in Light*. It's one of my favorite records, because there's only one groove the entire time and all the choruses and verses are based around it; all the other sounds and the melodies coming in are built on top. When I heard that I was like, "Ahh, just one thing."

Like *Remain in Light*, "River" is just one beat and one pulse. Different layers on top of the original pulse, instead of chord changes, delineate the parts of the song. That was the record—*The Sun Awakens*—that was going to be just one drone, and then a couple songs came out of it and I thought, "Fuck, I can't have two songs at the beginning of the record and a sine wave for the bulk of it," and then more songs came and seemed to want to be included. So to have it all make sense I thought, "All right, I'm going to do it like Pink Floyd's *Meddle*. I'll do 'River' like 'Echoes.'" Because on *Meddle*, "Echoes" was side B. That's how *The Sun Awakens* constructed itself.

Actually, the two songs I was talking about, it was the *Grizzly Man* soundtrack, hearing the theme, that inspired those.

DT: Which pieces were those?

BC: "Torn by Wolves" and "Wolves' Pup."

DT: Is it true that your guitars are called Black Wolf and White Wolf?

BC: The drummer for Comets named them that, Utrillo [Kushner]. I had a Stratocaster and that was White Wolf and then the Telecaster became Black Wolf. They were named that way before the wolf epidemic hit.

DT: With longer pieces like "River of Transformation," or maybe "The Six Stations" from the 2004 *Manifestation* reissue, is your writing process much different?

BC: Well, with "River," I just had this riff and I wanted it to last for a long time. It was a matter of, "How can I make this last for twenty minutes and be interesting? Where would it cut off? Where are the solos?" I just planned it out.

"The Six Stations" was more complicated. Originally, *The Manifestation* was a one-sided twelve-inch, where the second side was an etching of the sun. What I wanted to do for the reissue was incorporate that etching side, as in "Oh, you could play that. Play the etching." So what I did was, I flipped one of my copies over and I made markings on it corresponding to where the [first six] planets would be if the label was the sun. I used this thing called Bode's Law, where you can figure out how far away the planets are in relation to each other. So I just marked where Mercury would be and went outwards with the planets, and then I dropped a needle for about three minutes on each one so it played the etching. And then I took all those different recordings of the etching and then found the Greek modes for each respective planet. I tuned the guitar to those modes, and then I played in those modes for each planet's recording. Once I had all six pieces I just edited them so they flowed together. But that's why Earth had to be the vocal piece, without guitar, because Earth, being the center, doesn't make a sound in the original concept of the harmony of the spheres. So I just had the voice of a man.

That was a piece I wanted to do. It wasn't just, "I want to do a twenty-five minute piece." It was very personal.

DT: Is that the most structured thing you've done?

BC: The most analytical thing. I don't know, I was just excited about the idea, reading about the modes. We were talking about [Gaston] Bachelard before [the interview], like the poetic truth of things. That was sort of the idea behind it.

DT: Did playing in those Greek modes give you any insight into how they were connected to the planets they were named for?

BC: No, but it was really fun, like some Leonardo da Vinci flying machine that doesn't work but it's beautiful. You know what I mean? And that was the point of it.

DT: I wanted to ask about the process you underwent in combining the acoustic/folk and electric/noise sides of your style. Not to be stereotypical about it, but it seems like there were a few Japanese bands that could have been relevant in that.

BC: I think that's totally true. Those guys Kan Mikami, Tomokawa Kazuki are fucking amazing. It's so not folk at all, and they're so aggressive with the way they play the guitar and sing, and the stuff that Kan Mikami did with Haino in Vajra and some other projects, it's hugely influential on me.

Ghost definitely helped out too, because they did a lot of that, joining those forces. Actually, it's funny, because you're talking to [Michio] Kurihara, and he was a big part of it, before he was a full-time member and he was just a soloist. On the first Ghost record, some of their songs would be strung in acoustic guitar and then on some of them they'd be chanting in a cave and then on some Kurihara would be ripping an amazing solo. So, yeah, that was one of the bands that kind of helped me kind of put things together.

DT: How smooth was that process for you?

BC: I don't know. Even when I did the first record I didn't know what I was going to do after that. I didn't see it going anywhere. It wasn't until I started doing the second record that something started to click with how melodies go together with finger picking and drone, and how other sounds can be incorporated.

They're two pretty different elements, and it's difficult to take different genres and make something cohesive. It was hard to make it so it didn't seem like it was just sewn together. I think now I've developed my style to the point where it's not such a challenge. But I remember after trying to work on that first record wondering, "How am I going to do this?"

DT: On those first couple of records, it seemed like there was more of an Eastern feel.

BC: I think that came from the fact that I didn't do a lot of chord changes; I was constantly just droning.

I've always felt like the more you use chord changes, the more people are going to relate those changes at least unconsciously to other music, for good or bad. Because a lot of chord changes have been used. And I've always felt if you just continue with one thing and don't change the chords, then the thing that the brain is going to relate to is, you know, probably Indian music, because they use that a lot. But if you do just one constant thing you're not going to be sucked into it like, "Oh, this is a Carly Simon song." So the drone came from not pulling out a lot of chord changes or being very minimal with them, just avoiding that sort of thing. I don't know if that makes sense.

DT: It makes sense. But what is your concept of the drone?

BC: When I say a drone, it is because generally I work with scales around a single root note. It's not exactly a drone, and I imagine there are many definitions of that word. But as I was saying, mostly what I work with is a lack of chord progressions as opposed to just one constant note. If I want to work with one specific mood, I will employ that idea of a drone.

DT: What is a riff as you use that term?

BC: I use that because if you took out the rest of the parts on a lot of the things I do—if you took out the bass and the middle strings—it would be a riff, just really high up but constantly repeated. That kind of repetition is very important to me, and that goes directly back to the *Remain in Light* record, just one repeating thing and then other things get built on top of it, you know. It's just in my brain to want to do that.

DT: So for you, what is the connection between riff and a drone?

BC: Well, because of the way I make music, the riff can go over a drone at the same time, and that has to do with fingerpicking. When I'm droning on a lower string, I consider the treble strings to be the riff. So I guess that's it.

DT: What about your primary alternate tuning—how essential is that to Six Organs?

BC: It's definitely helped shape the sound. Sometimes I feel it is more of a crutch and I try to break out of that mode and play in standard or a much different tuning, but throughout all these years that tuning has made its mark.

DT: What is that tuning?

BC: It's D-G-D-G-A-D, which would be a Gsus2, I guess. That's my standard tuning that I use.

DT: Where did you get that?

BC: It was actually in this book of alternate tunings. It was a Nick Drake tuning, and it was the only Nick Drake tuning I could get without snapping strings. I don't know what he was doing, but every time I tried one of his tunings, it'd snap, and I'd get pissed off, and this was the only one I could do. And then I figured that out and I was like, "I'm going to learn this inside and out." So I made my own charts and I graphed out all the scales by myself. And I would just practice. And it was really exciting to learn it by myself too, to not have somebody just say, "Learn this, learn this." I was like, "Well, here's this whole world. I can graph up the scales by myself and practice."

DT: It seems like one of the things that makes Six Organs work is how you're able to combine all the different styles and techniques we've been talking about, like the band succeeds as a concept in a way, which seems like a big part of the challenge nowadays. There are so many subgenres and so much music out there, a contemporary musician could be trapped in terms of how to find something new.

BC: See, I think that is one of the biggest problems. Too many people are trying to find something new, as if new music has more validity than good music that isn't new. That's why these bands become popular for three seconds, because they discovered something new, but the fact is that things are moving so fast that new only lasts for a week now. And I think it has to do with the way people are obsessed with how fast they can collect music, with speed. They correlate one with another, new music and new sounds, and they need it faster and faster. I think it's a big mistake.

Shit, I like new music, too. But I think if you're just worried about finding something new you're never going to find it at all, ever. You're just going to end up creating some sort of pastiche rather than any type of transcendental form. You know what I mean? It's just going to be this patchwork.

DT: I hear you on all of that. But given that you're about as big of a music fan as it gets, did you ever find yourself wondering where you could go?

BC: As a guitarist I don't think that got to me, because once I started learning, the fingers took over and it just sort of developed into what it was. But there was definitely a time when it was like, "What am I going to do?" before it started jelling in a certain way. But yeah, it's crazy to think about growing up nowadays; maybe you're sixteen and you can listen to anything you want now—I mean anything. It's really curious what's going to start happening. Hopefully, people will just go with being sincere in what actually moves them and won't listen to other people. Because another thing is, we're living in a culture of not exactly critique but comments. You can comment on anything from your Amazon order to your restaurant, and I'm just afraid kids are just going to be, like . . . negative.

I don't know, the future is going to be really strange. You know what I mean? It's going to be strange for the people in it. I hope that there are kids who are strong enough to just be inspired to do something.

Acknowledgments

I would like to thank the guitarists for their patience, their hospitality, and their insights. For his translation of the Michio Kurihara transcript, I'd like to thank Eric Ozawa. For their images, thanks to the photographers and designers credited throughout, especially those who went beyond the call of duty. Of course, this book wouldn't exist without the help of many managers, press reps, and contacts, or without the feedback of Alan Licht, Paul Trynka, Brandon Stosuy, and more than a few others. My gratitude to them all. For making this happen, thanks to William Clark of his literary Associates, and to Yuval Taylor, Devon Freeny, Mary Kravenas, and everyone at A Cappella/Chicago Review Press. Lastly, for their generosity and guidance, thanks to my own underground network of atonal friends.

INDEX